ADVANCE ACCLAIM FOR

e-Enterprise

"NO MATTER HOW SHARP your vision of the future may be, success depends on being able to invent the business model, implement the technology, learn with every step, and start the cycle again. It takes a robust e-Enterprise methodology to do that."

—DON TAPSCOTT
Author, *The Digital Economy* and *Growing Up Digital*

"THE E-ENTERPRISE METHODOLOGY described in this book is providing essential guidance as we develop strategy and implementation plans to transform CompUSA to an e-Enterprise. This stuff works."

—HONORIO PADRON
Executive Vice President and Chief Information Officer, CompUSA

"THE AUTHOR EXPLORES the rich and rapidly evolving landscape of electronic business—a journey well worth taking."

—VINT CERF
Internet Pioneer

"WHETHER YOU'RE CREATING a new e-Business or using e-Technology to add bandwidth to your existing business, this book is a must-read. Faisal Hoque provides an excellent conceptual framework and marries this with proven systems concepts employed by high-performing organizations. This is the recipe for rapid development of highly scalable e-Systems that maximize return on investment. It should be required reading for e-Business decision-makers and technologists alike."

—RON GRIFFIN
Senior Vice President and Chief Information Officer, The Home Depot

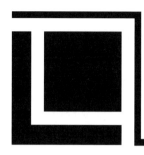 e-Enterprise

Breakthroughs in Application Development Series

David Orchard, Series Editor
Cambridge University Press
New York, New York

and

Solutions Architect
IBM
Burnaby, British Colombia

The Breakthroughs in Application Development series is dedicated
to providing hard knowledge in the form of detailed practical guides
to leading-edge technologies and business models in modern application development. This series will identify, define, and stimulate
emerging trends in the industry, covering such rapidly evolving areas
as electronic commerce, e-Business, Inter/intranet development, Web
architectures, application integration solutions, and the intersection
of business and technology. Each title will focus on a new innovation
in the field, presenting new ways of thinking and demonstrating how
to put breakthrough technologies into business practice.

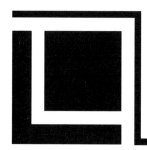

e-Enterprise

Business Models, Architecture, and Components

FAISAL HOQUE

CAMBRIDGE
UNIVERSITY PRESS

SIGS
BOOKS

PUBLISHED BY THE PRESS SYNDICATE OF THE UNIVERSITY OF CAMBRIDGE
The Pitt Building, Trumpington Street, Cambridge, United Kingdom

CAMBRIDGE UNIVERSITY PRESS
The Edinburgh Building, Cambridge CB2 2RU, UK   www.cup.cam.ac.uk
40 West 20th Street, New York, NY 10011-4211, USA   www.cup.org
10 Stamford Road, Oakleigh, Melbourne 3166, Australia
Ruez de Alarcón 13, 28014 Madrid, Spain

Published in association with SIGS Books

First published in 2000

Design by Susan Ahlquist
Composition by David Van Ness
Cover design by Andrea Cammarata

Printed in the United States of America

A catalog record for this book is available from the British Library.

Library of Congress Cataloging-in-Publication Data is on record with the publisher.

ISBN 0 521 77487 X

Dedicated to

- Christine, the reason I live.
- Reaz, the most talented person I know.
- My parents, the reason I persevere.

ABOUT THE AUTHOR

Faisal Hoque, author and entrepreneur, has founded three pioneering Net commerce companies and blazed new trails in business process automation for Fortune 1000 companies.

He is the founder and CEO of **enamics**, an e-Enterprise modeling company. **enamics**, an affiliate of META Group, offers objective tools and operating models to its customers to define, visualize, simulate, and to architect an evolving e-Enterprise. In 1997, Mr. Hoque founded EC Cubed and pioneered e-Commerce Application Components. In 1995, as a GE Capital divisional product head, he implemented for that company one of industry's first comprehensive B-to-B Net commerce initiatives. Over the last 12 years, Mr. Hoque has worked with corporate giants like Dun and Bradstreet, Pitney Bowes, General Electric, MasterCard, American Express, Transamerica, Chase, and CompUSA. Mr. Hoque is also a META Group Research Fellow. More information is available @ hoque.com and enamics.com.

CONTRIBUTORS

Contributions to this book were made by Ryan J. Sheehan, Christine M. Hoque, Frank Ovaitt, Todd Certer, Niaz Adel Khan, Leon Reis, and Lance Sperring.

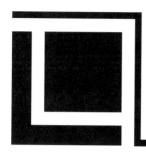

Contents

PART 3   e-Enterprise Methodology and Architecture

PART 4   Enabling Components

Multiply, vary, let the strongest live and weakest die.
—Charles Darwin

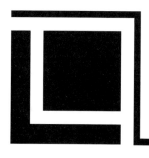

Foreword

Whoever invented the button didn't need much of a business architecture model to cope with the change he unleashed. The button, a thirteenth-century invention, took 400 years to achieve widespread use. The bicycle appeared in 1818 and took 50 years to catch on. The telephone, invented in 1876, needed 35 years to find the beginnings of a mass market. Television took 26 years; the personal computer, 16 years.

Those adoption rates seem pretty leisurely by today's standards. The unyielding environment of speed in technology-induced business change is so pervasive that a CEO (or any C*O, responsible for operations, finance, human resources, technology, marketing, or any other function) who doesn't occasionally get a sense of panic perhaps doesn't get a lot of other things either.

And speed is only one element of the profound paradigm shift that is happening in how business is transacted as a result of the Internet. The e-Revolution is on and—as is the tendency of revolutions—things can be a bit confusing while the participants sort themselves out.

Maybe it was acceptable that your company created its first Web site to "keep up with the Joneses"—whoever they are in your industry. You didn't need much of a model or architecture for that decision; the Joneses, after all, were equally unsure about what they were doing and why. Maybe you made your first forays into electronic commerce and electronic business in the same fashion. Maybe you're not even sure how e-Commerce differs from e-Business, and e-Business from e-Enterprise. If the Joneses don't know either, does it matter?

Faisal Hoque and this groundbreaking book argue that it does. Because with so many businesses recognizing the strategic imperative of "catching the wave" of electronic commerce, sooner or later the Joneses may get it right. Worse, they may read this book before you do, and discover how to develop and implement (and re-develop, and re-implement) a dynamic iterative strategy for true e-Enterprise transformation.

For the first time, Hoque's book offers a robust and *repeatable* way of thinking about strategy in this sense. He demystifies the principles of electronic commerce, electronic business, and e-Enterprise, starting with a history and an explanation of the critical differences among these three concepts. He covers the strategic challenges faced by enterprises as they embrace this new way of doing business, and examines the business drivers that are smashing old value-chain models in industry after industry. Most importantly, he introduces tools that allow business leaders to replicate—even automate—business architecture and technology architecture analysis and decision making. The ultimate outcome is a repository of reusable strategic assets that allow your e-Enterprise to evolve as rapidly and continuously as today's fluid markets.

Transforming an enterprise from a bricks-and-mortar structure to a clicks-and-mortar organization is not easy; virtually any of my peers among Fortune 100 chief information officers can attest to that. The business strategists as well as the technologists must understand the market trends of e-Applications and the dynamics of business-to-business versus business-to-consumer opportunities in your industry sector. Sometimes one needs to push the "reset" button in the executive brain to recognize and capitalize on real differences in such areas as branding and the customer experience. These in turn have a profound effect on what are the right technological infrastructure choices.

Hoque analyzes all of these subjects and makes them understandable through case studies and business models. He explores the practical implications of such business-to-consumer concepts as one-to-one marketing, online community building, e-Tailing, self-service, auctioning, and branding. He also examines the fundamentals of business-to-business concepts such as the virtual marketplace, resource management, extended value chain, and customer relationship management. He explains why the answer is usually *not* switching your business model totally to the Internet, but engaging the Net as a subset of a larger e-Enterprise model—truly clicks and mortar. For companies that too often have put the technology horse before the business cart, learning how to articulate an appropriate and doable business vision and strategy for e-Enterprise before placing expensive bets on technology will be enlightening indeed. To be able to *reuse* these assets and models, iteration after iteration, to stay abreast of your markets and ahead of competitors, is truly breakthrough stuff.

The transformation of business to e-Enterprise is inevitable. To lead that transformation requires a journey through a number of business and technology crossroads. These intersections are not easy, but they are predictable—as are the profound effects of the various decisions you must make there. The final section of Faisal's book provides guidelines for safely traversing these crossroads.

After the battle of Waterloo, Wellington gave us a memorable quote that ought to be posted on the wall of every business strategist's office: "For every problem there is a solution," he said. "Where there is no solution you have no problem, only fact."

In this book, Faisal Hoque certainly provides facts that some businesses need fear as they enter the Net economy. More importantly, he provides problems, solutions, and dynamic tools for building the future of your e-Enterprise.

—Tom Trainer
   Executive Vice President and Chief Information Officer
   Citigroup

Acknowledgments

This book could not have happened without the creative contributions, encouragement, and endless feedback from a wide variety of people. These are people who *believe*—certainly in Net commerce and the creation of next generation enterprises, but also in me. It was my great fortune to have access to some of today's most talented industry leaders, who helped me to formulate the very basis of this book; and to have the support of many special individuals who have long shown the knack for bringing forth my best efforts. My sincere gratitude goes to the following people:

- Ryan J. Sheehan for doing the lion's share of research for this book, for listening to and trying to organize my brainstorms, and for four years of being the most loyal research assistant any author could have. Without Ryan, this book might never have been started.

- Frank Ovaitt for endless time spent editing, for putting complex concepts into simple terms, and for taking over the management of all communications regarding this work. Without Frank, this book might not have been finished.

- Thomas Trainer for being a mentor and true supporter, even to the point of contributing the foreword of the book.

- Dale Kutnick for believing in my concept of e-Enterprise modeling, and for honoring me by contributing the introduction to this book.

- Honorio Padron for being a friend and supporter, not to mention a test case for many of the concepts described in this book and rolling them out in his own organization.

- Folks like Don Tapscott, Vint Cerf, Ron Griffin, Bert Ellis, Gordon Kerr, Clinton Wilder, and Edward Brginsky for honoring me by taking the time to review the manuscript.

- Terry Waters, Paul Berg, Marty Bell, Bob Edwards, Bruce Barlag, and Sathish Reddy for being personal friends, for helping me think through these concepts, and for sharing with me their own experiences.

- Todd Carter, Niaz Adel Khan, Leon Reis, and Lance Sperring for contributing critical elements of the finished product.

- All the folks at Cambridge University Press and SIGS Publications involved in making this book a reality, especially my editors Lothlórien Homet and Mick Spillane for pulling it all together.

- The dedicated staff of EC Cubed for making e-Commerce Application Components a reality, thereby validating my ideas about Net commerce architecture.

- Leaders who are striving to be the great e-Enterprises—companies like General Electric, MasterCard, American Express, Transamerica, Chase, CompUSA, Home Depot, General Motors, Citigroup and all others mentioned in this book—for sharing their vision and experiences as relevant knowledge for this book.

- Paul Daversa for being my closest friend, for supporting me on every new project over the last nine years, for being there through the ups and downs, and for introducing me to most of the people who are part of this book team.

- My bother Reaz Hoque, an accomplished author himself, for inspiring me to write this in the first place; and my parents for instilling in me the perseverance and drive required for any project of this magnitude.

- Lastly, and with my greatest gratitude, my wife Christine Hoque for spending countless hours with me discussing the content of this book, for contributing many ideas and drafts, and for inspiring me like no one else can.

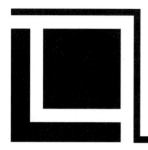

Introduction

In an era of e-Everything, there is no shortage of books proselytizing the benefits of participating in the e-Universe and warning that the failure to develop and execute a Net commerce strategy threatens your company's survival. There's no shortage of vendors and consultants offering to sell you Net commerce solutions and presenting themselves as experts with broad strategic scope and knowledge of "how to do it right." While most of these purveyors talk a good game at the information and strategy level, they lack a rigorous approach in putting it all together.

The reason there are so many claims is because the underlying value proposition and the opportunities are enormous. Enterprises that develop a business strategy that perfectly integrates traditional real-world operations with a great Net business model, and that are able to simulate its implementation and test its assumptions before investing millions, will have a major competitive advantage. A rigorous, continuously fine-tuned approach to execution will also be on the critical path.

It's not an easy thing to do. Furthermore, it has to be done fast the first time, the second time, the third, and the nth time. Your markets—*everybody's* markets—are changing that quickly. But major winners will determine how to innovate, sustain, remain, and then re-innovate.

Faisal Hoque has developed a robust methodology that enables an enterprise to develop its electronic commerce vision and strategy; to architect and simulate the business processes and technology applications that operationalize the strategy; and to create the repository so that every architectural component can be reused in the next iteration (and the next, and the next).

Hoque's unique insights into these processes were nurtured during e-Space pioneering efforts as strategist and practitioner. His six-plus years of intense involvement in electronic commerce already make him one of the most experienced gurus. He is a seasoned entrepreneur who has now founded three ventures relating to e-Commerce and worked with industry giants like General Electric, Mastercard, AMEX, TransAmerica, and CompUSA.

META Group itself has extensive experience in this space. Based on that experience, it's my view that no single factor could be clearer or more relevant than that customer demand will continue to evolve in real time. That's the only time frame in which your competitive response can possibly be successful anymore.

So the only question that matters is, do you have an operating model that will enable you to be that fast and flexible?

Hoque's e-Enterprise methodology is aimed at ensuring your ability to integrate traditional strengths with a Net-based business model. At the end of the day, that's what will make you are a far more viable competitor than companies at either end of the spectrum—Net-based or "bricks and mortar"—who fail to integrate. His operating model is based on objectivity, simulation to verify strategic decisions before pouring in millions, and re-use of both business and technology architecture assets.

The Internet has produced a handful of spectacularly successful new companies that came out of nowhere. But 25 to 30 percent of the more traditional companies—those with real assets, real profits, integrated channels, and an array of other real strengths—will exploit the e-Commerce transition to become even more dominant in their industries. Meanwhile, a small percent of the Net-only wonder businesses will successfully integrate back in the other direction.

Together, these leaders will be remembered as the great e-Enterprises.

—Dale Kutnick
  Chairman, CEO and Co-Research Director
  META Group

PART 1

—

The e-Enterprise

From Net Commerce to e-Enterprise

I don't think there's been anything more important or more widespread.... Where does the Internet rank in priority? It's No. 1, 2, 3, and 4.[1]
  —Jack Welch, Chairman & CEO, General Electric

When Jack Welch makes the Net his top business priority you can be sure that the Internet and Net-based business have taken the critical step from possibility into reality. In fact, General Electric and countless other Global 2000 companies are quickly investigating and applying the newest Internet technologies. These companies seek to gain and retain competitive advantages in new and evolving markets through highly adaptive Net-based enterprises. Everywhere you turn, both the mainstream and business news media are focused on the Net Revolution. Both alluring and critical reports about the Web, the Information Superhighway, and Internet ventures abound.

The Net is the backbone for the new digital economy that is radically changing business models around the globe. These new business models have become differentiators that redefine market winners and losers. No one is safe from the changing tide. Past critics of the Internet have said that it's a gadget for hobbyists and computer geeks—not a valuable tool for business. It's all hype, they said. As evidence they pointed to the astronomic market capitalization of so-called Internet stocks. They said that conventional enterprises are safe from these over-publicized startups. Put simply, they were wrong then, and they're wrong now. As *Business Week* says "You are Merrill Lynch when Schwab.com comes along. You're Barnes & Noble when Amazon.com hits big. You're Toys 'R' Us when eToys shows up."[2]

For some companies, the Net Revolution may have begun a new era of unrivaled prosperity. For others it has probably begun a descent toward extinction. The Net Revolution, however, isn't just about setting up shop on the World Wide Web. Instead, it's about realigning business models around global, dynamic value chains by leveraging Net technologies to survive, to compete, and to succeed.

A spring, 1999 survey of cross-industry manufacturers conducted by AMA Research and Ernst & Young revealed that 50.9 percent of the 766 respondents currently use some form of e-Commerce in their business activities. In addition, 92.3 percent of the respondents that were identified by the overall survey results to be "ultimate manufacturers" reported that they are using e-Commerce.[3] The forms of e-Commerce that were surveyed include: 1) Supply management/buying/auctioning 2) Internet order, status, and availability tracking 3) Placing Internet orders with suppliers and 4) Accepting Internet orders from customers. The survey also showed that the average percentage of manufacturing revenues presently attributable to e-Commerce initiatives is 8.6 percent, however, that figure is projected to increase to 27.1 percent in five years. Among the "ultimate manufacturers," average revenues from e-Commerce are currently cited at 15.1 percent of total revenues, jumping to 34.4 percent in five years.

This survey clearly shows that Net commerce has already begun to touch both internal and inter-organizational business processes in every part of the enterprise. These processes form the heart of "what the business does." On the supply side, they include essential inter-organizational activities such as material, repair and operations procurement, and logistics. Internally they include manufacturing and distribution. On the demand side they include internal activities such as order entry and external activities, and catalog management and customer care functions among others.

The frightening reality, however, is that many of these initiatives are destined to fail. According to META Group, "By 2000, corporations will waste from $35 to 40 billion of the money spent on IT services due to providers whose services underperform or do not perform at all."[4] The analyst firm Gartner Group predicts that "By the end of 2001, over 70 percent [of companies] will have failed to plan a coherent approach to electronic business, leading to a significant loss of competitiveness. These e-Business failures will be a result of disconnects between the CEO, operating/line of business units, and IT departments around the strategy to create new competitive advantages and the technology required to implement this strategy."[5]

This book is about defining the next generation enterprises that will undergo the transformation from e-Commerce to e-Business to e-Enterprise. Many business leaders refer to this transformation as "e-Transformation" and to e-Enterprises as "clicks and mortar." These organizations will leverage their existing asset bases with Net business models. This book postulates that there is a coherent operating model you can adopt that embraces the unique competencies of your business. Using this model, you can successfully plan and execute your own e-Enterprise strategy. It is about the convergence of business and technology that is critical to achieving success in creating e-Enterprises.

According to the analyst firm META Group, for companies aspiring to stave off threats and achieve sustained success from their investments in Net technologies, it will be necessary to integrate business architecture and information architecture into enterprise architecture, and the business technologist will play a critical role in overcoming the barriers and constraints of doing so.[6]

This book is designed to help business people understand the technology architecture needed to implement the desired business model, and to help technologists gain an understanding of business architecture. It is meant to bridge the gap in understanding between business leaders and technologists. The effective outcome of the relationship between these two camps will determine which companies will succeed in the next few years.

This book will not teach you how to become the next Amazon.com. Instead, it will teach you how your company, no matter what industry you compete in, can approach the Internet from the standpoint of converging your company's Net business model with your existing real assets. It will prescribe a method of doing so that will provide you with the building blocks to win and win again. These building blocks are meant to provide an operating model that should be explored for your particular e-Initiatives. It should be made clear that it would be impossible to have a complete discussion of all aspects of this operating model in just one volume. Instead, this book attempts to introduce the most important concepts as your road map to the future.

Before I launch into the how to's of this operating model, it is important that you understand fully the evolution of Net commerce. You should also understand the nuances of business-to-consumer (B-to-C) and business-to-business (B-to-B) models and applications, and how they are converging. It is the convergence of these models and applications that form the underpinnings of an e-Enterprise, the entity that will dominate the digital economy.

In this chapter I will introduce the transformation that Net commerce has undergone in its brief history. I also will discuss what the future holds for it and the business implications associated with that. Chapter 2 will introduce you to e-Application models and how the Internet has fundamentally altered the traditional value chain model. Chapters 3 and 4 will explore in greater detail the B-to-C and B-to-B e-Application models, respectively.

You will be introduced to an operating model for building e-Enterprises in Chapter 5, including a close examination of five key stages: strategy/vision, processes, applications, architecture, and reusable repository. Chapter 6 will explore in detail business and technology architectures, and Chapter 7 will introduce the concept of defining common business components to create reusability and speed. In Chapter 8 you will learn about technology components that enable e-Applications.

FROM BROCHUREWARE TO E-ENTERPRISE

There remains a great deal of confusion about what exactly electronic commerce means. For many corporations, it is still associated with Electronic Data Interchange (EDI), an established standard for corporations to transact business in the form of standardized electronic messages sent over private networks. To the general public, the term e-Commerce is frequently interchangeable with Internet commerce, Web commerce, or I-Commerce, all of which refer to buying and selling on the Internet, or more specifically the World Wide Web. Even many of the technologically illiterate, for example, would now recognize that purchasing a book from Amazon.com or a video cassette from Reel.com falls under the umbrella of e-Commerce. Both of these narrow associations, however, fail to convey the magnitude to which electronic devices, computers, and networks have redefined and will continue to redefine business as we know it.

The fact that even industry experts shy away from pigeonholing e-Commerce into any particular niche speaks volumes about the wide range of its potential. According to the Association for Electronic Commerce, e-Commerce is simply "doing business electronically."[7] By this definition almost any business activity—from a simple telephone call to a complex EDI message exchange—can be categorized as e-Commerce. CommerceNet, an industry consortium of companies that "use, promote, and build electronic commerce solutions on the Internet",[8] includes in its definition of e-Commerce "the use of internetworked computers to create and transform business relationships. It is most commonly associated with buying and selling information, products, and services via the Internet," CommerceNet continues, "but it is also used to transfer and share information within organizations through intranets to improve decision-making and eliminate duplication of effort. The new paradigm of e-Commerce is built not just on transactions but on building, sustaining, and improving relationships, both existing and potential."[9]

This book will provide a fresh perspective of what electronic commerce means. I refer to the evolution of commerce over the Internet as Net commerce because despite its relatively short history, Net commerce has in fact evolved into different phases, so to speak: Brochureware, e-Commerce, e-Business, and e-Enterprise. I define each phase according to the business models and e-Application categories associated with it. You will see as I drill down from those business models and e-Application categories that there exists various e-Application functionalities. Here I will briefly introduce each of

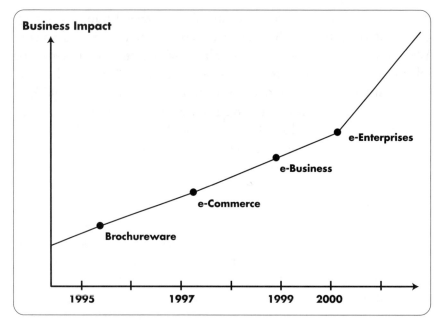

FIGURE 1.1

the phases and their associated business models and e-Application categories and functionalities.

As Figure 1.1 depicts, the emergence of these phases has occurred only over the last five years. It is important to note that the date indicated for each phase is the begin date and there is no end date associated with any phase. In fact, these eras may actually overlap in the greater business world, so that while some companies are operating in the Brochureware phase, other companies may be operating in the e-Business phase. A few leading firms are already integrating different phases' business and e-Application models in a cohesive fashion. These companies will be known as e-Enterprises.

Brochureware

Despite the early technological limitations of the Internet, companies were quick to recognize the value of the Internet and the World Wide Web in particular as a medium to reach out to customers around the world. In almost no time at all, the Net became a key medium for global marketing that provided a low-cost repository of product and service information. According to Forrester Research, by the end of 1995 some 34 percent of Fortune 500 companies had established a Web presence. Only a year later, this figure had risen to nearly 80 percent.[10] Today, it is difficult to find a corporation of any size that isn't yet on the Net.

Most first-generation sites consisted of little more than static documents and simple multimedia. Customer interaction was often limited to reading text and viewing pictures. Actual transactions and customer interaction were still conducted over traditional media such as phone or fax. These information repositories are commonly described as brochureware in reference to their similarity to conventional print publications, and are presently considered a primitive and largely inefficient use of the unique resources of the Internet.

e-Commerce

Initiatives in the e-Commerce era have focused on consumer applications that allow transactions and interaction between the company and the consumer over the Internet. Most of the successful online ventures have been pure Net plays—a brand new business model designed specifically for the purpose of buying and selling to consumers online. With the invention of new B-to-C business models for selling to and servicing consumers over the Internet, several e-Application categories supported by many different application functionalities have emerged. The dominant ones include e-Tailing and Consumer Portals, Bidding and Auctioning, Consumer Care, Customer Management, and Electronic Bill Payment (EBP).

Many successful e-Tailers and Consumer Portal companies have nearly become household brands. There's CDNOW, Planet RX, MS Expedia, and Amazon.com to name a few. Some of the common e-Application functionalities utilized by these ventures include online catalogs, personalization, advertising, shopping carts, and online communities. Brand name Bidding and Auctioning companies such as eBay, Priceline.com, and Onsale all use similar functionalities such as online catalogs, bid boards, account management, and notification applications.

Companies known especially for their Consumer Care and Customer Management abilities over the Internet, such as eToys, E-Trade, and Reel.com all utilize functionalities that enable personalization, self-service, immediacy, and information. e-Application models used by such companies as MCI Worldcom and AT&T, which allow consumers to pay bills electronically, utilize bill consolidation, analysis and reporting, payment processing, and integration functionalities.

The e-Commerce era can further be defined by the culture of hype over ".com mania," where the existence of the technology itself is the catalyst for activity over the Net. The e-Commerce era is characterized by content-aggregation business models that focus on the consumer and that have organizations that are driven by the founders and are typically managed from situation to situation. In the B-to-C e-Commerce world, the most important factors impacting a company's success are the company's abilities to successfully brand its .com initiative(s), to market to each consumer individually, to personalize the information and transactions for each consumer and to create a community environment that welcomes consumers back again and again.

e-Business

Initiatives in the e-Business phase have focused on business-to-business applications that allow transactions and interaction between the company and its business customers and partners over the Internet. Most successful B-to-B ventures online have been those developed by well-established bricks-and-mortar companies seeking process improvement. As with the e-Commerce phase, there are unique e-Application categories and functionalities associated with e-Business. For example, Virtual Marketplaces, Procurement and Resource Management, Extended Value Chain, and Customer Relationship Management (CRM) applications are frequently used e-Application categories found in e-Business.

Cisco Systems, General Electric, and Dell have all successfully developed Virtual Marketplaces, which include catalog, buying tools, integration, and payment option functionalities, among others. Common functionalities used by MasterCard, Chevron, and General Motors for their Procurement and Resource Management e-Application initiatives include request for information, request for proposal, requisitioning, purchase orders, payment, and supplier management. Corporations that have developed successful e-Applications aimed at extending their value chain include Federal Express, TransAmerica, and GE Capital. In doing so, they have utilized demand and supply planning, logistics, and production planning functionalities. Finally, to develop successful CRM e-Applications, notable firms such as Hewlett Packard, Dell, and General Motors have utilized self-service, solution-center, personalization, and account management functionalities.

The e-Business era is characterized by initiatives that are proactively focused on the organization's core competencies and whose business model is oriented toward process aggregation. Organizationally, an e-Business czar is often appointed to "make it happen" for the company and it is brought about in a process-driven fashion. Accepted technologies serve as the driver of these initiatives.

For e-Business initiatives to be successful, there are a number of factors that must be considered when developing and launching the initiative. For instance, creating the right processes and being able to improve upon and integrate them is of utmost importance. Additionally, having agile applications and the ability to integrate applications and data is also necessary. Furthermore, the organization must be structured in a way to support the business model of the e-Business initiative, and there must be a means of overcoming political obstacles in order to achieve success.

e-Enterprise

So far we have reviewed B-to-C and B-to-B e-Application and business models, and have been introduced to some companies that are presently making use of them.

We also see that there is a convergence happening among companies who find that their markets contain both business-to-consumer and business-to-business segments. These companies are implementing common functionalities across different e-Application categories in order to serve both market segments. A few companies at the leading edge of this convergence include financial services giant American Express, Dell Computer in the high-tech world, and Healtheon in the health care industry.

This convergence leads Net commerce to yet another phase: the era of the e-Enterprise. In an e-Enterprise, the whole value chain—from procurement of raw materials on the supply side to consumer retailing and customer management on the demand side—happens by combining traditional bricks-and-mortar assets with the efficiency of cybermediation. Hence the term "clicks and mortar." Because these organizations consist of complex combinations of internal and external business processes and relationships (with customers, suppliers, distributors, partners, and competitors), e-Enterprises are quickly emerging as co-opetitive virtual organizations.

In the world of the e-Enterprise, organizations across different industries will have certain unique commonalities. For instance, business models will be based on people aggregation and applications will focus on mission-critical, inter-organizational business processes. The company's CEO and business partners will drive the organizational changes needed to carry out the initiatives. Its people will be concerned with ROI analysis, and results will come about through iterative, methodical efforts using technology that is viewed as an enabler and as a commodity.

The unique value proposition for e-Enterprises isn't solely about using the most effective manufacturing techniques or having retail outlets with prime locations. Instead, the competitive advantage of each e-Enterprise is embedded in the speed and agility gained by establishing Net business models that leverage its existing asset base. Compared to conventional enterprises, the e-Enterprise is agile, smart, and deadly.

As Clinton Wilder explains in his article "E-Transformation," these e-Enterprise models have just begun to emerge. He provides some excellent examples of the types of models that I refer to. For example, AutoNation, the largest auto dealership network, has built an online infrastructure that enables the company to market on the Web and channel leads to its physical infrastructure of nationwide dealerships.[11] This year's sales from this endeavor are expected to reach $750 million, or 12 percent of total revenues. And, in order to bring about this kind of success, organizationally the endeavor required a change in the sales culture of dealerships and the way sales representatives manage leads.

Another prime example Wilder cites is Timkin Corp., the world's largest producer of tapered roller bearings. Timkin deployed an Internet-based customer relationship management application that is now used by 40 percent of the company's distributors. The application links them to Timkin's back-end inventory database and enables customers to find self-service answers to their most common concerns: availability and price. As a result of the success of this initiative, the company "has redeployed 15 percent of its service reps to sales, where they make proactive sales calls instead of fielding rote queries."[12]

In many ways, e-Enterprise initiatives are an extension of the Business Process Reengineering (BPR) movement that appeared during the late 1980s and early 1990s. In the early 1990s, Michael Hammer and James Champy warned American corporations in their seminal work *Reengineering the Corporation* that to survive in an increasingly hyper-competitive business environment they "must undertake nothing less than a radical reinvention of how they do their work."[13] Today, in the face of radical market changes fueled by the growth and maturation of the Internet, the same maxim holds true.

Conventional BPR advocated the abolition of centuries of industrial management "best practices" including specialization of labor and optimization of individual tasks (at the expense of customer-facing processes) in favor of end-to-end business processes focused solely on delivering maximum value to the customer. The re-centralization of the enterprise around the customer in many ways was a direct result of the technological revolution enabled by the personal computer and network computing. At the simplest level, the computer revolution enabled business managers to automate existing business processes. Hammer and Champy, however, advocated a far more ambitious role for technology. By recognizing that technology investments enable the enterprise to completely reengineer rather than simply automate business processes, Hammer and Champy rephrased the question "how can we use technology to improve what we do" to "how can we use technology to allow us to do things we are not already doing?" Because of technological limitations, the immaturity, and in many cases non-existence of standards for inter-company electronic business, the first BPR revolution was focused on internal company processes.

Today, a new generation of process engineering has begun. With the emergence of the World Wide Web and standards such as Open Buying on the Internet (OBI), Secure Electronic Transactions (SET), and Extensible Markup Language (XML), managers are beginning to turn their attention to engineering and reengineering outward facing business processes to unite buyers, suppliers, and trading partners in dynamic, real-time information sharing partnerships. The impact on the traditional producer-consumer relationship is profound; by providing real-time, up-to-the-minute information across the entire value chain, companies can complete the move to a customer-centric business model by placing the customer firmly in control. The result is a fundamental shift in the focus of business from optimizing and refining internal processes and strategies to refocusing the core, central nervous system of the enterprise outward to business partners.

Fundamentally, e-Enterprise is about engineering and re-engineering inward and outward facing business processes by leveraging the unique strengths of the Net. Industry boundaries will crumble, antiquated industries gradually become extinct, and new industries will be born to take their place. More than being about technology such as XML, CORBA, or Java, e-Business is about repositioning brands and companies, cannibalizing distribution channels through disintermediation, establishing new markets on the Net through re-intermediation, segmenting the needs of customers, marketing products one-to-one, empowering customers with customer self-service, and building communities of interest to promote goods and services.

Competition between firms that cling to traditional processes and best-practices and next-generation e-Enterprises may be bloody, but the outcome will be decidedly one-sided. Corporations that operated in the physical world—in person, through paper communication, or by telephone—dominated the twentiety century. The twenty-first century will belong to the e-Enterprise.

E-ENTERPRISE: WHERE TO BEGIN?

Whether you are a Global 2000 "bricks-and-mortar" company or a start-up .com pure Net play, the fact that you have picked up this book suggests that you are scurrying to morph your company into the next phase of Net commerce. If the ultimate goal is to become an e-Enterprise, how do you get there? All too many attempts so far have been characterized by wasteful chaos, confusion, and a lack of strategy and planning. The approach seems to have been "Ready, Fire!…oh, Aim?"

Instead, you can develop a more productive and efficient operating model that enables you to follow an iterative "Ready, Aim, Fire!" sequence. This means being able to plan and prepare for a launch based on a new business model within a very short cycle time (for example, three to six months for a new business model as opposed to 24 to 36 months). Rather than taking the time to fully learn and then launch, this operating model enables a company to launch and learn, and then incorporate those lessons and launch again. Whether the learning process drives you to a tweaked version of the same business model or an entirely new model, the key is to be ready to fire another round very quickly.

In today's breathtakingly competitive environment, this can be accomplished only if you have an agile operation based on a reusable business and technology infrastructure, and supported by a knowledgebase of market data, research, simulation and modeling tools, and objective methodology.

Nowhere in this book is it argued that this is easy. Your business is complex; why would this be less so? In fact, it probably will involve more complexity that your existing business. That's because the transformation to e-Enterprise means marrying traditional enterprise strengths with a Net business model. Or, if you began with a Net-only model and now enjoy a market cap that was unimaginable when you started, it means building or acquiring traditional bricks-and-mortar resources to sustain your current success when the old-line companies finally strike back.

I do argue in this book that this is essential, and that it is doable. But it takes a methodology that allows you to harness all that your

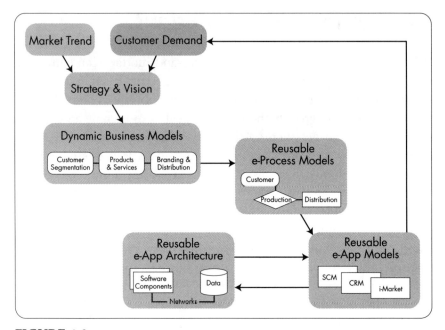

FIGURE 1.2

business is today, and all that your customers will want it to be as
e-Enterprises increasingly are recognized as the great enterprises of
this age. It takes an operating model—the product of this methodology—that lets your e-Enterprise live and breathe and reinvent its
business models over and over.

As this operating model unfolds through the chapters of this
book, you should detect certain themes emerging again and again.
Figure 1.2 summarizes these themes.

*The first of these themes is the importance of defining an
e-Enterprise strategy and vision that brings all of your real-world
and virtual-world strengths together in a powerful constellation.*

It starts by knowing your markets, your customers, and your
competitors as completely as possible. What are your core competencies and your credibility in those areas? What about your people,
your culture, and how these relate to both the real world and the virtual world?

Where and how will you seek to add extraordinary value, alone or in connection with business partners? And how will you measure return on your e-Enterprise efforts—financial return, of course, but also analyses based on responsiveness to customer needs, branding, mind/market share, time to market, cost reduction, and so on? But you cannot expect to create your e-Strategy/e-Vision one time and then let it go untouched for years. This stage of creating your e-Enterprise, like all other stages, must be iterative and rapid fire.

The second theme encompasses the business models, processes, and applications—in other words, the business architecture that will let you move from strategy and vision to reality.

Put simply, business architecture gives an enterprise a distinct shape and defines its high-level functionality in much the same way that a skeleton gives shape to and defines the support and motion of an otherwise amorphous body. You must lay out the flows of products, services, and information between actors who add value by playing specific, defined roles. Conventional business process reengineering (BPR) is simply the process of identifying, dissecting, and then reassembling these components to add more value for customers. Viewed as an extension of conventional BPR, the transition to e-Enterprise can be defined simply as leveraging the Net to knock down boundaries and improve coordination between enterprises rather than simply departments. Out of business model and process definition come e-Application models, (for example, a picture of your complete supply chain or your approach to customer relationship management). At this stage, you will also articulate more clearly how your physical stores and sales force relate to Net-based sales and service. Some of these processes will seem to be very specific to a particular offering, but many more will prove to be common functions that enable many different offerings. But properly designed and stored, they begin to provide a catalog of resources that enable rapid re-load to support your rapid-fire approach to e-Enterprise.

The third theme entails a corresponding technology architecture that allows flawless implementation of the business models and processes.

The e-Application functionalities identified in the business archi-tecture must now be embodied in technological systems and compo-nents. Before defining the technology architecture, a technology audit must be performed to identify cross-organizational integration points, extendibility, and inter-operability.

The final stage of e-Enterprise development is the actual imple-mentation of the technology framework and specific applications that mirror the business architecture. By fusing technology architecture with the business architecture, enterprises can ensure that e-Enterprise applications reflect carefully designed and modeled processes at the same time that they leave the door open for change.

The fourth theme is that a reusable infrastructure of both busi-ness models and technology applications will allow you to recycle every piece of learning, time after time, and in as little time as pos-sible.

Nobody would undertake construction of a 100-story skyscraper today without first using computerized simulation tools to visualize and test every aspect of the structure. Every building ultimately con-sists of parts, materials, and systems. But vision and functionality are what makes it a great building.

Today, it is also possible to design a great enterprise this way. In doing so, you develop a series of business processes and technology components that are as reusable as the basic plans for elevator or elec-trical systems, which a building architect may use repeatedly with appropriate tweaking. For 40 or 50 years of systems development, we couldn't do this. Now the technology is here to enable repeatable, reusable business processes, because they ultimately are embedded in reusable software components.

Industry analyst META Group predicts that by 2001, most global companies "will use a 'software factory' model to implement new application systems, requiring developers to move from a 'craftsman' approach to a culture of assembly and reuse."[14]

In an e-Enterprise, this idea applies not only to technological implementation, but equally to business direction and planning. Fur-thermore, your repository of components and processes becomes more valuable all the time, as you populate it with objects that are more and more specific to your own business—even though all of the individual components may be off the shelf. When market conditions demand a change in your business model, you don't have to start from scratch. Instead, you start with known processes and components, do "what if" analysis, and put together your new business operating model in far less time than a competitor who doesn't know what you do.

This is the ultimate source of agility, which allows the enterprise to respond to real-time customer demand. Best of all, if you've won this way once, you're likely to win again and again.

PART 2

—

Business and Application Models

2 e-Application Models

NET FOR BUSINESS?

Not only has the basis of computing changed, the basis of competition has changed too.[1]
—Andrew S. Grove, Chairman, Intel

L et's start out by taking a moment to ask—and answer—the most obvious of "e" questions: why do companies that are already successful at selling their products via the more traditional distribution channels (retail locations, catalogs, television, and even the telephone) feel the need to sell their wares online? In short, what is the appeal of the Net?

First and foremost, the Net enables businesses to interact personally and directly with customers without incurring the overhead costs of building a larger sales force, opening new retail locations, or hiring and training new customer service representatives.

At first glance, this seems a bit absurd. How does the World Wide Web—largely just a repository of text and images—increase personal interaction? The answer lies in the capability of computers to gather, store, and transmit mountains of data in the blink of an eye. By always utilizing this information in real time, enterprises can focus on building personalized, long-term relationships with each and every customer, such as was done before the days of strip malls, superstores, and direct-mail catalogs. In many ways, this is a better way to do business. Let's pick a simple example to illustrate.

Say you want to read *A Tale of Two Cities*. Today, you'd probably just head down to the local branch of a national bookselling chain and buy a copy. Except for checking out at the register, you probably wouldn't need any assistance. With any luck, the process would be quick and easy, and in an hour you'd be settled into your favorite easy chair ready to begin reading.

If it were a hundred years ago, however, things might have been a bit different. First, you probably would have made your purchase at a local store owned by a proprietor who knew your name and had at least a rudimentary idea of your tastes and buying habits. He would have helped you select your book, and perhaps would have recommended one edition over another on account of, say, the excellent illustrations. He might have inquired whether your husband was enjoying the copy of *Moby Dick* he purchased last week. If so, he would probably recommend another selection for your husband when he was finished. Maybe, if you were a frequent, valued customer, he would give you a discount to show he appreciated your business. Eventually, you would pay, he would thank you for your business— again by name—and you would be off.

Superficially, the result is the same: the "you" of today and "you" of one hundred years ago both ended up with the book you wanted at (we assume) a reasonable price. There is, however, an important distinction. The "you" of today has been part of a transaction. The "you" of yesterday is part of a business relationship. What's the difference, you ask? "Transactions are the equivalent of buying coffee at a 7-Eleven," Peter G. W. Keen of *Computerworld* explains, "Relationships are much more: collaborating with a trusted financial adviser or having your hair cut by your favorite barber."[2]

How, then, do the Net and e-Enterprise facilitate business relationships rather than transactions? By accessing massive banks of customer information and buying histories, online businesses can recognize and provide custom services to each customer individually, the same way that local businesses did a century ago. Because of this "greased" information that moves invisibly across the Internet, even the largest enterprises can once again begin to focus on individual customers and provide services that build strong, long-lasting business relationships.

It's not difficult to see that although an efficient transaction may please the customer, it is these successful business relationships that are an infinitely more valuable commodity. The difference from the enterprise point-of-view is one of focusing on the product versus and focusing on the customer.

In successful businesses, the shift from product- to customer-orientation is well underway, and customer information and relationships are becoming absolutely critical to success. As Regis McKenna emphasizes in his 1997 book *Real Time*, what matters most is meeting customer needs according to their own expectations.[3]

For companies doing business in the twenty-first century, owning the customer—if possible the whole customer—is a keystone for a successful business relationship. Today, many retailers focus on owning the product and pushing it to market segments. In the next century, however, companies will position themselves to meet every buying necessity of valued customers, even if it means pulling offerings from unlimited numbers of suppliers to meet those customer needs. Through the Net, e-Enterprises will become aggregator business portals that collect products and data from multiple suppliers to offer a complete solution to customers and focus entirely upon individual relationships.

In fact, nearly every business of every size should take a careful look at how the Internet might improve their chance for success. In some cases, such as Barnes & Noble, which opened a virtual marketplace to compete with Amazon.com, the motivation for moving business online is obvious. In other cases, businesses have built new and exciting competitive advantages using the Net, even in markets that don't seem immediately suited to the Information Superhighway. For example, who would imagine that dry cleaning services—seemingly a bastion of the neighborhood retail business—could be transacted over the Internet? By taking orders over the Net and receiving and shipping clothes via Federal Express, however, that's exactly what New York City-based Village Tailors & Cleaners has begun to do.

If even the corner dry cleaning store is moving online, are there any businesses that can afford not to? Maybe the answer lies in a comment made recently by an Amazon.com executive, who was asked what the retailer would *not* sell. Her answer: cement. The shipping costs would be prohibitive, she explained.

What is it about the Net as a medium for buying and selling that makes it so attractive? First, the Net is a global market, and it's open for business 24 hours a day, 7 days a week, 365 days a year. The Net never goes dark.

This enables even local, family-owned businesses, such as a dry cleaner, to do business around the clock. Unlike employees, a Web site continues to deliver information on cleaning package deals, provides customer service, and even takes new orders for cleaning on Christmas morning. Customers rushing off on vacation the day after a holiday can arrange on the Net for their clothes to be hemmed and dry-cleaned while they are away, and Village Cleaners would have them ready and waiting upon their return.

Despite Amazon.com's reluctance, it isn't difficult to imagine a zealous contractor taking a break from College Football Bowl games on New Year's day to order cement—perhaps side-by-side with roofing tiles, nails, and work gloves—to prepare for the coming week.

In fact, he might not even have to get up off his couch—a difficult proposition after a holiday meal—because it's not just PCs that can connect to the Net. Right now, Microsoft's WebTV combines the Net with traditional television in such a way that enables couch potatoes to check their stock quotes *and* watch financial news at the same time.

In the near future, through the growth of technologies such as Sun Microsystems's Jini, almost any electronic device will be able to exchange information over the network. Take, for example, the family refrigerator. Electrolux has in fact already debuted its Screenfridge model with Internet access. Using the Screenfridge's built-in monitor, consumers can surf the Net, send and receive e-mail, and even place orders for groceries from online dry goods sellers such as NetGrocer. Forget scouring shelves of thousands of products looking for "red dot specials" or waiting in long lines to check out; grocery shoppers of the future won't even leave their kitchen—except perhaps to open the front door and sign for the FedEx box to receive their goods.

Whatever device customers use to connect to the Net, when they do get online they can be presented with service that is attentive, personal, and economical for businesses.

In the 1970s TV drama *The Waltons*, Ike Godsey owns and operates a general store where grocery goods are stored behind the counter, away from the reach of customers. When customers want a pound of sugar or a stick of candy, they must ask Ike to collect the items for them. Meanwhile, other customers wait their turn until they can read off their grocery list and have Ike dutifully run after all the items.

Ike's general store is an outstanding example of the limits imposed on one-to-one service in the physical world. Ike's service to his patrons is personal to be sure, but he is unable to serve more than one customer at a time without hiring more help. Consequently, customer service comes at a high cost for Ike and ironically his customers too; although they receive one-to-one attention, they must dutifully wait to be served.

The Internet model for one-to-one service rips out the counter between Ike's goods and his customers, allowing shoppers to select goods themselves and check out with ease. This customer self-service model empowers consumers with more control than ever over the buying process. At the same time, it enables enterprises to reduce customer care expenditures.

Internet banking pioneer Security First National Bank gives customers direct control over their checking accounts, permitting them to issue stop-payment requests and see digital images of canceled checks. By eliminating the middleman through customer self-service, Security First National Bank is able to reduce costs and pass savings directly on to consumers.

If doing business online is this easy, one might be tempted to conclude that enterprises that have won in conventional marketplaces will simply move online and begin to win in cyberspace as well. However, being successful on the Net requires enterprise-wide knowledge of unique business characteristics and technology drivers.

Successful e-Enterprise initiatives must include the capability to market, demonstrate, and configure products and services, serve as negotiator and settler of transactions, and integrate real-time information from the Net into the existing back-office systems of both the enterprise itself and all its trading partners. Often these new requirements brought on by the Internet shake the foundations of even top business giants whose position in conventional marketplaces seemed untouchable.

Let's take, for example, Wal-Mart Stores. As the 1999 holiday season approached, Wal-Mart began to move frantically ahead with plans to expand its Web site and provide competition for online "e-Tailers" such as Amazon.com and eToys.

In the conventional marketplace, Wal-Mart's incredible logistics brilliance had earned its position as the No. 1 retailer in the United States. Online, however, conventional logistics designed to deliver bulk goods to a network of large stores don't play as important a role, and Wal-Mart began to worry that it was falling behind.

Instead of risking a disappointing holiday season performance from its Web site, the Arkansas retailer looked for outside help from an e-Application expert, Federated Department Stores' Fingerhut Companies, to help fulfill its orders from the Net. Similarly, it decided to take advantage of bookseller Books-A-Million's experience online to handle its book sales.

Clearly, Wal-Mart's conventional business practices weren't suited to the Net. Rather than rely on its conventional—and up until now successful—logistics system, the retailer wisely chose to tap a business partner adept at providing services more tailored for Net-based retailing. Instead of building an online bookstore from scratch, Wal-Mart incorporated the experience and expertise of a seasoned e-Tailer into its Web presence. On the Net, conventional best-practices don't always lead to success, and smart companies must be flexible and innovative to engineer new business models to tap into co-opetitive partners in order to complement their existing business models and leverage their core competencies as they move toward the virtual corporation.

Even more than in conventional marketplaces, a moment's delay online can place an enterprise at a significant disadvantage in its market. Ironically, one important source for this hyper-competitive business environment is the very reason many businesses move to the Net in the first place: the death of distance.

By breaking down boundaries of time and space, the Net enables potential customers and business partners across the globe to do business as though they were located next door. At the same time, it exposes even local businesses to cutthroat competition from around the world.

To a large degree it is this fact that makes the Net so chaotic. Entry barriers are low enough that nearly anyone can jump them and establish an online presence with the creation of a simple Web site. A dry cleaner next door and the one on the other side of the city are equal competitors on the Web, differentiated only by the quality and price of their services and their ability to market to their customers. In the most simplistic terms, if even a single competitor gains a competitive advantage, the entire industry must evolve immediately or die out. This notion of competitive advantage must be considered in terms of mindshare, marketshare, and process efficiency.

Granted, there are exceptions to the maxim that the Net makes geography irrelevant. Village Tailors & Cleaners in New York City, for example, isn't very likely to do much business with overseas customers—the cost of shipping dry-cleaned clothes internationally makes the proposition silly. Conversely, it's not likely to lose business to other dry cleaners in Sri Lanka or Madagascar.

On the flip side of this phenomenon, e-Enterprise enables companies to compete in geographic areas they wouldn't have even considered in the past.

Let's consider the wholesale-distribution industry. To reach markets across the nation, distributors of similar products often cooperate to extend their geographic strongholds. By utilizing information technology to communicate and appear as one to customers, these distributors can expand their reach from disjointed regional markets bounded by constraints of land, air, and sea shipping to a national or even global market bound only by their ability to coordinate and cooperate with business partners.

Although the initial barriers to creating a global Net business model can be high, companies are ultimately finding that an investment in e-Enterprise—if done right—will radically reduce the cost of providing goods and services and provide excellent ROI. Without bricks-and-mortar stores, the cost of maintaining a physical inventory for walk-in customers becomes superfluous. Instead, businesses can coordinate their supply and logistics to furnish merchandise on a just-in-time basis.

Michael Dell, in his bestseller *Direct from Dell: Strategies That Revolutionized an Industry*, explains how his computer company saves money by minimizing the time it holds products. "Inventory velocity has become a passion for us," he writes. "In 1993, we had $2.9 billion in sales and $220 million in inventory. Four years later, we posted $12.3 billion in sales and had inventory of $233 million. We're now down to less than eight days of inventory and we're starting to measure it in hours instead of days."[4]

Success on the Net isn't just about optimization and execution, however. The Net and the World Wide Web in particular offer unique advantages that enable e-Enterprises to market their wares like never before.

In the B-to-C market, Volkswagen and Amazon.com are excellent examples. By enabling customers to build a virtual dream car on its Web site (photos of a particular model change to reflect a visitor's choice of an exterior color, and features and add-ons can be added and subtracted at will), Volkswagen of America adds a measure of interactivity to the buying process. At Amazon.com, customers are accustomed to reading reviews—good, bad, and indifferent—of books, music, and movies by fellow patrons. Of course, they also have the opportunity to submit their own reviews. In addition to making the site more interesting—and taking some of the burden off the shoulders of Amazon's own literary review staff—this builds a sense of community among consumers with common interests, and fosters repeat buying and long-term business relationships.

This move towards mass-customization is vital for building effective Business-to-Consumer (B-to-C) marketplaces. Music e-Tailer CDNOW, for example, recommends CDs based on past purchases in an area of its site called "My CDNOW." It also permits users to build a gift registry, which friends and relatives can access by entering the user's e-mail address or simply clicking on a Web address provided to them. By doing so, CDNOW goes beyond the simple presentation of a static buying environment. Instead, it customizes its storefront for every visitor.

As e-Applications become increasingly sophisticated, the importance of mass-customization will continue to grow in customer-centric companies. Furthermore, the benefits of this movement have proven to self-replicate as more and more information is gleaned from individual buying behaviors in subsequent transactions. Databanks of individual customer information and buying habits enable marketers to develop a complete picture of each and every individual customer in order to target them for cross-selling.

In addition, marketers can track *biographics*, or temporal and long-term interests of individuals, to paint a complete picture of their habits as consumers. Of course, how companies use the data they have gathered can also impact their success in e-Space and beyond. Privacy issues are already a concern among consumers, and companies have both an ethical and financial obligation to responsibly use that data in order to maintain the trust and loyalty of their customers.

In the Business-to-Business (B-to-B) arena, companies have begun engaging the Net to enable buying and selling enhancements such as sophisticated product configurators, Computer-Aided Design (CAD) systems that enable engineers to collaborate on the product design process, and mediated discussion boards and branches that enable collaborative problem solving. Important information such as product specifications, bills-of-material, and production schedules can be shared across enterprise boundaries to streamline next generation value chains. The end result of these initiatives is an enriched buying/selling experience for enterprise users that contributes to the growth of long-term, mutually advantageous business-to-business relationships.

Branding in the virtual world is as important as it is in traditional business. Because of this, it is essential that companies create a branding strategy as part of their overall move into e-Enterprise. Quality and reliability are proven critical factors for the creation of brand awareness for bricks-and-mortar companies, and the same is true for the Internet. Cheaper hand tools may be available on the Internet, but skittish consumers may prefer to buy theirs online from Sears—if only because they know that a local store is nearby in case a problem occurs during the transaction. For the cheaper tool e-Tailer, some hard lessons may be quickly learned: The loyalty and trust of the consumer must still be earned in the virtual economy. Stories of bad experiences can spread quickly among consumers over the Net, throwing a monkey wrench into the most well laid e-Tailing plans.

In the past, some had argued that the Net is primarily the domain of anti-social teenagers, dyed-in-the-wool computer geeks, and science fiction fans, and that as such it should be approached cautiously as a medium for large-scale commerce. While this may have been a valid argument at one point, today the rapidly changing demographics of Internet users make a compelling case for enterprises to move their business online.

In its earliest days, Internet users were overridingly young, male, educated, and had a median income that was about 50 percent higher than the general U.S. population. More recently, however, the average Net surfer has begun to change. Women are venturing online in ever-increasing numbers and older Americans are expected to jump on the Net in the next great demographic shift.

As a result of these shifts, enterprises with traditionally non-Net demographics have begun to meet with success in cyberspace. The non-profit sector, for example, has begun using the Net to make it easier for donors to contribute to their causes as the Web's demographics shift to align with many of their long-time support bases. According to Michael Johnston, president of Hewitt and Johnston Consultants, a communications and fund-raising consulting firm specializing in the Internet and the non-profit sector, older women will continue to use the Internet in greater numbers and begin to feel comfortable with making online donations.

As important as age, income, race, and gender information are to the Internet merchant, bandwidth demographics, the demographics of which consumers have high-speed versus low-speed access to the Internet, will remain significant in the near term until high-speed phone and cable TV access is available to a majority of U.S. consumers. B-to-C e-Applications must be designed for users with slow modems. Not surprisingly, there's little tolerance for the delays often required to load multimedia files and large Java applets. Consumers with slow connections tend to abandon download-intensive sites and take their business elsewhere.

To avoid this phenomenon, Web sites must be kept simple and snappy, while still providing a graphical environment that is visually attractive and holds visitors' interest. Because business users often have access to higher speed connections at work, the bandwidth issue is much less of a concern for B-to-B merchants.

Just as people return time and time again to the same physical communities to build and retain relationships with neighbors, so do Net surfers tend to return to Internet sites that successfully build common community interest. Internet marketers have learned to leverage this tendency to build traffic at commerce sites and market goods and services to an audience of likely buyers.

Even when not actually buying books or music, Amazon.com customers often visit the company's site to review recent purchases, browse new selections, and get recommendations from their online peers. By developing a community atmosphere, this B-to-C portal cultivates loyal, longtime customers. Even though services such as free e-mail and discussion threads don't contribute directly to generating revenue, Amazon hopes that by encouraging customers to spend large amounts of time at their site they will increase impulse buying. In order to augment the services of their commerce-oriented site, Amazon.com is attempting to build an online community of users, a ready-made audience of customers whose attention is controlled by the e-Enterprise.

CNET, a network of World Wide Web destinations devoted to providing industry information to computer users and IT professionals, has taken quite an opposite approach. Whereas Amazon.com was established as a marketplace that became a community, CNET was originally developed as a community and later became a marketplace. Recognizing that many of its millions of viewers are regular purchasers of computer hardware and software, CNET recently introduced "Tech Auctions" that both generate revenue and encourage IT managers and computer enthusiasts to make CNET their home-away-from-home on the Web.

This is an example of an important trend in building e-Enterprises. Rather than focusing on providing narrow, specialized products to consumers, many e-Marketers are aiming to be *integrators* of complete customer needs.

In the e-Enterprise world, it's not enough for a bank to provide only mortgage loans; successful lending institutions in the digital economy will position loans as the drawing force and then add value by providing other goods and services—perhaps mortgage insurance and property inspections—that offer a complete solution.

In many cases, these related offerings are provided cooperatively by enterprises not involved in the initial transaction. In the example above, a local bank might cooperate with an insurance agency and network of local contractors to complete the solution. By acting as an aggregator of goods and services from multiple suppliers, the initial seller becomes a *cybermediary*.

The cybermediary's role, however, doesn't necessarily end when a consumer enters an order. With the exception of software and other intellectual property goods that can be downloaded over the Net, product delivery time and convenience play an important role in customer satisfaction. There is a false but widely held view that simply designing a cool Web site to hawk products and take orders will lead to global distribution success. We should consider that this is just part of the equation. What matters as much is the ability of the company to physically move the product to the customer. How the company does this is through a series of physical and electronic processes that can be reengineered for greater efficiency and gains in productivity. To achieve these gains, these processes should be revamped to include those that occur inside the organization as well as those that occur in its supplier/vendor relationships outside of the organization.

A somewhat more theoretical advantage of doing business on the Net is the promise of flexible pricing models. What if Stephen King's latest bestseller on Amazon.com or Barnes & Noble were priced according to demand? The $27.95 hardback might be priced at $16.95 in the middle of the night, when fewer people are buying books online. But the price might be $27.95—list price—during the network TV airing of a King mini-series, when millions of book readers head to the Net to buy his latest tome.

What if every online market behaved like the stock market? The Net makes such dynamic pricing possible by enabling corporations and consumers to examine costs and market demand in real-time. Some even go so far as to predict that the rise of the Net will bring about the death of fixed pricing. Regardless of the extent to which it is adopted, however, dynamic pricing still will be only one element of a buying decision: availability, perceived quality and service remain important factors in any customer decision.

The promises for Internet commerce are astounding, and few dare to predict anything but wild success for business online. However, before businesses move toward e-Enterprises, certain important barriers must first be overcome.

Tilburg University's Infolab in The Netherlands points out that e-Enterprise aims to support companies' complete external business processes, including the information stage (electronic marketing, networking), negotiation stage (electronic markets), fulfillment (order processing, electronic payment), and the satisfaction stage (after-sales support).

The broad range of this vision is without a doubt the strongest argument in favor of an aggressive e-Enterprise strategy. At the same time, however, according to Infolab the primary sources of most barriers to e-Enterprise success include:

- closed, self-contained markets that cannot use each other's services;

- incompatible frameworks that cannot interoperate or build upon each other;

- a bewildering collection of security and payment protocols; and

- the use of inadequate techniques to model business requirements and enterprise policies.[5]

To harness the many benefits of doing business on the Net while avoiding pitfalls, enterprises should aim to develop an e-Enterprise strategy that maximizes business return in the present while providing enough flexibility to adjust to constantly evolving and maturing marketplace dynamics.

Since at its core, moving toward an e-Enterprise is a strategic business issue rather than solely a technology decision, it makes sense that the move to the digital economy is guided primarily by business demands and goals. Forward-thinking enterprises recognize that the key to success is building an e-Enterprise model that is defined by the dynamics of both business and technology architecture, which will be discussed in detail in later chapters.

INTER-ORGANIZATIONAL BUSINESS PROCESSES

As was discussed in Chapter 1, the core of the e-Enterprise is a backbone of inter-organizational business processes. Because by definition an e-Enterprise is modeled with these electronic processes, a successful platform for e-Enterprise applications must involve not only customers and suppliers, but also internal processes, employees, and back-office functions, as well as external partners.

Processes that cross enterprise boundaries to include external stakeholders are referred to as inter-organizational processes. It is by engineering and re-engineering these external processes to integrate seamlessly with the internal processes and the external-facing processes of other stakeholders that e-Applications provide the most tangible benefits to the enterprise. Figure 2.1 illustrates this integration of inter-organizational, internal, and business partner processes:

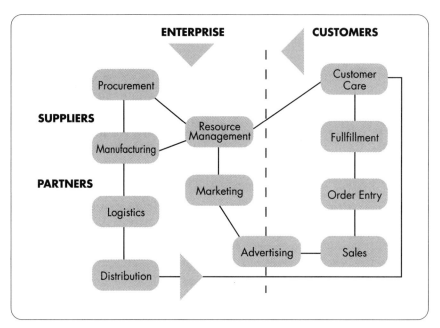

FIGURE 2.1

To demonstrate the role that inter-organizational processes play in an e-Enterprise, let's examine and compare the B-to-B and B-to-C purchasing processes.

B-to-C Purchasing Processes

In a B-to-C buying environment, individual consumers purchase goods from a virtual marketplace. Because the actions of the buyer drive the process, we look at the procedure from the buyer's point of view. Typically, the buying process consists of four phases: *product identification*, *catalog search*, *product comparison*, and *purchase*. While this is the typical process for most consumers, the Net almost encourages a random sequence through these steps whereby the customer may deviate from this sequence and still acquire the goods that he or she seeks.

The process begins with the *product identification* phase as the consumer instigates a search for a product or service that interests him.

Oftentimes, consumers do not have a clear idea of exactly what they are looking for from the get-go, and so they rely on advertising, marketing promotions, and browsing particular product classifications to determine an appropriate purchase. During this stage of the buying process, one-to-one marketing techniques and advertising are absolutely essential.

Once individual consumers have determined what type of good they wish to buy, the *catalog search* phase begins. Typically, this involves the buyer locating potential candidates for purchase in supplier catalogs or retail outlets. For some purchases—as in the case of choosing a particular brand of cereal—it is likely that the consumer will search only one catalog or store for products. In other cases—such as purchasing a new car—they are likely to be interested in products from a wide variety of suppliers, each with its own retail channel.

Eventually, the consumer will narrow his or her choices down to a short list of candidates and the *product comparison* phase begins. At this point, the buyer examines each candidate in some detail, and compares the features, price, and additional information such as warranty detail in order to select a final product. Consumers also often indicate that a total solution is a key asset for customer satisfaction and product selection.

Finally, the consumer is ready to make a *purchase*. Typically, the buyer pays with cash, a personal check, or a credit card and receives a receipt for purchase along with the product.

The process is easily illustrated with a brief case study. Imagine, for example, you are looking to purchase a new computer. When your product search begins, you may know only that you want a large hard drive, DVD-drive, and a relatively fast processor. Probably, you also have some idea of the price range you are willing to consider. To begin your product search, you would likely gather information from multiple vendors about memory configuration options, monitor sizes, software bundles available, pricing, multiple brand options, and special advertised promotions. You might consult PC manufacturer product information pages online, speak with friends who have recently made computer purchases, consult specialized publications such as *PC Week* or *PC World* for product reviews and comparisons, and examine advertisements for especially good deals.

Eventually, you would narrow your search to a couple of options. You would then need to determine what retailer offered the best price for each configuration, which features you were willing to pay for, and what type of bundled services you would choose. You might call your local electronics wholesaler, visit a specialty computer store, surf through online computer marketplaces, or even contact manufacturers themselves if they support a direct sales model. At this stage, you would be influenced by brand, customer service, and reliability reputation.

Ultimately, you would make a decision about which product at which price best suits your need. To make the purchase you would supply a credit card number and in return would receive some type of order confirmation. Eventually, your PC would arrive at your home—assuming you hadn't picked it up directly from a retail outlet—and the purchase would be complete.

B-to-B Purchasing Processes

The B-to-B buying process is predictably quite different than in consumer marketplaces. B-to-B procurement is typically divided into four phases: *requisitioning, request for quote, purchase order generation*, and *payment processing*.

B-to-B procurement begins with the *requisitioning* phase, where an employee in the purchasing department creates a requisition for materials they would like to purchase. Depending on departmental and corporate policies, the requisition may be subject to an internal approval process based on total cost, the type of goods ordered, or the profile of the purchaser. Larger corporations may also choose to engage in collaborative requisitioning, where buyers from different departments or geographic locations combine their purchasing efforts to obtain volume or frequency of purchase discounts.

Once a requisition has been approved, the process enters the *request for quote* phase, where the purchasing department allows potential suppliers to generate quotes to fulfill the requisition. Oftentimes, this stage includes a great deal of collaboration among suppliers hoping to win the contract. For example, if a large manufacturing corporation were to order 10,000 iron rivets for a new machine, two smaller rivet-producers could agree to supply 3,000 and 7,000 rivets respectively, and would thus be able to place bids for contracts that otherwise would be well out of their reach.

Many firms engage in some sort of bidding and auctioning to determine the most favorable quote delivered by suppliers. Other special pricing considerations include individually negotiated pricing for particular enterprises, and real-time, dynamic pricing of commodity goods.

Once the prospective buyer has settled on a particular supplier quote, the *purchase order generation* process begins. Typically, this is matched up with another, final approval process. Upon receiving the appropriate approval, the PO is processed and suppliers are notified to begin to fulfill the order.

Finally, payment is processed in the form of a corporate P-Card, Smart Card, EDI transaction, or simply a corporate check. When payment is made, the transaction is recorded in the financial/accounting systems of both the purchasing and supplying enterprises, and the order is completed.

FROM PROCESSES TO E-APPLICATIONS

Once inter-organizational processes have been defined and modeled in some detail, developers can build e-Applications that support particular processes. You will recall from the previous section that the B-to-C purchasing process was defined as consisting of four broad phases: *product identification, catalog search, product comparison,* and *purchase,* while B-to-B purchasing consists of *requisitioning, request for quote, purchase order generation,* and *payment processing.* This section provides two examples of application models that can be developed in the B-to-C and B-to-B areas (see Figure 2.2).

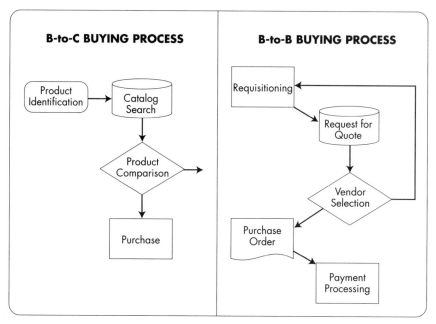

FIGURE 2.2

Chapters 3 and 4 will discuss these models in much more detail to provide an overall understanding of e-Application-driven e-Enterprises.

B-to-C e-Procurement

In keeping with this process-orientated definition of purchasing, B-to-C applications that support the consumer buying process would have to address and provide functionality consistent with these phases.

The *product identification* phase of a B-to-C purchasing application often involves a combination of online advertising and one-to-one marketing in virtual marketplaces. On the Net, advertising opportunities include banner ads on Web sites as well as inclusion in important content aggregation sites such as search engines, aggregator portals, and industry-specific content sites. According to the *eAdvertising Report* by e-Marketer, U.S. companies spent $1.5 billion on

Internet advertising in 1998. The research firm also estimates that this figure will increase to $8.9 billion by 2002.[6]

Despite these varied opportunities for advertising and marketing online, however, Internet sellers still must advertise in the physical world to succeed. Companies wishing to develop traffic at branded Web sites will find it necessary to continue to allocate most of their advertising budgets to traditional media such as television, radio, magazines, and newspapers rather than heavy concentration on Internet banner advertising and hyperlinks with the goal of creating awareness of their brand Web sites. Only after this awareness has been created in the marketplace will consumers begin to show up at the site and the company can begin interacting directly with the consumers.

Once advertising has driven traffic to virtual marketplaces, one-to-one marketing and content personalization become key factors. Frequently, successful marketing promotions aim to encourage buyers to not only make individual purchases, but also develop long-term business relationships with e-Tailers.

Focusing on current—and profitable—customers is an often underappreciated aspect of online marketing. Pareto's Law, also known as the "80/20 rule" describes the belief that 80 percent of profits come from 20 percent of the customers. Michael Meltzer, NCR Corp.'s director for financial services consulting, believes that too often this rule is ignored. "In the past, it was always easier to attempt to 'poach' your competitors' customers," he says. "However, studies have shown that companies spend five times more money on acquiring new customers as they do on retaining those they already have. Further studies demonstrated that as a customer relationship with a company lengthens, profits rise. And not just a little," Meltzer continues. "Companies can boost profits by 100 percent by retaining just 5 percent more of their customers."[7]

Cambridge Technology Partners also emphasizes the dividend that can be achieved by cultivating loyalty among the existing customer base and fostering increased spending and new customer referrals. Of course, this doesn't imply that the other 80 percent of consumers who visit virtual marketplaces should be ignored.

To provide personalized service that improves over time, e-Tailers often rely on individually targeted product promotions and advertisements for repeat customers. If possible, most retailers try to customize content from the very beginning by tracking a consumer's browsing and customizing content to fit his or her suspected tastes. Observing shopping patterns and then replicating them within the application makes a Web site easy to navigate—and brings back consumers for repeat business.

The *catalog search* process in a B-to-C purchasing application is not surprisingly focused on the product catalog itself. Because it is the primary repository for product and service offerings, the virtual custom catalog is an essential component of any e-Application system that hopes to provide goods and services to either consumers or other businesses. Whether it is hosted by the buyer, supplier, or an independent trading network, most catalogs include products and services with pre-negotiated prices from multiple vendors.

On the whole, B-to-C catalogs tend to be fairly straightforward. Consumers, for the most part, want virtual catalogs they can easily navigate and search, enabling them to browse specific areas they choose. If possible, most retailers try to customize content from the very beginning by tracking a consumer's browsing and generating content to fit their suspected tastes.

Observing these individual shopping patterns and then replicating them within the application makes a Web site easy to navigate—and brings back consumers for repeat business. However, requiring customers to register as a user and provide personal details before they can even browse product selections often drives consumers away and reduces the chance for random, impulse buying. At Amazon.com, for example, consumers are deliberately told that they don't need to register before making a purchase.

Virtual catalogs don't just carry the latest widgets. They also can offer services and other product information. For example, the U.S. General Services Administration's procurement catalog lists professional services like graphic designers, architects, and IT consultants; it includes their skills, experience, and pay rates.

When the *catalog search* phase crosses into the *product comparison* phase, features that enable consumers to navigate catalogs, compare similar offerings, and make product selections become essential. In some vertical markets, complex catalogs that also allow advanced searching abilities, collaborative filtering, and other tools are necessary.

The most complex catalogs dynamically generate catalog content from a collection of multiple supplier catalogs in order to facilitate and automate the comparison process. In many cases, each separate supplier catalog exists in a proprietary data format. Fortunately, new industry standards such as extensible markup language (XML) permit users to comparison shop and seamlessly integrate information from multiple data sources in order to compare offerings from multiple original suppliers.

The best virtual catalogs are also flexible, permitting companies to change their catalog sources as the market shifts and they begin doing business with new and different suppliers or begin to cater to a customer base with different interests.

When the customer is finally ready to make a *purchase*, the c-Application must provide authentication and encryption services to ensure that the transaction is confidential and accurate. The seller must also be prepared to accept some form of online credit, such as a credit card or cybercash. Once an order is placed, details about individual product preference and browsing habits can be stored under a personal profile, ensuring that the consumer's next shopping experience has a one-to-one feel.

Advanced virtual marketplaces can also be connected directly to back-office legacy applications and data sources in order to automate the vendor's fulfillment process and trigger third-party service providers. In consumer-focused e-Tailing environments, this link between a B-to-C front-end that provides goods and services to consumers and back-office systems that operate in a B-to-B environment illustrates an important component of complete e-Enterprise development: the integration of B-to-B and B-to-C, a subject that is tackled later on in this chapter.

Because many purchases also require at least some customer service in the post-purchase phase, many B-to-C applications hand consumer and purchase data off to a customer care/customer management application before completing the transaction and ending the purchasing process.

B-to-B e-Procurement

The B-to-B procurement/purchasing process tends to translate into applications that are more complex and tightly integrated with internal corporate systems than B-to-C initiatives. In the interest of brevity, let's review a brief description of a potential B-to-B procurement application.

The first phase of B-to-B purchasing, *requisitioning*, often consists of an online form containing product information, quantity, and cost that is filled out by the buyer and submitted over the Net for requisition approval. First, the application must determine the buyer's purchasing privileges and limitations based on a role-based profiling component. If requisition approval is required, a workflow component routes the requisition in the form of an e-mail message, fax, or pager message to the appropriate manager. When approval is received, the requisition is routed to the purchasing department—again in the form of an e-mail, fax, or page—and the appropriate purchasing agent begins the process of receiving quotes.

The *request for quote* phase begins when the purchasing agent notifies potential suppliers that the enterprise is interested in making a purchase of specific goods in specific quantities at an approximate price. Typically, this information, or *request for quote*, is posted at a message board in an online community of buyers and suppliers, or delivered to pre-identified suppliers through e-mail or fax.

Potential suppliers can then immediately begin to place bids for the newly posted RFQ at online bid-boards. Supplier collaboration can be facilitated through private bid-board branches as well as communication techniques such as online chat, instant messaging, and e-mail. When a contender is prepared to submit a bid, the contender can either post it in a private page on the Net or deliver it securely through e-mail or fax to the purchasing manager.

Upon closing bidding, the purchasing manager must choose a supplier to fulfill the purchase in order to begin the next phase of B-to-B procurement, *PO generation*. In simple auction applications, where the lowest price wins, this is an easy step. In more complex requisitions, however, where delivery time, volume discounts, prenegotiated markdowns with particular suppliers, and logistic expenses must be taken into account, picking the right quote can be a difficult process.

Luckily, through the integration of disparate bid information through a data translation component, the process of weighing advantages and disadvantages of each option can be automated, and the buyer can select a supplier in a relatively short time.

As soon as the chosen supplier has been notified—again through e-mail, fax, or a pager message—the supplier can begin to fulfill the order. Ideally, this happens automatically when the winning bid notification triggers events across the value chain of the supplier's internal inventory and logistics systems that begin the shipment of the order. If the supply were to run low, the application would automatically detect it, and an electronic message would be sent indicating that inventory should be delivered to the distribution center as soon as possible.

Finally, the application begins the *payment processing* portion of the transaction. The data transformation component transmits payment information in the form of corporate P-Card or smart card information, or an EDI transaction to the supplier in a format customized to integrate with internal supplier accounting systems. Simultaneously, the application adjusts internal buyer systems to record the transaction.

As more and more of these processes begin to be automated and integrated across enterprise boundaries in real-time, corporations will begin to do business almost entirely in the virtual world. In essence, the members of the value chain become virtual companies that think and react as one entity and communicate around the clock in real-time. The result is the deconstruction of the linear value chain into dynamic value grids that provide the latest, up-to-date information to all participants and optimize the transaction of goods and services between partners from suppliers of raw materials to end customers.

E-APPLICATION MODELS

When people talk about Internet commerce, they're usually referring to B-to-C commerce Web sites such as Amazon.com, eBay, and CDNOW. This isn't surprising, because purchasing a new bestseller, a unique piece of memorabilia, or a collection of rare CDs is a far more interesting topic of conversation than say procuring 100,000 paper-clips at a really great price.

It's not surprising then, that consumer *virtual marketplace* initia-tives have in many ways been the public face of the e-Revolution. In addition to being high profile, they are accessible to a wide audi-ence and are far more likely to create a buzz among non-technical users than B-to-B applications. The announcement that a Fortune 500 company such as Dell uses the Internet to reduce inventory to a couple of days' supply, elicits barely a yawn from all but die-hard industry gurus. When a familiar and well-respected name such as Wal-Mart shifts millions of dollars and important resources to selling on the Net, however, it provides a clear sign to the general public that B-to-B e-Applications are exploding.

The vast majority of B-to-C e-Application initiatives are e-Tailers and consumer portals that aim to add value to businesses and con-sumers by breaking down barriers caused by time, distance, and form.

In a conventional marketplace, buyers and sellers are restricted by regular hours of business. Purchases can be made only when a seller and buyer can interact directly, and companies that are not "open for business" when the consumer is ready to make a purchase often lose out to a competitor. Similarly, a seller and buyer must meet face to face to conduct the transaction. This places obvious geographical restrictions on potential sales. The transaction is also limited by form, in that a physical infrastructure must be in place for the transaction to occur. An obvious example is that a retailer must have retail space of some kind, must stock an inventory of goods that are attractive to buyers at any given time, and must have a particular good to exchange with a customer upon a transaction.

On the Internet, however, the barriers of time, distance, and form are broken down, and businesses are able to transact goods and serv-ices 24 hours a day, 7 days a week, 365 days a year with consumers all over the world. In certain cases it is possible to even deliver the product over the network, and convert a physical good (CDs, pack-aged software, a newspaper) to a virtual good (MP3 audio, download-able software, information in HTML format).

By lowering these barriers, the Internet enables businesses to concentrate on building customer relationships and providing valuable goods and services rather than focusing on the logistical demands of making a transaction. A successful e-Tailer lowers seller costs at the same time that it enables one-to-one marketing to build customer loyalty and eventually long-term customer-enterprise relationships.

B-to-C e-Applications can reduce the cost of selling goods and services to contribute directly to the enterprise bottom line. For example, empowering consumers with customer self-service reduces customer service costs and improves the efficiency of the buying process. Similarly, the importance of customer support centers, which repeatedly answer the same questions over the telephone, can be reduced as help functions are moved to the Web. Answers to frequently asked questions are also posted online, and consumers can use e-mail to ask specific questions not covered in FAQs.

The crown jewel of most B-to-C virtual marketplaces, however, is the ability to build individual, personal relationships with customers on a massive scale. According to Don Peppers and Martha Rogers, Ph.D., this one-to-one revolution will enable marketers to "communicate directly *with* customers, individually, rather than shouting *at* them in groups."[8] The result is customers who feel that the enterprise has taken a personal stake in their satisfaction.

Online, this can mean as little as greeting customers by name as they enter the site and as much as tracking customer behavior and preferences in order to present completely customized interfaces and content. Yahoo, for example, allows consumers to customize their personal "My Yahoo!" pages with favorite sports team scores, stock prices, local weather, and other customizable data.

One-to-one marketing also enables retailers to target customers for individual promotions and super-targeted marketing campaigns that increase dramatically the instance of impulse buying.

Often, this personalized attention encourages customers to return to the site for information and interaction with other online community members even when they don't intend to make a purchase. When content in a virtual marketplace is focused on a particular type of product or service—say healthcare, bidding and auctioning, or Electronic Bill

Payment (EBP)—e-Tailers often choose to extend the marketplace's functionality in order to position the site as an informative and useful destination as well as a transaction-orientated marketplace.

The ultimate evolution of such a community-based marketplace is a complete consumer portal that attracts customers with engaging content and well-organized links to related destination sites. While viewers peruse information, the e-Tailer can target potential consumers with one-to-one marketing campaigns based on personal profiles, buying history, or surfing patterns.

Take, for example, a healthcare destination site. When a consumer chooses to read the latest article from a scholarly journal on migraine headaches, an application could extrapolate that the reader would be a favorable target for a product promotion advocating extra-strength painkillers. This type of intelligent, one-to-one marketing campaign proves quite effective in transforming simple content viewers to active consumers.

In the B-to-B arena, however, buyers have different priorities. Business professionals spending their companies' money want to know how a purchase will add to the bottom line. They are less concerned with being identified as a special, unique customer as with the extent of the savings it can achieve.

According to Forrester Research, U.S. electronic business-to-business transactions are projected to rise from $43 billion in 1998 to an astounding $1.3 trillion (or over 9 percent of total U.S. business sales) by 2003. In addition to the computer and electronics industries—which already have a strong sales presence on the Internet—the aerospace and defense, petrochemicals, utilities, and motor vehicle industries are predicted by Forrester to lead Internet-based sales by this time.

"Industry adoption of Internet commerce will be driven by the network effect, in which the value of participating increases dramatically as more and more companies join in" explains Forrester. "Internet trading initiatives generally start small, as early adopters use their industry clout to pull suppliers and customers online. Once these companies realize the efficiencies of Internet trading, they will persuade their business partners to join them online."

The four categories of B-to-B applications—*virtual marketplaces, procurement/resource management, extended value chain,* and *customer care*—are quite different from B-to-C commerce applications.

The ultimate goal of a B-to-B *virtual marketplace* is the same as it is in the B-to-C area: sell goods and services. That, however, is where the similarities end.

Marketing to business professionals in a *virtual marketplace* requires more than simply providing a means for obtaining information, placing orders, checking on the status of orders, and getting help, according to Patricia Seybold, author of *Customers.com: How to Create a Profitable Business Strategy for the Internet and Beyond.* "To win over business customers, you need to understand exactly where your product fits within customers' business day (or night!), how they need to use it, and how you can make it easier for them to do so," writes Seybold.[9] Her key ingredients for marketing to business customers include:

- Develop a deep understanding of how your customers do their jobs.

- Refine your business processes continuously to make it easier for your customers to do their jobs.

- Give customers direct access to your inventory.

- Give customers the ammunition and tools they need to make purchasing decisions.

- Prepare bills the way your customers need them.

- Make it easy for your customers to satisfy their customers.

Besides simply purchasing finished goods at fixed prices, B-to-B *virtual marketplaces* enable companies to turn to online auctions to procure custom-made parts, near-commodity coal and steel, and other specialty products while driving down prices and lowering overhead costs.

Unlike in conventional auctions, however, where the seller is bound to transact with the highest offer, in a reverse auction companies aren't contractually obligated to accept the lowest bid, but can instead evaluate the lowest bidders in terms of quality, trust, and other decision-making factors before awarding the sale. Companies like Freemarkets Online advocate using their products and services for substantial corporate purchasing savings in both cost and time. Freemarkets Online is an example of a partner sourcing model where organizations can partner with one another to take advantage of e-Applications and e-Facilities.

Procurement/Resource management applications aim to streamline the procurement process for non-production as well as production goods and services. They provide a framework for establishing strong supply-side trading relationships in the dynamic value chain while maintaining the company-specific purchasing processes that provide unique value to the individual enterprise.

The heart of *procurement/resource management* has traditionally been Maintenance, Repair, and Operations (MRO) Procurement. Today, many companies have successfully implemented MRO Procurement applications to reduce the cost of purchasing non-production materials. A successful example of such an installation is General Electric's use of its Trading Process Network (TPN) to automate the purchase of over $1 billion in supplies in 1997. By 2000, General Electric expects to inflate this figure to over $5 billion in procurement purchases.

Procurement/Resource management applications, however, have the potential to affect the bottom line in a far broader scope than simply streamlining MRO purchasing. In Global 2000 companies, for example, 35 percent of expenditures are earmarked for the types of non-production goods and services that are streamlined by an MRO procurement applications. Clearly, this represents a significant opportunity to automate procurement and reduce costs. An additional 22 percent of expenditures, however, are devoted to production materials and general outside procurement. Combined, a total of 57 percent of expenditures are devoted to external procurement, a far greater opportunity to reduce the outflow of corporate cash than the automation of MRO procurement alone.[10]

Extended value chain applications seek to extend the functionality of traditional Supply Chain Management (SCM) applications by integrating customer demand planning, supplier supply planning, and inbound/outbound logistical constraints to optimize performance and profits. In a typical SCM environment, suppliers and customers are linked via expensive and tightly integrated extranets, traditional SCM installations, and tightly coupled Electronic Data Interchange (EDI) applications. Historically, these applications have been both very technologically complex and expensive to implement. As a result, Small to Medium Enterprises (SMEs) are very infrequently able to make the technology and financial investments required to be included in such systems. "Supply chains used to be exclusive affairs," Gartner Group analyst Mathew Schwartz explains, "the playthings of corporate giants who arm-twisted a few of their bigger supply-chain partners into following along."[11]

This coercive supply chain model, however, is a poor substitute for an Internet-based *extended value chain* application. By incorporating information from customers and their customers, suppliers and their suppliers, and newly connected SMEs, *extended value chain* applications replace monolithic supply chains with dynamic supply grids containing real-time business process facilities and shared data warehouses of information for decision support. As a result of this paradigm shift, enterprises are able to bring inventory levels down to improve responsiveness to market conditions.

Fundamentally, *extended value chain* applications differ from traditional SCM systems through their ability to integrate easily and inexpensively with external suppliers, trading partners, and customers. Through this new integration, enterprises are able to extend their investments in legacy SCM applications to span the entire value chain, from the procurement of raw materials on the supply side to the delivery of finished goods to customers.

Customer care applications serve an essential, if simple, purpose. As the dynamics of personalized product and service offerings continue to take hold in the Internet age, the customer has assumed ultimate control in the marketplace, and building comprehensive customer relationships has become the critical byword for success.

This represents a dramatic power-shift from the past dominance of production efficiency as a yardstick for prosperity. According to Kevin

Kelly, the executive editor of *Wired* magazine and author of *Out of Control: The New Biology of Machines, Social Systems and the Economic World* and *New Rules for the New Economy*, "the central economic imperative of the industrial age was to increase productivity. The central economic imperative of the network economy is to amplify relationships. Because a relationship involves two members investing in it, its value increases twice as fast as one's investment. The network economy is founded on technology, but can only be built on relationships. It starts with chips and ends with trust."[12]

These applications do not aim to simply facilitate a single transaction or deliver a particular piece of information to the customer. Instead, the goal is to build long-term relationships with customers. *Customer care* is about a conversation, interactive dialog, and shared know how—not simply a transaction.

Distinctions such as B-to-B and B-to-C and application types such as *virtual marketplaces, procurement/resource management, extended value chain,* and *customer care* are useful for describing the landscape of the e-Enterprise. In the real world, however, distinctions between such artificial vernacular aren't usually obvious. And, as the evolution of the digital economy progresses, the lines will only continue to blur.

THE CONVERGENCE OF B-TO-C AND B-TO-B

Despite the many differences between selling to consumers and to businesses, these formerly distinct practices are increasingly beginning to converge into a single, inclusive model for e-Enterprise. Led by a rising number of small business and home office workers who blur the line between a business and home user, enterprises are recognizing that a measure of common functionality exists that supports both B-to-B and B-to-C applications.

Take, for instance, American Express. At the company's home page, links lead to three distinct customer areas: "For individual card, financial & travel needs"; "For entrepreneurs, small business owners & merchants"; and "For businesses & merchants with over 100 employees."

Superficially, this would lead one to believe that the services offered in each area are entirely unique. In fact, the crossover in functionality is significant. Different credit options that are targeted to specific markets are available in each area, but the fundamental goal of each is the same: display recommended options for the individual buyer, encourage them to order goods and services, and record buying behavior and preferences to improve the user experience down the road. In fact, the Web site also acknowledges the crossover implicitly by introducing goods and services from multiple sections to a single buyer: a corporate employee, for example, might be offered individual and small business services that they may require at a later time.

Similarly, Dell Computer Corp. offers a front-page menu listing selections for home/home office, small business, large business/health-care, education, and government customers. Clicking on a menu item takes users to a Web site within the site, which focuses on meeting unique customer needs in addition to the site's core functionality: configuring and selling personal computers.

For businesses, Dell offers individual "Premier Pages" where pre-negotiated prices and pre-approved PC configurations are listed, and order status, technical assistance, and other information that can be easily accessed by corporate employees. "Your Premier Page will help make business activities even more effective by reducing time and costs, and increasing productivity," Dell claims. "And you'll enjoy multiple levels of user access that can be managed and controlled by your organization." Consumers, on the other hand, are offered core product configuration and order processing facilities, and the option to bundle related consumer goods and services through cross- and up-selling.

The emergence of the online healthcare industry provides us with many examples of the convergence of B-to-C and B-to-B e-Application development. Such applications are pulling the industry toward the realm of e-Enterprise.

As the number of online pharmacies and health-care information Web sites increase, consumers are becoming empowered in an area where, until recently, knowledge has been tightly controlled by large corporations that are often perceived as hostile to customer inquiry.

Ultimately, B-to-C healthcare applications will fundamentally change the way that companies provide healthcare for employees and their dependents. Today, most medium-to-large companies administer healthcare benefit plans for their employees. As a result, when employees change employers they are unable to maintain the exact same coverage over the long term and usually must switch plans and providers.

According to leading consumer healthcare application provider Healtheon, the mission of B-to-C healthcare providers online is to "leverage advanced Internet technology to connect all participants in healthcare, and enable them to communicate, exchange information, and perform transactions that cut across the healthcare maze. This will simplify healthcare, reduce costs, enhance service, and result in higher quality and more accessible healthcare."[13]

Like the exploding healthcare market in general, the sheer size of the online market for consumer healthcare services is simply astounding. By 2003, online healthcare is projected to be a $1.7 billion market. To give some perspective as to the size this represents, this is an amount higher than what is spent on the Net for books, CDs, and other consumer items today.[14]

Generally, online healthcare initiatives offer services to three distinct customer bases: recipients of care and their families, doctors and healthcare professionals, and insurers.

For patients, services often center around purchasing prescriptions for over-the-counter drugs from vendors such as Drugstore.com and PlanetRX. In addition to this core value, however, consumers can turn to informational Web sites like drkoop.com to learn about diseases and treatments, review personal insurance coverage information, check on the status of claims, and research topics in health-orientated dictionaries and encyclopedias of disease information and treatment descriptions. In addition, many consumer sites include support communities for patients afflicted with particular diseases and their families in order to share experiences and mitigate their suffering.

From the B-to-B perspective, doctors and other medical professionals have begun to use the Net for a number of important functions. One high-profile application enables doctors to search databases of previous symptoms, diagnoses, and analyses in order to make difficult diagnoses. Also, doctors and hospital workers can access patient charts and histories stored in locations around the world. Care providers can also compare medical test results with repositories of other information stored in databases, determine the eligibility of patients to receive tests or undergo procedures not covered by some insurance policies, and submit claims to insurers for payment.

Finally, the Net allows insurers to examine patient history to determine eligibility for particular coverage plans, and also allows them to deliver billing information in real-time to doctors and clients.

Going forward, benefit management agents will move online in order to maintain healthcare coverage independently from employers. In the near future, consumers will be able to maintain their healthcare coverage through job and company changes in much the same way that today they maintain their 401k plan. Hence, the convergence of B-to-C and B-to-B toward the e-Enterprise.

Clearly, the distinction between B-to-C and B-to-B isn't always crystal clear. However, it provides a useful framework to compare and contrast these two models. In the next two chapters, I will examine both B-to-C and B-to-B e-Applications in the context of the business case and inter-organizational processes for a number of e-Application models.

B-to-C
e-Application
Models

The whole concept behind virtual integration is to use direct connections, enhanced by technologies like the Internet, to bring your customers virtually inside your business so you can meet their needs faster and more efficiently than anyone else.[1]
—Michael Dell, Chairman and CEO, Dell Computer Corp.

The early stage of transactional e-Applications, which have focused on marketing and selling goods and services to the consumer and have created new distribution and global reach, is giving way to the e-Enterprise model. To understand the fundamentals of e-Enterprise, we must first go back to further analyze the early stages of B-to-C e-Applications, which many people refer to as ".com mania". In this chapter, I will focus on explaining the different types of B-to-C business models and e-Applications that have prevailed, and I'll discuss the critical success factors associated with them.

Although some of the case studies presented may seem obvious, it is necessary to begin with an intentionally basic analysis of these models and e-Applications in order to compare and contrast them with the B-to-B discussion that will follow in Chapter 4. In this way, we will start to see the distinction between the business models and applications. A key strength of the Net is its ability to treat every customer like she is the only one that matters. Nowhere is this more apparent—or important—than in the B-to-C retail environment. e-Applications that focus on the consumer share a common goal: to attract potential buyers, transact goods and services, and build consumer loyalty to own customers through individual, courteous treatment and engaging community features.

The first—and simplest—examples of B-to-C platforms were catalog-based retailers that began to display product information and take orders over the Net. For the most part, these pioneers aggregated and presented content in the same manner as in conventional print catalogs: product selection was typically limited to a single supplier, and order processing involved manually entering credit card numbers and customer shipping information into internal computer systems. Gradually, however, the Net became more than just brochureware, and multiple revenue models began to evolve for doing business with consumers online.

The primary focus of most B-to-C e-Applications is generating revenue by selling goods and services. An example of this strategy is outdoor retailer REI, which offers a visually appealing—if rather straightforward—site on the Net. REI's intention is clearly to move merchandise online much as the company does in its physical stores.

Although REI makes some effort to include other features—for example, a local store locator that provides information about area hikes and a "How to Choose" section that helps consumers select gear to purchase—REI's site is largely geared toward presenting product information and taking orders.

At the other end of the spectrum are sites that concentrate on providing content and community services and that derive earnings from advertising and subscription fees. Time Warner's Pathfinder is an example. Although the site doesn't transact goods and most content is free to even non-subscribers, Pathfinder is an example of an e-Application that attempts to move the company toward becoming an e-Enterprise. It extends core internal resources—magazine articles and multimedia from *Time, Entertainment Weekly,* and *Fortune* among others—outward to a new customer base for the purpose of generating revenue. To cover the costs of potential lost subscriptions to online viewers, Time Warner maintains a few specific sections of the site for print-subscribers only and collects revenue from targeted advertisement banners that are displayed on each page of content.

A third type of B-to-C initiative focuses on providing services that, although they don't directly generate revenue online, add value to traditional business models by improving interaction between retailers and customers to reduce costs. Shipping company Federal Express is a prime example. FedEx's core logistics business is largely unaffected by the Web. Shipping packages, after all, is done with delivery trucks, cargo planes, and freighters—all decidedly non-virtual forms of transportation.

FedEx's interNetShip application enables users to pinpoint drop-off locations and then track packages as they are shipped from city to city around the world. Because the services it provides are free, FedEx.com doesn't contribute directly to the company's revenue. However, by maintaining user profiles, enabling customers to track packages, targeting users for special promotions, and improving response to customer inquiries about shipping progress, FedEx has upped customer experience a notch and in the process reduced its costs dramatically. Moving its business online, in fact, has fundamentally transformed FedEx's primary business from simple logistics to customer relationships.

The most successful B-to-C e-Applications don't opt to only sell goods and services, build online content and communities, or reduce customer interaction costs. Instead, they do all three at once. No matter how they embrace these models, however, a few key drivers form a backbone for most B-to-C e-Applications. To succeed, B-to-C e-Applications must focus on .com branding, building one-to-one relationships with customers, aggregating online communities of users, advertising both on the Net and in the conventional world, and providing unparalleled customer care.

As more and more consumers with wider and wider ranges of interests begin to use the Net, new and different models for B-to-C e-Applications will be developed to meet their needs. In order to partially segment and provide some relevant examples, during the course of this chapter I'll present five distinct examples of vertical B-to-C e-Application models:

- *e-Tailing/consumer portals:* e-Tailing/consumer portal applications are what most consumers widely associate with e-Commerce and B-to-C e-Applications. They aim to aggregate consumers, market goods and services, and make transactions from simple, static catalogs with mostly fixed prices.

- *Bidding and auctioning:* Bidding and auctioning sites sell products and services with non-traditional, flexible pricing models. Often, the host of the auction or bidding application is a third-party cybermediary who operates as a link between the buyer and the seller.

- *Consumer care/customer management:* Consumer care/customer management applications aim to provide services to customers that add value to either transactions that already have taken place or long-term customer relationships between the end user and the host of the application.

- *Electronic bill payment (EBP):* EBP applications streamline the process of collecting, presenting, and paying repetitive consumer charges such as credit card, telephone, and utility bills.

E-Tailing/Consumer Portals

Most e-commerce sites that immediately come to mind when considering B-to-C e-Applications are examples of e-Tailing/consumer portal applications. Amazon.com, CDNOW, PlanetRX, and Microsoft Expedia all fall under this category. Like retailers in conventional marketplaces, e-Tailers aim to sell goods and services to consumers—only over the Net. Put simply, e-Tailers have two main goals: increase revenue through new sales and aggregate a community of buyers at consumer portals for targeted, one-to-one marketing campaigns that increase the instance of impulse buying.

e-Tailers have several key advantages over their counterparts in conventional marketplaces. One of the most important advantages is that well-designed consumer portals can deliver multiple revenue opportunities through selling products supplied in-house, co-marketing and selling products from competitors, and delivering targeted advertising.

e-Tailers can establish an upper hand over conventional retailers by providing a consumer portal that enables it to reach new customers without investing in costly new retail outlets. Online, Web sites are available to a global audience 24 hours a day, 7 days a week, and provide access to a virtually unlimited supply of new customers with just a point-and-click.

In general, e-Tailers also provide customers with better access to a company's products and services. Even massive retailers with thousands of products can include their entire catalogs online, and consumers can find any item they want in a matter of seconds through a combination of browsing, parametric searching, and keyword retrieval.

Marketing to consumers in a B-to-C consumer portal is not unlike marketing to the traditional retailing world. Typically, consumers can be enticed with coupons, contests, and other promotions to explore and use Net shopping sites. In their battle in the burgeoning and increasingly competitive arena of online pharmacies, for example, drugstore.com and PlanetRx are aggressively courting customers by offering "one-cent" items and "three-for-free" promotions. Although they are likely to take a bath by offering name-brand products for a penny, these types of promotions help to develop consumer loyalty. e-Tailing also provides an environment that is ideal for up-selling and cross-selling opportunities that expand product lines and offer a wider range of goods and services to consumers.

The real-time nature of the Net also provides companies with supply and demand information that enables firms to better manage their pricing strategies. The fixed pricing in consumer markets that is the norm today is gradually being replaced in certain markets by "dynamic pricing," which constantly changes to reflect the ebb and flow of supply and demand.

Auctions, which already have proven quite popular on the Net, are examples of this dynamic form of pricing. Because of the exciting, stock-market-like atmosphere, Auctions often prompt consumers to bid and pay higher prices for goods than they normally would consider. We'll discuss Bidding and Auctioning commerce sites in more detail later in this chapter.

Above all else, e-Tailers are able to build customer loyalty by combining personalized service and complete customer care offerings. For example, some sites enable customers to enter their payment data only once, after which it is stored for "one-click purchasing" in successive visits. Loyal users of consumer portals such as Lands' End and Amazon.com are likely to spread the word about their experience online, eventually attracting exponentially more customers without necessarily expanding investments in marketing and advertising.

In addition to building the revenue opportunities already mentioned, e-Tailers have the extra advantage of decreasing the cost of making a sale. These cost savings can come in several different forms. Most obviously, the automation of inter-networked computer systems reduces the cost of processing sales transactions.

By communicating in real-time with members of the supply chain, the costs of warehousing, shipping, and maintaining inventories can also be reduced—and even eliminated outright in particular cases. Soft goods such as software, music, and text, for example, can be transferred through a digital supply chain, sold by an e-Tailer, and delivered to the customer all over the Web for nearly no cost at all.

As we mentioned in Chapter 2, selling to consumers on the Net involves four steps: *product identification*, *catalog search*, *product comparison*, and *purchase*. In order to support this process, e-Tailing/consumer portal applications support a wide base of common functionality. Some examples of the activities supported in such an application include:

- *Catalog management:* e-Tailers must integrate product and service information from multiple vendors into a single, cohesive catalog that is intuitive to navigate and that presents products in an attractive manner.

- *Parametric searching:* Consumers often search for product categories (i.e., detergents) rather than specific product names (i.e., Tide or Wisk). Parametric searching enables buyers to search product categories incrementally to determine product selections that meet their needs.

■ *Personalization/profiling:* Consumer portals should identify visitors individually wherever possible in order to collect personal information about the types of products they research and ultimately buy and their overall surfing behavior at the site.

■ *Advertising/targeted marketing:* e-Tailers can dramatically increase the instance of impulse buying by targeting advertising banners and special promotions to consumers with identified interests and buying habits.

■ *Shopping cart:* Most e-Tailers use a virtual shopping cart metaphor to allow customers to collect and manage products that interest them before actually checking out.

■ *Payment processing:* The site must include some form of payment processing to enable users to make purchases using credit cards, online payment methods, etc.

Generally speaking, the first three steps of e-Tailing, *product identification*, *catalog search*, and *product comparison*, can be described as the information-gathering phase. Typically, this stage begins with catalog creation and site development on the part of the e-Tailer. Once the site is operational and the catalog populated with a compelling cross section of products, the e-Tailer begins to advertise to establish .com branding.

Eventually, when the retailer succeeds in aggregating an audience of prospective customers, the functionality of the site must begin to deliver. At this time, customers identify, compare, and select products that they are interested in purchasing by navigating through and utilizing the features available in the marketplace application.

When the consumer is ready to actually place an order and move from the information-gathering phase to the *purchase* phase, the application must respond immediately to begin to process the transaction. This is accomplished by ensuring an intuitive process for the consumer to place items in a virtual shopping cart where they can be reviewed and, if the customer chooses, discarded. Ultimately, when all items have been selected, the process moves to the "checkout lane," where the items are finally purchased.

During the electronic transaction stage, information including credit card or other payment data is collected from customers. Once authenticated and authorized (if appropriate), this data is immediately passed on to the transaction processing portion of the application and payment information is saved along with the buyer's personal profile so that it is available for use the next time the buyer comes to shop.

Of course, once the order is made and processed, it must be delivered to the customer. This fulfillment stage can be as simple as "picking" merchandise from the shelves in a warehouse or as complex as coordinating the delivery of products from many different inventory locations.

Finally, the order process moves to settlement, where money actually exchanges hands and is transferred to the seller.

At any and every point in this process, the e-Tailer must make sure that extensive customer service features are available for buyers to check on the status of their order, make arrangements for changing/updating the order, and returning items that don't meet their expectations.

Conventional "bricks-and-mortar" companies that don't recognize these advantages of setting up shop and beginning to sell online quickly find that new, virtual competitors can appear overnight and steal business directly from their traditional customer base. Take, for example, Toys "R" Us and eToys. Content that their infrastructure and expertise in conventional marketplaces would protect them from online competitors, Toys "R" Us was slow to develop a strategy for becoming an e-Tailer. This hesitation gave start-up online toy retailer eToys the edge it needed to establish itself as the market leader in online toy sales. Today, despite a concerted effort to establish an e-Tailing presence online, Toys "R" Us continues to lag well behind eToys in terms of both market share and .com brand recognition.

Net consumer portals, of course, will never completely take the place of conventional retailers because—with the exception of soft good sales—they will never be able to deliver the hands on, instant gratification that the customer receives when making a purchase and taking home a new product from a bricks-and-mortar store. Net consumer portals will make, and are already making, however, huge dents in traditional markets. For the few conventional retail powerhouses who have not yet set up shop on the Net, the time to act is now. Only by developing a two-pronged strategy of bricks-and-mortar and Web sales will they be able to fend off .com startup threats.

BIDDING AND AUCTIONING

Led by market pioneers such as eBay, Priceline.com, and more recently Amazon.com, bidding and auctioning have become prime examples of how the unique capabilities of the Net have created a new and exciting business model.

Traditionally, bidding and auctioning have been exclusively the domain of niche markets where it is difficult to put an objective value on the products being sold. Some examples of established markets for bidding and auctioning include estate liquidation, antique and refurbished novelties, and procurement of custom-designed, business-to-business production goods.

The Net, however, has made the advantages of these dynamic pricing models available in mainstream Net shopping venues from airline tickets at Priceline.com to PCs and computer peripherals at ONSALE.com. The real-time excitement of supply-and-demand pricing and the elusive quest for a bargain are only a couple of the many factors that have fueled their success. Others, although perhaps less exciting, speak directly to the Net's contribution to the auction model.

For one, it's easy to post goods for sale on a Web site. Unlike in conventional auctions, goods for sale in Net auctions don't have to be physically transported to a marketplace at all until the auction ends and a successful bidder has been determined. Also, almost *anything*, no matter what it is, can be sold in an online auction.

With millions of users, the Internet is arguably the only marketplace with a pool of buyers diverse enough to support the broad spectrum of goods needed to propel an auction hosting platform towards critical mass. Even in an auction environment as diverse and large as eBay, for instance, it's easy to search for very specific goods. By using the tools of the Net, the auctioneer can create an environment that is both massive and simple to navigate—a combination that often isn't possible in the physical world. Online communities also can be used to steer targeted users to auction items that may interest them, and one-to-one marketing can predict the auction items they'll likely want.

Successful bidding and auctioning applications must support a common core functionality in order to provide the basic features and services that customers expect in an auction environment. Some examples of this functionality include:

- *Catalog integration and management:* Because bidding and auctioning often involves the sale of excess supplies or unique goods from multiple suppliers, applications must maintain a catalog of individual or limited quantity goods for auction that is flexible enough to integrate new items from new suppliers on the fly.

- *Chat:* Because evaluating a product in an auction setting is a dynamic and often subjective process, many bidding and auctioning sites include some sort of chat functionality to allow potential buyers to discuss the relative merits of available products.

- *Bid boards:* When consumers are ready to place a bid on a good or service, they must be able to post their bid information on a public bid board to keep other potential buyers up-to-date on the auction process.

- *Personalization/buyer seller account management:* Many auction sites concentrate on matching buyers with multiple sellers in a buyer-cybermediary-supplier model rather a simple buyer-supplier model. Because the cybermediary often cannot guarantee the reliability of disparate, unrelated buyers and sellers, it is essential to maintain transaction histories in order to ensure that unreliable buyers and sellers don't compromise the integrity of the system.

- *Notification:* Auctions are driven by a series of events (i.e., new item posted for bidding, new high bid received, auction closed). To ensure that all potential buyers have access to up-to-date information about auctions, the application often utilizes an event notification component to deliver updates by e-mail, fax, pager, etc.

Online auctioning has moved beyond its earliest, immature stages. Right now, a number of e-Tailers are using a bidding and auctioning format to deliver a completely unique buying experience online.

At eBay, for example, an amazing 35,000 new auctions are started each day. Many individuals have even quit their jobs to auction goods over the service on a full-time basis. Entire companies are springing up whose sole distribution strategy is auctioning their wares on eBay.

In addition to eBay, there are other successful models for B-to-C bidding and auctioning applications. Already, hundreds of Web sites have begun to provide auction environments for consumers. Most of the volume is generated by a few large Web sites, however, including eBay and those run by ONSALE, of Menlo Park, Calif., and uBid, based in Elk Grove Village, Ill. These sites serve as high-volume movers of merchandise for vendors, which often are manufacturers or retailers faced with the need to dispose of computer equipment and consumer electronics that have been replaced by newer models. Both ONSALE and uBid illustrate a growing trend in the online auction market: many large auction sites specialize in selling surplus merchandise and services.

uBid supports several different payment models, and gives vendors a choice of which model they would like to embrace. One option is to allow uBid to share in the proceeds from goods sold in auction. Another is to sell merchandise outright to uBid, who then auctions it off as its own. In the latter case, uBid does its own warehousing, packaging, and even refurbishing of goods. The company says that although this adds significant costs, controlling the entire process allows it to provide better customer service and to reduce the instances of fraud.

More recently, B-to-C auctioning has gone beyond simply distributing surplus goods. Priceline.com is a prime example of how specialized services can be sold in a bidding environment. Priceline began by selling airline tickets in what is essentially a reverse auction: buyers name their price and airlines are sought who are willing to accept it. Gradually, Priceline has expanded into hotel rooms, home mortgages, new cars, and other areas. In the future, it plans to extend the franchise to sell telecommunications, cruises, insurance, and credit cards.

Priceline's business model is simple. Their core product base is surplus airline tickets and hotel reservations. According to Priceline, it makes more sense for an airline to auction off extra seats at, say, half price than it does for them to fly with a plane that is only half full.

As more and more bidding and auctioning markets open in special niches online, many predict that static pricing will become less and less relevant. Some even go so far as to predict that the Net will ultimately make every market behave like the stock market. Whether this is true or not remains to be seen. In any event, bidding and auctioning will continue to capture market- and mind-share online.

Consumer Care/Customer Management

With vast amounts of information and technology at their disposal, consumers are becoming more educated and empowered than ever before. Customers in the digital economy are rarely forced to settle. Instead, they are continuously comparing new and better offerings, causing retailers to scamper to keep up with their every move. In the digital marketplace, it is the educated consumer that holds absolute power.

Not only do consumers demand the best price, but they also want the best service. No longer is retailing just about transactions. In the digital economy, and on the Net especially, it's about interacting with the customer and sharing knowledge about products and services.

Describing this shift to the customer and the need for enterprise customer management, EDS vice president Bob McCashin says, "We are entering a new era—or perhaps it is the rebirth of an older one—in which the individual customer is central. It is an era of understanding, or intimacy, with the people we serve—even when they live on the other side of the world. It's a time when we can know hundreds of thousands of customers well—particularly our best customers."[2]

"And," McCashin continues, "we can show them that we appreciate their business in meaningful ways. It's called 'enterprise' because market leaders today realize that all forms of interactions with their customers—whether through sales, service, or delivery—affect their customer relationships. These interactions can help you acquire the right customers—retain them by meeting their individual needs—and maximize the lifetime value of the most profitable customer relationships."[3]

Customer care/Customer management applications must support a wide range of consumer processes and functionality in order to deliver a robust, relationship-building experience. Some examples of common features of a customer care application include:

- *Profile management:* Because customer care typically includes accessing information that is unique to individual customers, the application must keep track of individual user profiles to ensure that each user has access only to information that pertains to him.

- *Custom content delivery:* Similarly, the customer care application should be able to identify and deliver support information directly to users for whom it is intended. For example, if a software update is made available for a particular program, all users who have purchased the program should be notified that the new version is available.

- *Account management/product feedback:* e-Tailers should aggregate user experiences with products in order to deliver real-time feedback about each customer's use of the product to design teams. Ultimately, this information can be used to automatically provide custom product configurations for individual buyers.

- *Information gathering:* The site should attempt to aggregate a knowledgebase of user experience in order to enable customers to engage in self-service and self-support.

- *Interactive community building:* Often, customers who have experienced similar problems are the best source for solutions and advice. By enabling users to interact through online bulletin boards, FAQs, and chat rooms, enterprises can reduce support costs at the same time they improve service.

The first stage of good customer care online begins during customer acquisition and relationship building. In fact, at this point in the sales process customer care should be the top priority. Later, once customers have made a purchase, it is essential to continue to provide only the best and most attentive service. A consumer's decision about whether to become a repeat customer is based a great deal on her first and last impressions of the site's service.

Customer care applications not only improve customer service while reducing costs; they also place the customers in control by allowing them to answer their own questions through customer self-service. Used in conjunction with the telephone and face-to-face communications, the Net can strengthen e-Tailers' relationships with customers like never before.

To succeed, these interactions with customers must be done right. "If these [customer] dialogues are designed properly, they will allow a wide range of people with varying needs to find their way through the system easily to get what they come for," says Rich Melmon, partner in The McKenna Group. "From the user's point of view, the dialogues will integrate four basic elements:

Personalization: I want it my way, with my particular needs driving the system's responses to me; *Self-service:* I want to explore on my own, select on my own, and troubleshoot on my own; *Immediacy:* I want the information now; I want the product now; *Intimacy:* I want it to feel like a two-way process; I want to know that my actions are being used by the company to learn what I want; I want my feedback to register with the company; and I want tangible evidence that I'm in the loop."[4]

The balance between effective customer self-service and blatant information overload, however, is a delicate one. While self-service does empower customers to take service into their own hands, it doesn't mean dumping a limitless amount of information on them. Instead, by taking the time to learn their individual needs, e-Tailers can present consumers with the data they need to make a buying decision or service products they have already purchased.

Given the right information, self-service also can become self-selling. Leveraging the right knowledge and technology can turn customers into a company's best sales force. For instance, eToys balances knowledge and technology to help parents and others find their way through the often mystifying world of toys and games. The Web site permits searches by age, category, and price, and also provides toy recommendations and lists of "favorite toys by age." eToys also provides a "low price guarantee" and explains, in simple terms, the latest toy fads for otherwise bewildered parents.

Customer care e-Applications even enable real-time support. E-Trade Securities, for instance, uses a chat function to give customers access to support representatives during certain hours of the week. And it provides account holders with online access to the forms they need to transfer individual retirement accounts and perform other tasks. Other e-Tailers are using technology to replace the human customer care or sales representatives that consumers have traditionally turned to for help in a retail environment. For instance, Reel.com invites customers to type in the title of their favorite movie, promising to list "similar films that cover the same subject, appeal to the same audience, or provide a similar movie-going experience." The company also knows from where a good chunk of its customers come: it provides a link that creates a special version of the site for America Online users.

ELECTRONIC BILL PAYMENT (EBP)

A key emerging B-to-C application is electronic bill payment, or EBP. The benefits of EBP are twofold: first, consumers are able to organize, keep track of, and pay all of their bills through a single electronic interface; second, the cost of paper and postage is eliminated for billing agents, along with customer complaints that bills weren't delivered correctly. A growing number of consumers already are paying their bills electronically, and soon the trend is predicted to explode.

According to a Netroscope study, 96 percent of consumers have heard about electronic bill payment, 18 percent are already using it, and 27 percent plan to pay bills electronically within the next 12 months. Even more astounding, only 34 percent of respondents don't expect to utilize some form of EBP in the foreseeable future.[5]

EBP encompasses a wide range of potential applications. Many, however, share common elements. Some typical features of EBP applications include:

- *Bill consolidation:* To offer a complete solution for EBP, sites must be able to integrate, present, and collect payment for bills from multiple billing organizations. Typically, this involves customizable data translation through standards such as XML.

- *Payment processing:* EBP applications must be able to accept multiple payment methods including credit cards and cybercash.

- *Analysis and reporting:* Consumers should be able to automatically analyze and summarize billing information in charts, graphs, and other useful formats.

- *Integration with biller accounting systems:* When a consumer makes a payment, it can be automatically integrated with the internal accounting systems of the biller to reflect the latest, up-to-date information at all times.

There are a number of reasons why EBP is beneficial to businesses and consumers. Using their PCs, consumers can pay their bills electronically whenever they want, often right from an integrated interface to the personal accounting and financial software they already use.

Moreover, the growing popularity of Internet banking makes checking account balances and bill payments available to consumers wherever access to the Internet is available. Customers can manage and track expenditures in real-time in order to avoid double payments and improve understanding of their expenditures.

Using one-to-one marketing techniques, bills can be customized for consumers based on their personal preferences. For businesses, EBP can mean a reduction in late payments because bills often are scheduled for payment at the same time each month. By staggering due dates for payments, companies that are habitually short of cash on hand can mitigate the possibility of missing a payment. Companies also find that there are substantial savings in the costs of processing bill payments.

By automating a good deal of the process, businesses cut down on manual accounting expenditures and improve employee efficiency.

EBP has the added benefit of improving customer service by automatically integrating charges made, removed, or altered after a bill was initially presented. The real-time basis of electronic billing allows consumers to always see the correct amount that is due. When a payment is made, it is reflected in the outstanding balance immediately. Consumers know where they stand at any given moment.

As more and more companies make EBP available, savings will skyrocket for businesses and customer service will improve as consumers feel they are once again empowered with self-servicing information.

Long-distance service providers MCI Worldcom and AT&T are among the largest corporations that are attempting to move billing online, where savings can be enjoyed while implementing features that increase customer service. Both telecommunications companies provide billing statements on their Web sites, and both allow customers to view detailed accounts of calling activity in order to analyze phone charges and prevent unauthorized calls. Ultimately, both AT&T and MCI Worldcom aim to entirely eliminate paper billing for their online customers.

In exchange for special, nine-cents-per-minute rates that are available only to EBP customers, the companies send users e-mail messages when monthly bills are posted online. Customers then can view their bills for the current month and for the previous 90 days or so. In the case of AT&T and MCI, customers' credit cards are instantly billed when the invoices are available. In the future, however, bill payment services will allow consumers to choose whether to pay for bills by using their credit cards, checking accounts, or through some other means.

Electronic bill payment services devoted entirely to aggregating and presenting bills are beginning to pop up on the Net. Paymybills.com is among this new breed of EBP Web sites. It handles all aspects of bill presentment and paying, from notifying companies to send the bills, to sending e-mails to users letting them know on a regular basis that bills have been received and are due. Paymybills.com also permits users to analyze their bills from month to month and lets them see scanned images of the paper invoices.

These types of online billing schemes can help strengthen customer service because consumers are provided the resources to both serve themselves and manage their billing with simplicity. Finally, the growth of EBP opens up a myriad of other possibilities and add-ons to the service, including, for example, the ability of customers to request credits for individual bill items.

Ultimately, EBP will mature to the point where a consumer can have bills from multiple companies and billing agents consolidated at a single site for review and remittance. The payment process will then mimic conventional bill presentment and payment and support customized activities such as delaying payment and pre-payment.

CRITICAL SUCCESS FACTORS

Despite the seemingly broad scope of these categories, every B-to-C platform relies on three strategies to bring value to online consumers: *.com branding*, *one-to-one marketing*, and *online community building*. Going forward, success in these three areas will be the critical factor that separates B-to-C winners from losers.

.com branding

In the past, branding was almost exclusively about positioning in advertising in order to build a public perception about a product. Michael Jordan eats Wheaties? It's the "breakfast of champions." That truck can climb a mountain? Sure, it's "built Ford tough."

Advertisers told us what to think, and we listened. Not because we're gullible or easily influenced, but because conventional advertising media are decidedly one-sided. When we read a newspaper, watch television, or listen to the radio, we are passive participants. By design, the reporter, sitcom actor, or talkshow host entertains us with what they want to say rather than necessarily what we want to hear.

"On television," as Chuck Martin describes conventional advertising and branding, "it takes high-speed action and catchy jingles to capture a couch potato's attention. On billboards, it takes quick

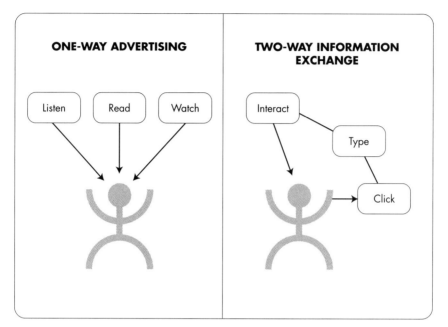

FIGURE 3.1

messages and appealing images to grab the eye of passers-by. In magazines, newspapers, and radio, it takes a combination of high-impact messages with a clear value proposition to reach an audience quick to turn the page or flip the dial. In each of these cases, the consumer is the passive recipient of the message."[6]

The Net, however, is a two-way medium. Rather than read, watch, or listen, we click, type, and interact. On the Web, .com branding is as much about listening to customers as it is telling them what to believe. Figure 3.1 illustrates this two-way information exchange and how it differs from traditional, one-way advertising:

"Once brand was simply about product differentiation," marketing guru Regis McKenna describes, "successful brand names commanded unquestioned loyalty, and they were created chiefly by advertisements broadcast by mass media. These one-way messages were absorbed—often subliminally—by consumers who took them to be virtual instructions on what to buy and where to buy it. But all that is now history. Branding of a new and entirely different kind is being born—brand as *an encapsulation of actual, experienced value.* The nature of that experience is increasingly determined through customer preferences expressed in dialogue with producers or service providers—an exchange made possible by technology, and one in which the consumer has the upper hand."[7]

The age of static, push-based advertising to build brand recognition is over. In the new economy, advertising will be about establishing a dialogue with the customer to begin to build a profile and enable one-to-one marketing. Don Peppers and Martha Rogers predict that in the interactive age, advertising will take one of three forms: *invitational* advertising where companies invite customers to learn more about their wares, *solicited* advertising where customers initiate a dialogue with e-Tailers when they're looking to make a purchase, and *integral* advertising where product placement becomes an essential part of everyday entertainment and information.

.com branding, however, must extend into conventional advertising media to be truly effective. In order to capture the mindshare of the hundreds of millions of customers who haven't yet ventured online, B-to-C e-Tailers must establish an advertising presence on television, on the radio, and even in traditional print media.

Brands that have succeeded online include a curious mix of the established and the unknown. Acknowledged leaders in the traditional economy such as GE, Barnes & Noble, and Dell walk hand in hand with .com startups such as Amazon.com, AOL, eBay, and eTrade. For each, the secret to .com branding success is different. All, however, take advantage of the two-way communication of the Net to listen to customers, respond to their needs, and build brands based not upon catchy advertising, but instead upon the valuable products and services they provide for their customers through one-to-one marketing.

One-to-one marketing

In the retail world, customers have developed a highly evolved set of expectations for personal, courteous service. They demand attention from knowledgeable salespeople. They expect product displays that are organized, attractive, and intuitive, so that they can shop without assistance if they prefer. They count on post-sale service and support to ensure that their purchase meets their expectations. In short, they expect to be appreciated for what they are: far and away the consumer retail industry's most important asset.

Customers are powerful, and they're not afraid to express their displeasure with retailers by taking their business elsewhere. Shoppers in a department store who receive service that doesn't meet these expectations, for example, will often walk next door to make a purchase at a competing retailer before patronizing a place of business that doesn't "appreciate their dollar."

Sometimes, the nearest competing retailer in the conventional marketplace isn't simply next door or even just across the mall. Maybe it's at the other end of town, across the state, or even a different part of the world. In some cases, customers will stay put because it's just not practical to switch—no matter what kind of service they get.

Online, however, this isn't the case. In B-to-C business models, there are rarely long-term contracts, volume discounts, or pre-negotiated pricing that insure customer loyalty as there are in the B-to-B process. Unlike business purchasers, consumers are fickle. At any given moment, even your most valuable and loyal online consumer is just a URL and a click away from belonging to someone else. Not surprisingly, then, successful e-Tailers have recognized that more than anything else B-to-C online marketplaces are about using one-to-one marketing to meet and exceed consumer demand for personal, courteous service.

One-to-one marketing enables e-Tailers to replicate the intimacy of shopping at the corner general store, where the owner knows the customers' names and their favorite fruits and vegetables. It's about personalized service, about knowing the customer's preferences and buying habits. It's about delivering content, marketing promotions, and even the latest news to the individual customers that value it most. It's about having an intelligent salesperson guide the customer through every stage of the buying process.

In the real world, providing this personalized service would require tremendous overhead, and might actually detract from the shopping experience. Imagine, for example, the men's section in a department store crawling with as many tailors and shoe salesmen as customers. On the Web, however, invisible personal profiling and the lightning speed of computers enables e-Tailers to greet customers personally and adjust their shopping experience to their individual preferences and tendencies.

The trick is to make it appear as though the online store has been customized and exists solely for the person who is currently shopping. Although the e-Tailer's customer database may hold ten million names and sets of data, only the person viewing the site counts. Marketing on this personal level allows e-Tailers to bring individual products directly to the customers that are most likely to want or need them. The result is an increase in impulse buying, a higher return per-dollar spent on marketing promotions, and improved loyalty from customers who believe the e-Tailor holds their personal interests at heart.

In a conventional retail store, emphasis is on selling the maximum number of products; salespeople are rewarded based on the volume they sell and suppliers reward outlets who sell the most products with volume discounts. Often, there is very little if any recognition of individual customers, much less appreciation for customer loyalty. That's because in product-driven conventional marketplaces it isn't important; a sale to a loyal, long-time client means the same as a sale to a first-time buyer.

To attract customers to buy more and more products, retailers must continuously broaden their customer base and attract new buyers through marketing promotions and advertising. Because by definition the targets of these campaigns are new and unknown, they are often largely ineffective. As a result, retailers begin to spend more and more money to attract fewer and fewer new customers.

Take the example of a pizza delivery business. In conventional markets, chains such as Dominos, Little Caesar's, and Pizza Hut are continuously spending money to attract new customers and increase marketshare. They're willing to offer outrageous discounts—two for the price of one, half-price pizzas, etc.—in order to gain a new customer.

Say it's Monday, and, too tired to cook, you see a coupon in the TV Guide from a local delivery chain. Even though this isn't the chain from which you usually order, the coupon is for Canadian bacon and onions—your favorite combination—and you decide to clip the coupon, take advantage of the special promotion, and place an order.

Next Monday, you're again looking to order pizza, however, you see that the coupon in the TV Guide is for anchovies. You don't like anchovies, and at just about any price, you're not going to order a pizza with them as a topping. Not surprisingly, you go back to your usual delivery chain, and order something you like.

Now let's consider an online pizza delivery business with a somewhat different strategy. Because the store's Web site recognizes your unique profile every time you place an order, it quickly is able to ascertain that you like Canadian bacon and onions, and that you don't do a good job of getting around to cooking dinner on Mondays.

Eventually, you receive an e-mail on a Monday afternoon offering a special deal—Canadian bacon and onions, of course—for half price that evening only. Are you likely to order? Probably. Are you likely to notice that they appreciate your needs as an individual customer? Absolutely.

This contrast demonstrates three important tenets of one-to-one marketing:

- *Aim for economies of scope rather then economies of scale:* It is more important to own a single customer's whole business than to have one-time relationships with many customers. Close, long-term relationships enable retailers to listen to the needs of their customers and respond directly, as well as prevent defection to competing offerings.

- *Manage customers individually:* Consumers have individual and highly variable tastes. No single product can appease everybody, so don't even try. Instead, treat customers as individuals. This can be done by collaborating with customer service representatives or even by talking with customers directly. Be careful, however, not to threaten consumers' privacy. Don't require too much information, and be forthright about what you are collecting and how you plan to use it.

  Collecting small amounts of data volunteered by the customer at various times will help to build trust. Make sure they know that you use information you collect to give them better options as buyers. Not only are promotions more likely to appeal to them, but at the very least they'll appreciate the attention to their personal needs.

◼ *Bring products and services directly to targeted consumers:* Consumers are highly subject to impulse buying. If you've got something that you think they want, don't wait for them to come to you. Instead, take it to them and let them refuse if they're not interested.

Consider the previous example of the pizza delivery business in light of these ideas. The first promotion was initially successful according to its goals; by instigating your otherwise improbable purchase, it increased pizza sales by one, improved overall marketshare, and contributed to building an economy of scale. Advertising in the *TV Guide* reached a large but unfocused target audience with a single message rather than targeting potential consumers on an individual basis. Finally, rather than take their product directly to consumers, they waited for your call, hoping the promise of a bargain would incite you to act. In short, their marketing strategy was decidedly not one-to-one.

In the long term, this promotional campaign failed to establish you as a repeat customer. If you don't see a similar promotion next time, you probably won't do business with them again. And, although the campaign increased sales temporarily, it is likely the revenue gain from your one pizza was more than offset by the cost of placing the print advertisement in the first place.

Now consider the online pizza delivery. Their promotional campaign was not designed to attract new customers from a pool of largely uninterested consumers. Instead, it aimed to generate repeat business from an existing customer, a clear economy of scope rather than scale. Second, it addressed your needs as a customer individually—not only what toppings you like but also your tendency to order at a certain time of the week. Finally, it delivered the special promotion directly to you in the form of an e-mail. You didn't have to even leave your desk to take advantage of the special offer.

Successful e-Tailers are beginning to recognize—like the online pizza delivery service—that one-to-one marketing strategies are

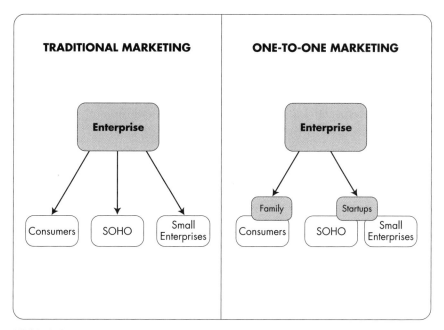

FIGURE 3.2

turning conventional ideas about marketing and advertising on their heads. Why does it work? It's simple: the more you know about your customer, the better you are at giving them exactly what they want. And the better you are at giving them exactly what they want, the more likely they are to buy. One-to-one marketers concentrate their efforts on targets likely to deliver the highest ROI: their best, most profitable customers. Figure 3.2 illustrates the difference between marketing one-to-one to achieve share of the customer and traditional marketing to achieve share of the market.

Conversely, the more you know that customers are unlikely to make a purchase, the fewer resources you can allocate towards persuading them to buy. No matter how catchy the advertisement or how much money the special promotion can save, a customer with no interest in the product isn't likely to buy. Save special promotions for customers who want them. Don't bother to offer them to consumers who will only be annoyed by the intrusion.

Already the principles of one-to-one marketing are appearing in typically mass-market media such as news, where online publishers have been enabling readers to choose the type of content that they are presented for some time. Consider again the example of Yahoo!'s personalized "My Yahoo!" feature. In addition to choosing local news and types of special topical interests, users can completely customize the sports section to display only stories about their favorite teams, the weather section to give a detailed report about their hometown, and the stock ticker to keep track of their personal portfolio. This type of customization and individual focus is about placing the exact information that customers want directly at their fingertips. It is about minimizing choices while maximizing exposure to relevant information. Instead of overwhelming consumers with a myriad of choices in order to offer the widest range of information possible, one-to-one marketing is about learning what they want and giving it to them directly.

Direct clothing merchant Lands' End recognizes this maxim and encourages customers to utilize special shopping features that provide far more personalization than a simple catalog. For instance, Lands' End's "Your Personal Model" feature enables female consumers to build a virtual model that mirrors their own dimensions. Clothes can then be "tried on" the virtual model, permitting customers to see how they might actually look in the new outfit.

Lands' End also encourages shoppers to register with the site in order to get automatic product recommendations, track orders, maintain an address book of people to whom you frequently ship gifts, and provide online personal reminder services for important dates such as birthdays and anniversaries.

Once an online merchant like Lands' End has collected—responsibly with consumer privacy concerns at the forefront, of course—this type of detailed personal information, cross-selling and other marketing opportunities become possible. In a traditional catalog, special prices and sales are usually determined on a product by product basis; this shirt if half off, or these slacks are two for the price of one.

An interactive marketer such as Lands' End can make recommendations and tailor promotions to fit particular customers at a particular time. The more information that is available about customers, the better the opportunities will be to build strong relationships with them. When a customer purchases a new shirt, for instance, the site can recommend a matching pair of slacks. When he buys shoes, a belt of the same color can be advertised. In short, focus shifts from selling individual products and services to selling a complete package to the individual customer.

Lands' End's attention to individual customers gives it a competitive edge over conventional retailers. Once shoppers take advantage of and derive value from individual promotions—say their virtual model helps them select clothes—they begin to forge a relationship with the e-Tailer that can be counted upon to encourage repeat business. Because it is typically five to eight times more expensive to gain a new customer than it is to sell to an existing one, relationships with customers that prompt them to turn to your business time and time again dramatically improves ROI on marketing investments.

Online communities

The idea of building communities of interest in order to generate consumer interest isn't purely a Net phenomenon. In fact, personal-interest and trade magazines, as well as local newspapers and TV stations, have been doing it for years—if not decades. Traditionally, these communities have been based around geographical locations (a local access cable channel), user demographics (the AARP, for example), or common interests (magazines dedicated to hobbies/sports/music).

Typically, however, communities have afforded members little control over the information to which they are exposed. Once they choose to be a member of a particular community, they are engaged in a one-way dialogue of programmed content.

But the Net is different. Because it is a two-way medium, the Web enables consumers to easily generate their own content and turn interviews into conversations, articles into discussions, and editorials into debates. Because the community itself often spawns content, it is by definition both relevant and engaging; the community generates the content that the community wants to see.

According to Robba Benjamin of Sprint in Don Tapscott's *Blueprint to a Digital Economy*, there are five requirements for successful online community building:

- *Shared space (i.e., a Web site):* In the real world, communities often are tied to a particular geographic location, such as a neighborhood association or a local chapter of national organizations such as the Boy and Girl Scouts of America. Because the Internet attracts a global audience, community builders must make a concerted effort to build a *shared space* for the community, which members can call their own and identify with the common values of the group. Just as neighborhoods have block parties, members of online groups should gather together in virtual shared space on the Net to build common interest and investment in the community.

- *Shared values:* Community members must have some sense of common appreciation and values in order to establish a foundation for discussion and productive interaction. Without the base of a common interest, interactions within the community add no more value than randomly bumping into someone on the street. If one member is an avid fisherman and wants to talk fly-fishing, for example, and another is an artist looking to find some new information about oil painting, they probably will find little in common to discuss and spontaneous dialogue is unlikely to occur.

- *Shared language:* Language is how we communicate. If we don't speak the same language, we can't talk. If we can't talk we're not going to get too much out of each other.

- *Shared experience:* Oftentimes, communities are based around a common experience that members share. Customers of a bookseller commenting in a message board on a title they have recently purchased are an example. Another is Web-hosting provider Geocities, which organizes customer Web pages into "communities" with common topics and similar virtual addresses in order to encourage interaction and dialogue between users with similar interests. Because these particular neighborhoods are visited by particular demographics of users with common interests and backgrounds, Geocities is able to sell specific, targeted advertising to individual neighborhoods.

- ▣ *Shared purpose:* Individuals visiting a community site must have a common purpose. In the case of a commerce-oriented consumer site, that purpose is often to discover new products, to find out about user-experiences with a product they are considering purchasing, to make a transaction, and to provide their own feedback to the community. If others share these priorities, discussions are likely to be focused and engaging. When users visit online toy retailer eToys, for instance, they most likely share either a common interest in toys or the need to purchase toys as gifts for someone else.[7]

Probably the largest and most successful attempt to create a virtual online community is America Online (AOL). By aggregating users from all demographics and walks of life, allowing them to select content from a number of different "channels," and then offering unique content including articles, shopping, and chat, AOL has built a reputation as not simply a service provider, but also a purveyor of some of the Net's finest content. AOL essentially uses "thick client" software to provide users with access to its features and services; in order to view the most content, users must be registered subscribers of AOL and must install the client software on their local machine.

Although they operate a closed, proprietary online service, AOL provides access to some information to non-subscribers through the Web at its homepage. Conversely, AOL users are able to view information from the Net on their own version of a Web browser.

Most online communities are located not in private, "thick client" environments, however, but instead have their home on the Web, where consumers use standard Web browsers, or "thin client" software, to access them. With the advance of technologies such as Java and XML, services that once were the sole province of AOL such as chat rooms and instant messaging have moved out onto the Net for the consumption of wider and wider audiences.

On the Web, Yahoo! is an early leader in providing online communities for consumers. Its Yahoo! Clubs offer virtual meeting places for individuals with dozens of different interests, from investing to antiques. Within each club, "members" can communicate via message boards, chat rooms, and even a calendar that alerts users to dates of common interest—say the date of an important auction for art collectors. Some of these clubs are extremely active, especially in the interest areas of investing. Followers of initial public offerings, for instance, may spend the entire trading day in a Yahoo! chat room, discussing the ups and downs of newly traded stocks with others who are passionate about the subject.

Some online communities make a concerted effort to target a specific demographic. An example of this casting is iVillage.com, which is entirely aimed at women. It, too, includes chat and message board features, but goes beyond those by providing original content from a women's perspective on parenting, relationships, personal finance, and other areas. iVillage.com also holds live author events, provides book excerpts, and operates real-time games.

For businesses to succeed in producing online communities, several goals must be met. First, the target audience's demographics must be determined. This helps provide the appropriate focus for content and create marketing campaigns that are targeted to the appropriate market. Secondly, community builders must determine how they plan on generating revenue from the consumer base. As we discussed before, this is typically a mix of online sales and advertising revenue. Lastly, individual members of the community should be segmented as much as possible in order to create opportunities for targeted one-to-one marketing opportunities.

Once it is determined those goals can be met, two processes must occur when building an online community. First, the site must make a concerted effort to generate traffic through advertising and targeted marketing campaigns. This is where .com branding comes into play. At this early stage, as moderators attempt to generate interest in a largely uninhabited and immature site, it is essential to maintain a content base that will encourage early users to continue to return to the site. Too often marketers make the mistake of luring potential users to a site that isn't yet interesting or useful. In doing so, they can lose the customer forever.

Also at this point, content providers must focus on generating information and services that cause community members to be "locked into" the site. This is often accomplished by tailoring content to individual users, providing services that are ongoing in nature, and by engaging users in interactive, one-to-one features such as chat areas and message boards.

By taking advantage of these three critical success factors (.com branding, one-to-one marketing, and building online communities), B-to-C business models will continue to turn heads and achieve long-term prosperity on the Net. Already, examples of *e-Tailers/consumer portals*, *bidding and auctioning*, *consumer care/customer management*, and *EBP* applications are redefining B-to-C e-Application models on the Net. However, many analysts and industry experts alike predict that in the coming years, it will be B-to-B (discussed in Chapter 4) rather than B-to-C e-Applications that will do the most to propel companies further toward next generation e-Enterprise.

The fundamentals of e-Enterprise as I have outlined in Chapter 1 suggest that e-Enterprises must leverage traditional business models and integrate its physical processes and its stakeholders. e-Enterprise success is then contingent upon the convergence of these models in both the physical and electronic worlds.

B-to-B e-Application Models

No man is an Island, entire of itself; every man is a piece of the Continent, a part of the main.

—John Donne, *Devotions*

Today, B-to-C business models seem to command more attention and generate more interest than do B-to-B business models. This is because relationships between consumers and e-Tailers are by nature less involved and customized than those between enterprises in B-to-B relationships. B-to-B commerce is dominated by long-term, symbiotic buyer-supplier-business partner relationships where stakeholders collectively work for common interests such as lower costs and improved product and service offerings.

The astounding success on Wall Street of Amazon.com, eBay, and Priceline.com provides strong evidence that B-to-C commerce has already arrived. We've just begun, however, to explore and exploit B-to-B business models. Due to the enormous volume of spending in the B-to-B sector (companies such as General Electric and General Motors each spend over a couple billion dollars per year), the next generation of .com success stories will be dominated by B-to-B product and service providers.

Adam Brandenburger and Barry Nalebuff explore this symbiosis in their popular book *Co-opetition*.[1] In the book, they introduce the concept of the "Value Net" in which customers and suppliers are both symmetrical, equal partners in creating value for the firm while competitors and "complementors" act as mirror images of one another. The Internet and its capacity for connecting organizations provides exciting new opportunities to explore and exploit the symmetries between customers and suppliers.

Simultaneously, e-Applications will enable firms to respond to competition with new revenue opportunities by helping to identify and promote complementary products and services online. Ultimately, the most successful B-to-B trading partners will be those who can recognize such symmetries and who will be prepared to collaborate electronically to maximize the new opportunities.

What kinds of businesses will be forced to move to the Net? Put simply, every kind. It's easy to assume that just because something exists on the Net, it must be composed entirely of bits, bytes, and tiny electrons whizzing through semiconductors at inconceivable speeds. In fact, it was this train of thought that once led business managers to believe that although soft goods and intellectual property such as music, text, and software might be suited to Net business, conventional, bricks-and-mortar industries had best stay grounded in the real world.

Today, managers know differently. Just as the telephone made it possible for enterprises to coordinate business processes across inconceivable physical barriers and the fax machine made exchanging important business documents as easy as placing a phone call, the Net will enable companies to do business in the virtual world.

But B-to-B commerce isn't just virtual or limited to cyberspace. It's real. The vendors are real and their products are real. The customers are real and the money they spend on Net transactions is also real. The benefits that e-Enterprises will reap in this virtual world will be real too.

The opportunity to make key strategic gains on the Net is there today, and it's only getting bigger. According to industry analyst Forrester Research, "as trade in every U.S. supply chain moves in some measure to the Internet by 2003… on-line sales will balloon from $43 billion to $1.3 trillion."[2]

B-to-B commerce on the Net isn't easy, however. Like any strategic business decision, it requires planning, careful ROI, and maybe even a little luck. Mostly, however, it requires a sound understanding of the four models for B-to-B e-Applictions: *virtual marketplaces*, *procurement/resource management*, *extended value chains*, and *customer relationship management*.

VIRTUAL MARKETPLACES

e-Applications that enable enterprises to sell goods and services to other businesses on the Net are referred to as *virtual marketplaces*. Superficially, virtual marketplaces share several common components with B-to-C e-Tailing environments, such as online catalogs of goods, marketing promotions, payment processing facilities, and post-sale customer care. Because business buying practices differ dramatically from consumer buying practices, B-to-B virtual marketplaces must offer services that are quite distinct from a simple e-Tailer.

B-to-B virtual marketplaces have a three-pronged approach to adding value to the enterprise: they aim to increase revenues and simultaneously decrease costs while they improve the customer buying experience. A well-designed virtual marketplace can go even further than providing this invaluable triple leverage. Not only can it increase revenues, it can also deliver multiple, completely new revenue opportunities; not only can it reduce the direct cost of sales, it can also cut multiple types of costs including structural expenses organic to the way the business is run. The double benefit of increased revenues and decreased costs is an attractive argument for any company to begin doing business on the Net. Not surprisingly, then, many enterprises choose to begin their e-Initiatives by building a virtual marketplace application to sell goods on the Net.

A study of major pharmaceutical companies' Internet strategies illustrates this common course of action. During the last decade, the explosive growth of the healthcare industry has driven pharmaceutical giants to get bigger and bigger through mergers to achieve greater economies of scale in their core activities—R&D and marketing.

As they grew, some began to use simple e-Applications to integrate information flows from multiple, geographically diverse divisions

in order to serve customers better. For many pharmaceutical companies, beginning to take orders directly on the Web to access global
markets was a logical extension of this digital enterprise-wide integration. By setting up shop on the Net in a virtual marketplace, they are
finding that they can improve sales and distribution at the same time
they dramatically reduce the inventory levels. According to the study,
one European company that made such changes to their distribution
system in Europe experienced both increased sales and a 35 percent
inventory reduction. For any company, holding dramatically less stock
means reductions in operational costs all the way from buying raw
materials, through production, to final sales in consumer marketplaces.

The healthcare companies' experiences in this regard are not
solely driven by the inherent advantages of virtual marketplaces; they
are equally derived from what B-to-B virtual marketplaces offer
today and from the expectation of what they'll be able to deliver
down the road.

In fact, this strategy of planning for today while looking toward the
future is common for most successful Web retailers. Just as
Amazon.com's first years of riches were share price-led while sales generated cash losses, the reality of many B-to-B virtual marketplaces is
that early cash losses may necessarily walk hand-in-hand with traffic
generation, full catalog population with compelling products, and
process refinement with learning from early mistakes. Ultimately, however, once buyers and sellers in a virtual marketplace have reached a
critical mass and economies of scale take hold, the three-pronged benefits forecasted for B-to-B virtual marketplaces will become a reality.

Virtual marketplaces can provide corporate giants and small businesses alike with a completely new distribution channel for access to
customers worldwide. In addition to attracting new customers, virtual
marketplaces also can offer many repeat customers improved access to
products and services and thus a wider choice of supply options. As
with any new sales channel, enterprises can expect some cannibalization in existing markets. However, through carefully targeted advertising and new customer acquisition strategies, successful B-to-B
retailers will more than offset cannibalization from revenue generated
by new customers.

When opening a new sales channel on the Web, businesses need to make some important strategic decisions regarding the relationship between traditional and virtual marketplace sales. There are no easy answers about how to resolve channel conflicts and maximize profitability. Instead, enterprises creating e-Initiatives must evaluate the impact of the Net on traditional bricks-and-mortar sales on a case by case, value-add by value-add basis. In many cases virtual marketplaces can work hand in hand with existing sales channels. In others, however, it makes sense to look to disintermediation to resolve conflicts and reduce inefficiencies.

In virtual marketplaces, the two-way interactivity and intelligent, one-to-one marketing capabilities of the Net can enable businesses to engage in complex up- and cross-selling to expand product lines and offer more complete total solutions to customers. Like B-to-C e-Tailers, successful virtual marketplaces aim to offer customers a complete solution in order to secure repeat business and increase long-term loyalty of buyers.

Let's take, for example, a manufacturer of hinges that has begun to sell its wares online. Because many businesses that purchase hinges probably will need to also purchase screws to attach them to, let's say, door frames and doors, the manufacturer may choose to suggest a set of appropriately sized screws supplied by a strategic business partner when an order of hinges is placed. This may not increase the hinge manufacturer's bottom line, but by demonstrating a clear understanding of the buyer's needs, the manufacturer is improving customer service and providing a superior solution for its customers.

In complex industries, instituting up- and cross-selling can mean either expanding the enterprise's own product lines or signing partnerships and strategic alliances with providers of complementary goods and services and including their offerings within the virtual marketplace. Even though product sales from external suppliers don't contribute directly to the bottom line, they can transform a B-to-B marketplace from a moderately useful resource in the eyes of buyers to a mission-critical source for goods and services.

Having created the ability to spot these opportunities, the virtual marketplace then comes into its own by making the public face of rapid business development easy, seamless, and inexpensive. Changing a Web site to incorporate a new product line or a totally new business direction is infinitely simpler than changing your offices, retail locations, the signs on your building, and so on. Certainly, underlying changes may be necessary to accommodate the new direction, but the virtual marketplace allows many of them to take place at the same time as, or after, the launch of the new business idea itself. Time to market becomes much shorter in this way, and payback on new ideas becomes faster than ever before.

B-to-B marketplace applications can also engage buyer profiling and reporting to monitor buying practices in order to create a selling environment that enables one-to-one relationships and individual buying behavior—especially with smaller customers whose business otherwise would not be worth the expense of customized selling and individual attention. This detailed, profile-based information represents a valuable tool for determining which customers contribute the most to the bottom line. Because buyer-seller relationships are usually long-term affairs, B-to-B virtual marketplace administrators that concentrate on the needs of their best customers reap greater rewards than even the B-to-C e-Tailer.

Through database and extended value chain integration (see "Extending the value chain" later this chapter) enterprises determine real-time costs and pursue cutting edge dynamic pricing policies. Because B-to-B purchases are usually high volume, are made by buyers with an established business relationship with the enterprise, and are generally more price sensitive than purchases in a B-to-C environment, dynamic pricing models are even more important in virtual marketplaces than they are for e-Tailers. In many virtual marketplace environments, sellers achieve dynamic pricing through the use of a bid/ask trading system, where potential buyers place bids on products and the highest bidder wins.

Finally, by supplying customers with digital planning and direct supply chain integration tools, virtual marketplaces can enable buyers to make forecasting and planning more accurate than ever before. These savings are then passed on to the B-to-B marketplace administrator in the form of increased purchases and long-term loyalty. While they increase revenue, virtual marketplaces can cut selling costs dramatically by automating important business processes involved in B-to-B selling. One example of a cost-saving opportunity in virtual marketplaces is processing transactions. By fully automating the transaction life cycle from requisitioning, to PO generation/processing, to fulfillment, enterprises can reduce customer support and sales staffing costs.

Another prime candidate for cost-cutting measures is the marketing and product promotion process. While some additional spending may be required to introduce your customers to your online presence, in a virtual marketplace distributing product information is essentially free. URLs for brochures, catalogs, and other product information can be distributed directly to potential customers via e-mail or through live links displayed within the marketplace. Furthermore, even when more and more customers become interested in particular products or promotions, the enterprise doesn't have to increase distribution costs.

Warehousing and inventory costs can also be reduced by providing real-time connections between virtual marketplaces and their dynamic supply grids (again, see "Extending the value chain"). Stockholding can be significantly reduced—which means warehousing can be too. In the case of corporations who choose not to manage the physical distribution of the goods they sell, warehousing can even be eliminated outright in some cases.

B-to-B virtual marketplaces build unparalleled customer loyalty and repeat buying through careful attention to customer buying experience and comprehensive customer care. Just like in B-to-C environments, shoppers in a virtual marketplace are identified and targeted with marketing and advertising campaigns on an individual basis. Once an order is placed, the virtual marketplace typically provides some type of support facility such as a knowledgebase of Frequently Asked Questions (FAQs) to ensure that buyers can engage in self-service to answer whatever questions about the purchase or product that they may have.

Many industry analysts would argue that the single most successful B-to-B virtual marketplace is operated by networking hardware manufacturer Cisco Systems. In fact, as of December 1998, Cisco conducted over 70 percent of its transactions, or $28 million a day over the Net, making Cisco Connection Online "the world's largest Internet commerce site."[3] Cisco's site enables corporate users to purchase routers, switches, and other hardware that enables customers to build high-speed information networks.

So what has made Cisco so successful? Some would argue that its market—networking hardware—is a prime product to sell online because the customer base is composed almost entirely of IT department staffers and consultants. To some degree, this is certainly true. On the other hand, competitors initially scoffed at Cisco's efforts due to the inherent complexity of its product. However, it's difficult to dispute that Cisco has built an online store with functionality and usefulness that is unparalleled in the B-to-B commerce world. Cisco was able to achieve success largely due to the variety of service offerings made available throughout its purchasing process. In addition to simply providing a catalog and transaction processing facilities, Cisco includes a personalized interface for buyers, an extensive customer support section with contact information, technical documents, software updates, product configuration tools, and even online training and certification courses for Cisco hardware. Also, Cisco provides direct integration with its internal back-end systems for frequent customers, and makes a set of APIs available that "customers can use to design custom software and links to their own line-of-business software from such players as SAP America, PeopleSoft, and Oracle."[4]

Cisco has also made a concerted effort to ensure that post-sale customer support is available to buyers of every kind. For most large corporations, this means diligent account management and dedicated support representatives to troubleshoot problems and aid in complex network design. For smaller businesses that may be installing their first routers or switches, Cisco includes recommended configurations and simple FAQs to get users up and running.

In order to maximize product sales from resellers, Cisco has also recently opened a site that allows VARs to share leads and engage in collaborative selling to meet large orders.

Like any fully mature virtual marketplace, Cisco Connection Online integrates directly with Cisco's internal applications and databases to automatically manage inventory and production. Cisco even allows ERP vendors such as HP, PeopleSoft, and IBM to exchange design data to enable easy network configuration troubleshooting online.

"Cisco has sped so far out in front with its electronic commerce efforts that the competition can't even see its dust anymore," *TechWeb* magazine gushes about Cisco's pioneering e-Application initiatives, "and it's still pushing the pedal firmly to the floor."[5]

The diversity within B-to-B selling initiatives is understandably daunting. However, all virtual marketplaces must emphasize four key processes to be successful: *catalog aggregation and creation, support for complex buying processes, integration with existing enterprise systems*, and *support for multiple types of payment*.

Catalog aggregation and creation

During the catalog aggregation phase of the virtual marketplace selling process, enterprises attempt to populate the online catalog with goods and services that interest and add value for the customer. Typically, this involves including offerings from outside the enterprise to round out product lines and provide a complete solution.

Because enterprises often store product information in data schema that are highly customized within a particular organization or department, virtual marketplace catalog developers must include some open data translation component to integrate incompatible catalog entries.

Once the complete product offerings are in the catalog, developers can focus on providing an interface to buyers that is consistent with the B-to-B buying process. Because this process depends a great deal on the type of good or service that is being purchased, catalog functionality can range from a simple keyword search to complex product category classification, parametric search functionality, automatic comparison product offerings, bid-boards for collaborative buying, message boards for posting buyer testimonials, real-time chat for negotiating flexible pricing, and even bidding and auctioning.

Support for complex buying processes

In order to support this wide range of potential buying processes, B-to-B sellers must incorporate a flexible workflow component. Although online selling is derived directly from the same see/buy/get life cycle of B-to-C purchases, in B-to-B environments there are almost as many marketplace life cycle models as there are products.

Furthermore, some virtual marketplaces cannot—or are unlikely to—complete their transaction cycles without the customer at least venturing briefly back into the "real" world for a particular step in the sales process. For example, many individuals and corporations have begun to purchase automobiles over the Net, but few do so without first taking at least one real vehicle for a test drive.

Even when enterprises do settle on a well-defined and modeled selling process, however, market instability can make changes to the process absolutely essential almost overnight. Developing and deploying a virtual marketplace isn't a one-time event. Instead, it is a continually evolving process of monitoring and responding to marketplace conditions.

As a result of this inherent variability in the B-to-B selling process, flexible workflow and application design are an absolute must for any virtual marketplace; no one model can work for every initiative.

It is easiest to look at the B-to-B selling process from the point of view of the buyer rather than the seller. When purchasing a simple item in a standard configuration and quantity, such as envelopes, the process is simply see/buy/get. For purchases of intermediate value and complexity, let's say personal computers, the procedure must take into account more in-depth comparison-shopping and financing techniques. Purchases of significant value but still relatively standardized configurations—let's say refurnishing a corporate office—begin to incorporate a dynamic pricing model in the form of limited negotiations over price. Finally, for custom-built, complex bulk industrial components, the process also oversees the design of the component, a testing phase, forecasting to determine exact short, medium, and long-term demand for the product, and robust bid/ask trading to ensure that the buyer

ENVELOPES (inexpensive business item)	COMPUTER (low/medium-priced business item)	OFFICE FURNISHING (medium/high-priced business item)	BULK INDUSTRIAL COMPONENTS (high-priced, customized business item)
See	See	See	Specify
Buy	Compare	Try	Design
Get	Select options	Evaluate	Forecast quantities
	Arrange finance	Compare	Forecast required delivery timescales
	Buy	Negotiate	RFQ (request for quotation)
	Get	Select product	Negotiate prices and terms
		Select supplier	Select supplier(s)
		Arrange finance	Establish ordering, quality testing, delivery and service procedures, etc.
		Buy	Agree to contract(s)
		Get	Place order for goods
			Receive and check delivery
			Receive invoice
			Pay for goods

TABLE 4.1

receives the most favorable price possible. Table 4.1 illustrates the distinction between these four virtual marketplace process models.

Integration with existing enterprise systems

By definition, virtual marketplaces connect multiple enterprises, each having distinct business architectures and buying processes. To interoperate seamlessly with these processes, virtual marketplaces must include a component capable of sharing information with internal company systems such as ERP applications, corporate databases, and custom-developed legacy systems.

Support for multiple types of payment

Payment for purchases made in a B-to-B environment is typically made either with a corporate check or for smaller purchases a corporate payment card, or P-card, maintained by a third-party financial provider such as Mastercard, American Express, or Visa.

In their early days, P-cards were used mostly by enterprises for what were considered to be trivial, low-cost purchases. Because of this attitude, many users failed to place purchasing requirements on P-cards, and because most had limited auditing and reconciliation features, users were able to make purchases almost completely without accountability. Gradually, as P-cards have become essential for electronic payment, safeguards have been developed to eliminate the problem of rogue and irresponsible purchasing.

PROCUREMENT/RESOURCE MANAGEMENT

The second application category for B-to-B e-Application is *procurement/resource management*, where enterprises use automated applications to streamline buying both production and non-production goods and services.

Traditionally, large enterprises have relied on seasoned purchasing departments to manage enterprise-wide buying. In addition to simply making purchases, these departments are responsible for aggregating and analyzing enterprise-wide buying statistics. Internally, this information is used to identify and curb excessive department spending, reward departments and individuals for efficient use of materials, and provide a basis for process engineering decisions made by executive management and consultants. Purchasing departments also use this aggregate information externally to negotiate volume discounts and special enterprise pricing with frequent suppliers and brokers. Because many enterprise purchases—such as buying specially designed and manufactured production goods—are done in a bid/ask auction environment, the purchasing department also is required to negotiate with potential suppliers and choose winning bids that will provide the most positive long-term reward.

Maintaining an expert purchasing department, however, has historically been quite expensive. Most enterprise purchasing relies heavily on time-intensive processes, and staffing costs in purchasing departments can quickly get out of hand. The Net, however, enables businesses to both maintain best-practice buying and dramatically reduce purchasing department labor and administrative costs. By building a procurement platform and making it available to the entire enterprise, companies can harness the productivity and expertise of a seasoned purchasing department for every purchase made by every employee—without spending a dime. According to the Aberdeen Group, choosing to automate purchasing through an integrated procurement/resource management application is "a slam dunk." Why is this so? Let's take a look at profitability strategies.

Most business strategies to grow the bottom line involve increasing revenues. Take, for example, a marketing promotion designed to deliver new customers, increase sales, and thus grow earnings. Before this gain reaches the business's final profit, the cost of the marketing campaign, manufacturing the new product, distributing the product to retail locations, and making the sale must be taken into account and subtracted from the total revenue gain. As a result, the effect on the bottom line becomes only a fraction of the total increase in earnings.

In a procurement application, however, cost savings go directly to the bottom line. Because of this, a dollar saved in procurement/resource management is the equivalent of increasing revenue by five to six times that. For example, a 4 percent cost savings achieved by a procurement application has the same effect upon the bottom line as an increase in sales of 20 to 24 percent.[6]

Traditionally, most procurement applications have focused on Maintenance, Repair, and Operations (MRO) goods and services. This is because MRO goods—goods purchased that are not for manufacturing purposes—are often standardized and well suited to automated, high-volume purchasing. An illustrative example of MRO goods is an office supply such as ball-point pens. Enterprises know they will be required to purchase pens for corporate use on a regular basis. Consequently, when they are purchased it is in volume. Also, their specific supplier often isn't particularly important. Most MRO purchases are made from a simple catalog with fixed prices, and automating very basic MRO purchasing usually requires little more than enabling an online catalog with order entry facilities.

This is in direct contrast with buying many production goods such as equipment, pre-assembly components, and real-estate and infrastructure supplies, which oftentimes are subject to highly specific design constraints as well as widely variable purchase volumes. In addition, production components are often subject to complex buying processes such as RFQs, co-opetitive supplier bidding, and long-term supplier contracts.

Already enterprises have begun to successfully implement both packaged and homegrown MRO procurement applications that have demonstrated impressive cost savings. Industry analyst Forrester Research indicates that implementing an automated, Web-based procurement application saves up to 15 percent of the total cost of making MRO purchases. According to packaged procurement application vendor Ariba, this represents a reduction in total enterprise costs of at least 5 percent. "At a $2 billion manufacturing company," Ariba describes, "savings [would] include $52.8 million due to supply chain economies of scale, $4.28 million due to more efficient business processes, and $2.6 million due to lower administrative costs."[7] This is a combined cost savings—and direct increase of profits—of nearly $60 million.

In order to transfer these efficiencies and cost savings to production and other non-standard supplies such as capital equipment and consulting services, e-Enterprises are beginning to bring Internet trading services and aggregation sites under the umbrella of procurement applications. These sites enable potential suppliers to engage in buying activities such as bidding and auctioning, collaboration in order to fulfill contracts beyond the means of smaller enterprises, and providing discounts to frequent buyers and repeat customers automatically.

The benefits of implementing an enterprise-wide procurement/ resource management application are dramatic:

- **Manage long-term relationships with suppliers**: Most important, Procurement/Resource management applications enable enterprises to build and manage long-term relationships with suppliers. These relationships can then be leveraged to create an enterprise-wide buying environment with the most favorable conditions possible. The long-term relationships forged in a vendor management system provide the foundation for every other potential benefit of installing such an application.

◼ **Lower requisitioning costs:** By automating the internal requisitioning process, buying organizations can reduce personnel costs and time inefficiencies normally associated with requisition approval and order processing.

◼ **Reduce supplier costs:** Integration with internal supplier inventory management and accounting systems reduces supplier costs and allows savings to be passed down to the buying organization in the form of ultra-competitive prices.

◼ **Increase accountability and control:** Procurement applications ensure that appropriate approval is secured before any purchase can be made. This reduces inefficient rogue buying and guarantees that employees whose purchases don't follow enterprise standards can be identified and held accountable for their actions.

◼ **Shorter cycle time/reduced inventory costs:** The automation and workflow facilities of procurement/resource management applications allow buying organizations to reduce the cycle time of purchases, decrease stocking requirements, and lower inventory management costs. Ultimately, internal inventory management applications are made available to suppliers and inventory control becomes 100 percent vendor managed; when new supplies are required, vendors instigate, process, and deliver the order automatically to replenish inventory level.

◼ **Optimize purchases:** Most important, enterprise procurement/resource management applications enable purchasing managers to monitor and analyze purchasing data in order to optimize order quantities and ensure business goes to selected suppliers. The single most effective technique for reducing buying costs, however, is collaborative buying, where multiple departments or even multiple enterprises can work together to meet sourcing needs and negotiate special pricing. For example, a medium-sized manufacturer may need to purchase 10,000 pre-assembly parts—a quantity not likely to warrant a volume discount. By collaborating on the Net to purchase this same part with multiple other manufacturers, the company can share in volume discounts that until now have been for only the largest enterprises.

It's easy to understand the appeal of a procurement application that promises to reduce the cost of goods ordered through supplier consolidation and diligent buying processes. An often overlooked component of purchasing, however, is the skyrocketing price of actually placing orders. In some industries, enterprises report that the cost of simply generating and processing a purchase order can exceed $300.[8] For typically inexpensive goods—most MRO purchases for example—this can exceed the actual cost of the order many times over.

In one particular example, a $2 billion dollar manufacturer of semiconductor equipment found that the cost of a single PO was $222. Of this total, $139 was devoted to processing the actual transaction, and the remaining $83 went to purchasing conventions such as approval and requisitioning. Because the company placed and processed over 31,000 transactions annually, the impact of these costs on the bottom line was substantial. By building a procurement/resource management application to automate the purchasing process, enterprises can reduce these costs dramatically and feel the effects of cost savings immediately throughout the enterprise.

Some corporations have expressed concern that by moving purchasing to the Net they will have to completely rebuild supplier relationships and redevelop purchasing department best practices. Nothing could be further from the truth. According to Forrester Research, over 86 percent of suppliers in new Net procurement environments are holdovers from conventional purchasing practices.[9]

That isn't to say that the buying process on the Net is identical to the real world. Because e-Enterprise is about process engineering as much as it is about technology improvement, new, streamlined procurement processes accompany new applications. In next generation purchasing environments, rogue purchasing by employees without purchase authorization and inefficient, low volume purchases from fringe suppliers have become a thing of the past.

This is not to say that rogue purchases would be completely prevented. In some cases, there are justifiable reasons for such purchases. There are e-Applications that will support rogue purchasing using control mechanisms and tight system integration. For example, it is possible to access spending data for individuals using P-cards that also provide for spending controls that are integrated into the card itself. Data from the P-cards are tied into the e-Applications of the overall purchasing system, enabling the spending to be reviewed and justified, verified, or validated. Already we see this blend from the partnerships between corporate credit card vendors and software vendors such as those between American Express and Ariba, MasterCard and EC Cubed (a company that I founded in 1996), and Visa and Commerce One. The trick to this solution is that it has to be open and interoperable so that the P-cards can work with either a packaged procurement application or a homegrown system.

Through enterprise-wide data integration and analysis, procurement platforms enable businesses to consolidate enterprise buying into a few, preferred suppliers to capture economies of scale. By leveraging these efficiencies to negotiate even more favorable pricing agreements, purchasing departments can ensure that every purchase made—from office workers restocking ballpoint pens to factory managers replacing an essential and customized machine tool—is at the absolute best price possible.

By relating individual purchases directly to the bottom line, procurement/vendor management applications allow purchasing managers and supervisors to analyze procurement as a strategic issue. When a procurement platform becomes fully functional, both the buyer and order processing department of the supplier can cut staff to further reduce costs. In fact, purchasing e-Applications will reinvent the concept and role of enterprise purchasing departments. No longer will purchasing employees be responsible for simply overseeing simple purchasing processes. Instead, according to Forrester Research, enterprise buying will become 70 percent relationship management: Paper pushers will be replaced by teams consisting of "relationship specialists for predictable demands, spot market and surplus gurus, and RFP [request for purchase] experts."[10] The primary goal of these teams will then be to communicate and coordinate with other purchasing departments in other organizations to organize efficient, collaborative buying.

Pharmaceutical giant Merck & Co. is an example of a Fortune 500 company that has implemented a procurement application that provides a tangible ROI. As of early 1999, Merck planned to allow purchasing agents from its more than 40 research laboratories in 17 countries to purchase over $2 billion annually on the system, which was built using an Ariba solution for MRO procurement. The platform will allow Merck to aggregate high-volume purchases such as laboratory equipment and other MRO goods with select suppliers who have pre-negotiated pricing agreements with the pharmaceutical giant.

Caltex Corp., a joint venture of Texaco and Chevron, is also installing a procurement application to consolidate over $1.2 billion in MRO purchases in a single online catalog. Because an installation of this magnitude is understandably complex, Caltex has elected to incrementally integrate the application with its existing SAP ERP environment during the next several years. Until the integration is complete, procurement managers hope that the application's primary value will be its ability to control rogue buying through the products included in the Caltex catalog.

In the application's first iteration, the system will be deployed at only a single Caltex location and buyers will have to actually place orders by e-mail or fax. A tremendous concern for Caltex is its ability to integrate small, local suppliers into the system. Because its supply partners are distributed around the world, it is essential for Caltex to establish the catalog component on the Net where users are able to browse product data and plan purchases from anywhere on the globe. Even though the system won't be fully operational without an expensive integration process, Caltex is confident that MRO purchasing efficiency will repay the company's investment many times over. "The massive savings of going with procurement today outweigh any concerns about integration,"[11] concludes John Conway, Caltex's director of e-Procurement.

Now that we've examined and validated the business case for procurement/resource management applications, let's take a look at the enterprise buying process in some detail. As we discussed in Chapter 2, the B-to-B procurement process consists of four distinct phases: *requisitioning*, *request for quote*, *purchase order generation*, and *payment processing*.

Requisitioning

During requisitioning, employees or purchasing agents identify which products they would like to buy in what quantity and at what price. In order to make these determinations, buyers must be able to search integrated catalogs of supplier offerings with pre-negotiated prices. Regardless of the number of suppliers that may be involved in the procurement process, advanced procurement/vendor management systems aim to integrate all product and service offerings into a single catalog with a unified user interface.

These catalogs can be hosted by buyers, suppliers, third parties, or in some unique cases no one in particular. Because of advanced data translation techniques available on the Net, product information need not actually be integrated into a single database in order to present a unified catalog interface. These catalogs that take back-end, raw information from multiple databases distributed across the Net are referred to as virtual catalogs.

No matter who hosts the catalog, however, application administrators must be able to share and integrate information from disparate sources such as industry consortia and third-party catalog integrators. As new suppliers begin to offer valuable new goods to enterprise buyers and old suppliers drop out of contention for sourcing contracts, administrators should be able to add and subtract vendors without disrupting the integrity of the catalog on the whole.

In MRO procurement, enterprises often make purchases from only a few preferred vendors. For example, a business may choose to buy PCs exclusively from Dell, copiers and printers from Xerox, and office supplies from Office Depot. This makes catalog integration a relatively painless process. In fact, some MRO procurement application vendors such as Commerce One and Ariba have gone so far as to provide their own catalog consisting of multiple vendors on the Web in order to allow buyers to source from a single location.

Production goods, however, are typically supplied by a wide variety of manufacturers and distributors who must place competitive and co-opetive bids in order to win contracts. In these applications, it is essential that the e-Application provider make a concerted effort to integrate suppliers of all sizes and capabilities into the sourcing catalog so that buyers can be assured of finding exactly the product that they need.

In this heterogeneous supplier environment, buyers must do careful comparison-shopping in order to choose the appropriate solution for their requisitioning needs. In order to enable advanced and seamless comparison as well as integration of catalog information from multiple suppliers, many catalogs support product metadata that includes standard industry definitions such as Universal Product Codes (UPCs), Thomas Registry's product headings, Standard Industry Classifications (SICs), and Dun & Bradstreet's Standard Product & Service Codes (SPSCs). This information can be integrated automatically using established standards such as eXtensible Markup Language (XML) to allow for seamless comparison of products even from completely different suppliers.

Over time, purchasing agents begin to make requisitioning decisions based on long-term relationship factors such as enterprise-specific volume discounts with preferred suppliers. In order to support these strategic buying decisions, procurement e-Applications must also aggregate individual supplier statistics such as specific contract pricing and records of service quality. Purchasing agents should then be able to analyze information in real-time in order to make decisions that are consistent with long-term, strategic enterprise buying goals.

As preferred suppliers emerge for particular types of purchases, buyers should be presented with shortlists of approved vendors to ensure that every purchase made by every employee contributes to volume pricing discounts. Some information that is typically used by purchasing managers to select strategic procurement partners includes quantities that must be purchased to secure volume discounts, supplier lead times, and customer care ratings.

Robust procurement platforms can then incorporate these decision-making criteria into the requisitioning component of the application. For example, if a buyer needs to ensure that a supply of raw production materials arrives at factories by a certain date, the purchasing agent can rate potential suppliers by their relative lead times in order to select a vendor who is likely to deliver on time. Once the transaction has been completed, buyers can then update this decision support information based upon their own experiences to incorporate it into future supplier selection and contract renewal decisions.

In cases where no supplier is a clear-cut choice, the catalog must support browsing, keyword/parametric searching, collaborative filtering, product configuration, and mediation/collaboration tools that enable purchasing agents to identify suppliers capable of fulfilling even the most unique, out-of-catalog orders. For these items, the requisitioning phase must include informal brainstorming, document interchange, and multi-supplier discussion.

When buyers select a good that they wish to purchase, they record the item in a requisition in much the same manner that a consumer places an item in a virtual shopping cart in B-to-C e-Tailing environments. When the purchasing agent completes the requisition, it must be routed for approval.

In most organizations, this internal approval process is subject to highly specific rules such as individual buyer purchasing limits. In order to correctly route requisitions to purchasing managers with the appropriate authority, the application must employ a robust workflow component. Authorization can come in many forms. Typically, a manager must simply visit a Web site where he can view the requisition, and then choose to either approve the purchase, modify the document to meet company standards, or reject the requisition outright.

Throughout the entire requisitioning processes, purchasing agents and managers must be able to check on the status of their request for purchase. A notification component can easily be configured to keep buyers and accounting personnel up-to-date so that they can incorporate the latest budgeting and inventory information into internal company systems in real-time.

Request for quote (RFQ)

Once the requisition has been approved, the process moves on to the Request For Quote (RFQ) phase. By automating the RFQ process, buying organizations can reduce human error, shorten the purchasing cycle time, and incorporate suppliers around the globe who otherwise would be unable to participate in the sourcing process.

When pricing is either pre-negotiated or fixed, the RFQ phase involves simply passing the requisition to PO generation. For items with dynamic pricing models, however, the buyer must begin the RFQ process by either posting an RFQ in a public, online bulletin board for open bidding or delivering the RFQ to only selected suppliers through e-mail, fax, or private bid boards. The RFQ must include all the information that a supplier needs in order to deliver an accurate, well-informed quote, including product configuration, quantity, and delivery date.

Ultimately, this bid/ask buying will occur in specialized online trading organizations that specialize in specific industries and market segments. In addition to simply hosting bid boards, these sites will enable enterprises to share purchasing experiences and exchange best-practice buying techniques.

Purchase order (PO) generation

Once a requisition has been approved and, if necessary, a winning bid declared, the procurement application must generate appropriate purchase orders. Advanced procurement/resource management applications customize electronic POs to automatically integrate with individual supplier order entry and accounting software. When suppliers collaborate to fulfill a single order of large quantity, the application must also be smart enough to deliver separate POs for each supplier.

In addition to being used externally to initiate a transaction, POs are used internally to help the procurement department manage outstanding orders and budget for purchases that have not yet been processed by suppliers. The application should also provide some type of reporting functionality at this stage to allow purchasing managers to view and track all outstanding POs. When suppliers fail to meet deadlines or deliver products that don't meet enterprise standards, the PO reporting component can notify future buyers for use in negotiating new contracts and prices with suppliers.

Payment processing

Finally, the procurement application enters the payment processing phase. At this time, the enterprise receives their newly purchased supplies and delivers actual payment for goods and services rendered.

The receiving process represents the actual hand-off of goods from the supplier to the buying agent. As the newly purchased supplies are integrated into existing inventory, internal inventory management and accounting applications must be updated to reflect changes in inventory level. For services, however, receiving is considered to occur not when the service is performed, but instead upon receipt of a confirmation of services to be rendered. Hotel reservations, for example, are considered to have been "received" when the buyer is delivered a confirmation number. Especially as the process nears receiving, both buyer and supplier must be able to track goods as they are delivered in real-time.

Payment for purchases made in a procurement/vendor management application is typically in one of the same common methods as in a virtual marketplace: either a corporate check or a corporate P-card for smaller purchases.

Procurement/resource management applications are also useful in extending internal payment processing systems directly outward to transaction partners. This allows suppliers to bill the enterprise directly for services provided, and payment information can be integrated in real-time into accounts payable, general ledger, and inventory control systems.

Once payment has been processed, the buying process is officially over. However, in order to allow managers to view purchasing data, monitor trends, and identify best practices, most robust procurement/vendor management applications support reporting features that operate independent of any particular step in the procurement process.

These tools allow managers to give feedback directly to pur-chasing agents, suppliers, and application administrators in order to select preferred suppliers, eradicate rogue buying, and continuously adapt new and more efficient purchasing practices. They also auto-matically generate purchasing summaries for review by executive management and enterprise accountants for tax purposes. Reporting capabilities enable enterprise purchasing departments to work effi-ciently and intelligently, and to focus on procurement/resource man-agement as an essential, strategic business process.

EXTENDING THE VALUE CHAIN

Unlike virtual marketplaces or procurement/resource management applications that operate in high-profile, outward-facing environ-ments, *extended value chain* platforms work almost entirely behind the scenes and are invisible to end consumers. The notion of the value chain is deliberately vague in order to accommodate and apply to impossibly broad markets: businesses buy something, add-value to it, and then sell it for a higher price. Extending the value chain simply means integrating isolated enterprise value chain environments to create a superior collaborative commerce infrastructure.

In the manufacturing industry, the idea of the value chain is prac-tically self-evident: the manufacturer buys raw materials such as steel, molds them into a particular device such as a hinge, and then sells the final product for more than the cost of the raw materials. In fact, the value chain applies to each and every company from the smallest family-owned and operated country store to the largest multinational conglomerate.

In some cases, there isn't any real need to actually buy goods to supply the value chain. Take, for example, an author. To actually write a novel an author needs only a pad of paper and some pens. The function of the author in the value chain is to take his or her ideas, experience, and imagination, add value by organizing them into a cohesive manuscript, and then sell the final product through a pub-lisher for a profit.

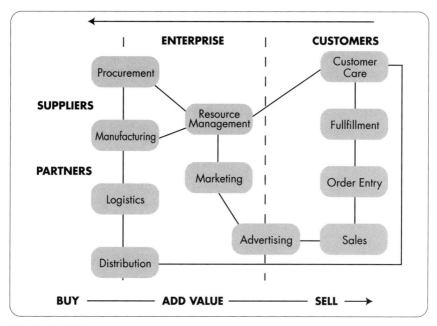

FIGURE 4.2

In other cases, the business need not physically modify the product to add value to it. A logistics company such as UPS or FedEx collects packages for shipment that start out in a particular location. They collect revenues from the package by delivering it to another city, state, or country. The value that logistics companies add to a product is its physical transportation.

The ultimate aim of extended value chain e-Applications is to share enterprise information with suppliers, buyers, and business partners to enable supply planning, demand planning, production planning, and logistics to occur in real-time. Eventually, the traditional, isolated value chain model breaks down and new value grids are created where enterprises of all kinds share information to provide each of them important strategic advantages over their competitors. Figure 4.2 illustrates how extended value chains unite buyers, suppliers, and partners.

In manufacturing industries—their most obvious and easily illustrated market—extended value chain platforms often aim to extend the functionality of conventional Supply Chain Management (SCM) systems by sharing forecasting and inventory data between multiple SCM applications.

Although many SCMs support some measure of data exchange for business partners directly, historically these applications have limited true, open information sharing because of technology constraints and high financial barriers to participation for enterprises. Most SCM applications require that all supply chain partners communicate either through tightly integrated EDI conducted over costly, privately owned and operated VANs or proprietary, closed application interfaces such as those provided by Manufacturer Resource Planning (MRP) packages from I2, Manugistics, or ERP players such as SAP, BAAN, and PeopleSoft.

This gave rise to what the Gartner Group describes as the coercive supply chain model for manufacturing, where dominant members of large supply chains would dictate that all participants adopt a single technology solution in order to communicate and make transactions electronically. Because these solutions are typically quite expensive and difficult to install and administer, supply chain automation has always been a viable option only for large manufacturers with complete coercive control over their partners.

Not surprisingly—considering the cost of technology investments that must be in place in order to operate successfully—the coercive model has been a largely ineffective means of promoting SCM integration. In fact, though it has been an acknowledged standard since the 1960s, even today only a small percentage of corporations utilize EDI in a supply chain environment.

With the rise of the Net, however, the advantages of integrated, SCM environments will be realized by manufacturers of all sizes. According to the Gartner Group, "Supply chains used to be exclusive affairs, the playthings of corporate giants who arm-twisted a few of their bigger supply chain partners into following along.... By 2003, however, eXtensible Markup Language (XML) will so lower the cost and technology hurdles to supply-chain automation that companies will no longer have to force their suppliers to adopt business-to-business e-Commerce ... collaborative extranets may be the wave of the future since they have the potential to spread standards far and wide ... (this) has the potential to drive costs lower and functionality higher by adopting standard (Internet) protocols such as XML and TCP/IP."[12]

The key difference between traditional SCM solutions and extended value chain applications is the ability to integrate information from suppliers and suppliers' suppliers and customers and customers' customers into a single databank for decision support. Extended value chain applications coordinate this exchange of information using open standards such as HTML, EDI, and XML to speed information between typical SCM, ERP, and other internal systems.

According to AMR Research, these internal systems deliver only about 20 percent of a complete, extended value chain solution.[13] The core advantages provided by conventional SCM applications are entirely internal: Bill of Material (BOM), Engineering Change Order (ECO), and Manufacturer Resource Planning (MRP) information.

Similarly, most ERP packages don't support the scheduling, planning, and inter-organizational information exchange required in dynamic supply grids. However, full-featured extended value chain e-Applications can aggregate data from multiple internal ERP and SCM applications and extend it outwards to all stakeholders in the supply grid. In an extended value chain platform, enterprises can view essential planning information from outside the enterprise as clearly as they can internal forecasts.

Extended value chain applications, of course, aren't limited to just manufacturing environments. In any industry the ability to coordinate delivery of goods and services with buyers and plan hyper-efficient supply of goods and services adds value to the business. For example, in the healthcare industry, care providers can share information about particular treatments to forecast costs.

Ubiquity and open standards driven by the business processes themselves are enabling every enterprise with Web access and a simple, thin client browser to become an integral member of even the most complex and demanding value grids. Because these new platforms for information sharing and collaborative planning extend the functionality of internal systems to every member of the value chain, they are often described as extended value chain applications. In the new, digital economy, supplier, buyer, and business-partner integration won't just be for the 500-pound gorillas of manufacturing. Instead, it will be a tool for every enterprise to maximize efficiency and lower costs.

By utilizing the Net to bring SCM, ERP, and other internal enterprise solutions together, next-generation extended value chain platforms can reduce costs. More important, however, they enable e-Enterprises to provide a unique competitive advantage over purely bricks-and-mortar competitors. Extended value chain applications offer the following four key advantages over conventional supply chain systems:

- **Improved cycle time:** Traditionally, changing market dynamics have had a slow, trickle-down effect on value chains; first consumer retailers were affected, and then their distributors and suppliers, and then *their* distributors and suppliers, and so on down the line. Extended value chains, however, enable corporations to reduce cycle time by sharing real-time supplier and customer planning data. The moment market demand changes, enterprise information is updated immediately throughout the entire value grid. Even organizations at the head of the value chain such as raw material providers can recognize the impact on their business at once and adjust accordingly.

- **Reduced inventory:** When planning production, managers used to face a difficult decision: minimize inventory and hope that market demand doesn't increase suddenly or overstock and gamble that product offerings don't become obsolete while sitting in a warehouse waiting to ship. By integrating information from every stage of the value chain in real-time, however, participants in extended value grids can eliminate this dilemma by choosing to reduce inventory and count on just-in-time reporting of market conditions to ensure manufacturing is ramped up immediately when demand increases. In today's fickle and often unpredictable marketplaces, a company's ability to respond to change is an essential competitive advantage.

- **Lower operating expenses:** Extended value chains offer manufacturers unique databanks of decision support information in order to streamline and automate the supply and demand planning processes. This improved planning is directly reflected in better operating efficiency and in a reduction in operating expenses. Additionally, in industries where the cost of suppliers is traditionally lower tomorrow than it is today (for example, the hardware technology industry), there will be a cost savings resulting from such tightly integrated systems functioning in a just-in-time manner.

▪ **SME integration:** Finally, Web-based dynamic value chains allow enterprises to incorporate electronic information from Small to Medium Enterprises, or SMEs. Typically, these small concerns are essential to even the largest companies because they offer niche goods and services that provide a unique competitive advantage. Although these SMEs can make up over two thirds of all value chain contributors, the cost of installing and operating most ERP and SCM applications has traditionally excluded SMEs from complete application and data integration. Extended value chain platforms, however, use open standards and defined data interfaces to enable efficient integration of SME homegrown systems and large corporate installations.

Dynamic value grids created with extended value chain applications realize these benefits through a combination of channel-wide data integration and inter-application process engineering. As market and supply conditions change, enterprises must also ensure that supplier models are flexible enough to integrate and disintegrate new and different business partners without installing and uninstalling complex software.

Successfully implemented extended value chain applications can then be linked with other systems to extend isolated solutions into channel-wide value grids that supply real-time information about production capability, pricing, and delivery dates from one end of the value chain to the other.

These grids give enterprises at every stage of the value chain real-time information about market demand and customer interest. This results in supply and demand planning that is driven not by vague predictions based on past market conditions, but instead by real-time monitoring of consumer buying habits and demands. The dynamic value grids of the future are designed to meet customer needs by querying direct customer input at every phase of the traditional buy, add-value, and sell process.

This aggregation of planning information into multi-department, multi-enterprise databanks for decision support requires new thinking about the relationship between the enterprise and its business partners. Gone are the days when individual members of the value chain collected planning information and optimized their businesses independently. Instead, entire value grids are collaborating in real-time on the Net to coordinate planning and production to match up-to-the minute market conditions.

In their article "The Seven Principles of Supply Chain Management," David L. Anderson, Frank E. Britt, and Donavon J. Favre write that for extended value chains in the manufacturing industry, the "real measure of success is how well activities coordinate across the supply chain to create value for customers, while increasing the profitability of every link in the chain.... Successes are typically broad efforts, combining both strategic and tactical change. They also reflect a holistic approach, viewing the supply chain from end to end and orchestrating efforts so that the whole improvement achieved—in revenue, costs, and asset utilization—is greater than the sum of its parts.... Unsuccessful efforts likewise have a consistent profile. They tend to be functionally defined and narrowly focused, and they lack sustaining infrastructure. Uncoordinated change activity erupts in every department and function and puts the company in grave danger of 'dying the death of a thousand initiatives.'"[14]

FedEx's logistic coordination solutions for manufacturing companies provide excellent examples of extended value chain applications in action. At its simplest level, FedEx aims to automate the transportation and warehousing of goods in order to reduce inventory and also costs.

According to FedEx, "through the industrial era, the ultimate corporate model was vertical integration—companies that owned their entire supply chains from manufacturing through assembly to marketing." In the new economy, however, FedEx argues that vertical integration will make way for virtual integration, "where value-leading businesses focus on a limited set of core competencies and outsource virtually every other function."[15]

To coordinate operations between an enterprise and its virtual business partners, FedEx has built a computerized logistics management system that allows users to schedule pickups, track individual packages, and integrate logistics information directly with internal systems. The system essentially provides an information bridge between business partners to extend the value of each one's internal inventory management and logistics systems.

FedEx calls this service "integrated logistics," and promises that it allows virtual corporations to build strategic advantages by reducing inventory. Companies can be assured electronically that their goods are "warehoused" in the FedEx transport system, thereby requiring less warehousing of its own. Not only are warehousing costs decreased, but the company is also able to respond in real-time to market changes and contend more successfully with the competition.

Extended value chain applications are by nature complex and can't be defined by any single task. In fact, the wide variety of important business processes automated by dynamic supply grids is limited only by the enterprise's ability to develop new ideas about how to manage the buy/add-value/sell chain. In most value chain applications, however, supported business processes can be divided into four key phases: *demand planning, supply planning, logistics,* and *production planning/fulfillment.*

Demand planning

During the *demand planning* phase of extended value chain applications, enterprises analyze shared information in order to anticipate market demand for their wares. Typically, this information is derived directly from up-to-the-minute sales data and end-market analysis. For example, consider a manufacturer whose primary product is an electronic component used in speakers. During demand planning, this corporation would be examining the production capabilities of its immediate buyers, speaker manufacturers. At the same time, it would be monitoring independent demand by carefully monitoring the sale of home stereo systems, televisions, and other markets where its product is likely to end up. Using statistics such as market share and unit growth, supply chain managers can predict with a large measure of accuracy the demand for electronic speaker components in the short, intermediate, and long term.

Making this type of prediction involves more than just gathering data, however. Accurate demand planning consists not only of analyzing facts and figures, but also incorporating known buying patterns of manufacturers as well as end users in particular market conditions. From this advanced information, extended value chain systems can make accurate aggregate, item, and group forecasts for industries as a whole, product niches, and particular products.

Because demand forecasting directly affects inventory levels in warehouses and distribution centers, most demand planning components either include or integrate with an inventory planning component to automatically trigger manufacturing ramp-ups and slow-downs to maintain favorable inventory levels. Demand planning applications also include reporting and analysis tools such as time-phased charts and graphical simulations that make analyzing these types of complex data intuitive and efficient for managers. Dynamic supply information is frequently made available in the value chain as soon as it is collected, so it makes sense that particular components of the application rely directly on input from other functional areas. In most value chain apps, demand planning results are used directly in all other phases to ensure a unified, holistic approach to value chain management.

Supply planning

In the *supply planning* phase, supply chain managers seek to position the enterprise to meet the demand forecasted in the demand planning stage. Unlike demand planning, which as a rule focuses down the chain toward end-user/consumer marketplaces, supply planning faces upward and incorporates information from immediate suppliers all the way to the collection of raw materials.

Supply planning consists of a number of distinct business processes, including strategic planning, replenishment planning, manufacturing planning, and also inventory/distribution planning in conjunction with the demand planning stage and logistics.

One of the core purposes of the supply planning phase is to outline purchasing requirements for production goods. This component of the platform must support advanced, best-practice sourcing techniques including multi-supplier and multi-site sourcing, supply allocation to multiple plants and distribution centers, and seamless integration with enterprise procurement/resource management applications if they exist.

Through the aggregation and analysis of information provided by immediate suppliers, inventory management systems, and supply grid databanks, managers can do accurate Available to Promise (ATP) forecasting. The purpose of ATP forecasting (where the enterprise is able to accurately commit to order specifications, prices, and delivery deadlines for goods before they have been prepared for sale) is to minimize time to delivery for orders without maintaining a large product inventory.

To support this extremely time sensitive process, enterprises often require a just-in-time procurement component to ensure that raw materials are available the moment the enterprise needs to begin fabricating the final good for sale. By shortening product delivery time, ATP forecasting improves enterprise agility in hyper-competitive markets.

Like demand planning, supply-planning components also require complex reporting and analysis tools for business managers to do advance enterprise-wide capacity planning and activity-based costing.

Logistics

The *logistics* component of an extended value chain platform plans and manages the distribution and receiving of materials, finished goods, and supplies. Logistics also includes managing existing inventory in warehouses and distribution centers.

Although seemingly a straightforward piece of an otherwise complex value grid, the logistics component must respond in real-time to dynamic market pressure in the transportation and storage industries.

This includes load control, mode and carrier selection, freight cost management, and shipping consolidation to take advantage of volume discounts. Robust logistic components must also include facilities to track supplies as they are transported and stored in real-time for customer service inquiries and general management of enterprise property.

In the past, logistics was often relegated to a second-tier concern. Today, however, as ever-shrinking margins and ultra-competitive markets push enterprises to take advantage of any and every possible cost cutting measure, logistics has become an important target for e-Enterprise automation.

Because logistics planning receives extensive input from production, demand, and supply planning, it often can be automated extensively to take advantage of optimum shipping/receiving conditions. Despite this relative simplicity, however, logistics can have a dramatic affect on the bottom line. According to software vendor Oracle, logistics cost American companies over $760 billion each year. Worldwide, enterprises spend an astonishing $2 to $3 trillion to ship and store goods.[16]

Production planning/fulfillment

The final stage in an extended value chain application is *production planning/fulfillment*. At this time, information from each of the three other phases of value chain automation is integrated to determine the enterprise's production strategy.

Production planning supports internal enterprise decision making such as requirements planning, order processing, costing, repetitive manufacturing, and capacity planning. Ultimately, the goal of production planning is fast, accurate delivery of products and services to buyers at competitive prices.

CUSTOMER RELATIONSHIP MANAGEMENT

The term *customer care* has typically been associated with problem solving. Can't figure out how to install a software application? Call the 1-800 technical support line. Want to return a purchase that is defective? Take it to the returns processing department. Can't find a particular product that meets your needs? Ask a knowledgeable sales representative.

By today's standards, customer care practices from just a few years ago seem primitive. Enterprises that employed a call center to automatically direct telephone inquiries or accepted customer questions by e-mail were considered cutting edge. In nearly every company, customer care was simply a passive process on the part of the enterprise; inquiries were always initiated by the customer and a day without customer interaction was a good thing—it meant nobody had a problem.

In most cases, a customer care process involved giving the customer some piece of information from the collective base of enterprise knowledge after the point of sale. Some examples of frequently queried information included product data, technical support, warranty information, and order status. Unfortunately, in order to get the right information, customers first had to determine which part of the enterprise to ask. For example, an enterprise buyer unhappy with the quality of a newly arrived shipment of products would have to determine what department handled returns before she could inquire how to send the goods back.

Because customer care often happened after the purchases had been made, it wasn't believed to materially affect the bottom line—except perhaps negatively. A customer care transaction was considered to be effective if it was short; long calls meant more customer care representatives would be needed to answer telephones, and personal service equaled an investment in high personnel costs with little hope for a direct return.

However, with enterprises shifting emphasis from commanding a share of the market to owning a share of the customer, the scope and magnitude of customer care has taken a dramatic turn. Today, dealing with customers after the point of sale isn't just about answering questions. Instead, it's about building relationships that transcend individual transactions and ensure customer satisfaction and repeat buying. What used to be simply customer care has become full-blown customer relationship management that improves service and reduces cost, gives customers individual personalized attention, and builds long-term relationships to own the customer's business forever.

Not surprisingly, it hasn't taken customers long to figure out their importance in new customer-centric marketplaces. In a few short years, customers have gone from being grateful for whatever service they could get to demanding prompt attention, courteous service, and quick results. In the new Net economy, customers have the power, and they know it.

To manage complete customer relationships, companies need to adopt a strategy that is about more than just problem solving. By creating and monitoring new customer touch points through automated e-mail responses, searchable databases of product support information, and full-featured Web sites with extensive product and service information, businesses can begin to track every customer interaction with the enterprise and build individual profiles for important customers.

This isn't to say, of course, that automated, profile-driven customer service will ever replace human interaction. But by anticipating and addressing common questions and complaints before the consumer even voices them, enterprises can improve service to the customer at the same time that they reduce costs.

The power shift to the customer has begun. To meet customer needs in the new marketplace, enterprises must make a concerted effort to deliver unparalleled customer care. This requires analyzing customer behavior in order to invest in relationships that will provide a sound ROI. "Since building relationships is not a cost-free proposition," Cambridge Technology Partners explains, "customers with the highest potential to perform should receive the most attention. For one-time customers as well as "churners," who display little loyalty despite all attempts to retain them, close relationships may represent losing investments. Personalized customer care makes sense if the customer's lifetime value sufficiently exceeds the cost of building the relationship."[17] In the age of long-term relationships with your best customers, customer Lifetime Total Value, or LTV, will become an important indicator of the strength of the enterprise-customer relationship.

Because it reaches from a customer's very first contact with the enterprise all the way through their last, the customer care relationship often manifests itself within other e-Enterprise models. Let's take, for example, an online consumer marketplace. We have already spoken about the importance of individual, one-to-one marketing in an e-Tailing environment. By integrating information collected for one-to-one product promotions and traditional customer care information, e-Tailers can build a complete profile for users that not only anticipates their buying patterns but also their service needs. If a user is new to the site, an interface with shopping instructions and generic contact information for pre-sales advice can be displayed. If the user is a long-term customer, however, the store can be customized to present products specially selected to attract his attention, and contact information for his favorite salesperson can be prominently displayed. If the user recently made a purchase, the site can even automatically include links to a FAQ and installation instructions for his new purchase in the event they need technical support.

In general, pervasive customer care/customer management applications provide three important benefits to the enterprise:

- **Improved care through individual treatment:** By tracking customer interactions with the enterprise and incorporating one-to-one customer service on the fly, businesses can answer questions before they are asked. In e-Applications that aggregate communities of users, the community can supply common know-how and hands-on experience to foster joint problem solving and customer self-service.

- **Reduced costs through customer self-service:** The vast majority of calls placed to customer service representatives are to ask a short and predictable list of questions. User profiles allow enterprises to anticipate customer support needs and prepare answers automatically. If a consumer has just purchased a VCR, for example, the next time she visits the Web site she could be directed to directions for setting the clock on that particular model. Because customer care dialog occasionally provides opportunities for cross- and up-selling, customer relationship applications can even increase revenues.

- **Increased repeat buying through long-term customer relationships:** Customer care/customer management applications require a significant investment of enterprise resources to function effectively. In return for the personal attention and superior service that this money buys, enterprises expect to receive customer loyalty. Today, 60 percent of an enterprise's business is repeat business. In the future, this number will rise as businesses fight to establish long-term dialogues with customers.

Even though the potential rewards for superior customer care are clearly identified, building long-term customer management success is still a difficult proposition. To be as successful as possible, enterprises looking to automate their relationships with customers should focus on a few key strategies.

First, and most important, successful customer management is about matching information from the enterprise and the customer. Too often when a customer contacts the enterprise for support, she is exposed to only a particular customer touch point—let's say a telephone call center. Holistic customer management means the customer must know as much about the enterprise as possible in order to find specific information—usually disseminated in multiple departmental data sources. If a customer only takes advantage of a particular customer management resource, then her understanding of the enterprise's overall customer care is limited to that particular resource.

Conversely, enterprises must resist the temptation to view customers simply in terms of their interactions with particular customer touch points. When a customer returns a new refrigerator because it isn't large enough, the marketing department should know immediately to target them with promotions for larger products.

This problem is especially important in enterprises with multiple, distinct customer care departments. Traditionally, large corporations have maintained individual customer service offerings focused on supporting particular product lines or distribution channels. In the new economy, however, these disjointed solutions must learn to work—and look to the customer—as one.

The solution to this problem is maintaining complete customer profiles in a single, centralized databank that all departments can access. Another potential advantage to this structure is that enterprises can reorganize or even eliminate particular departments with certain customer relationship responsibilities without compromising the integrity of the customer database.

To populate this database with complete customer information, Cambridge Technology Partners defines a process they call "zero loss learning," where the enterprise "views every point of contact with the customer as a potential learning experience. Every customer interaction—whether it is with a sales person, clerk, or customer support representative—yields insight into the customer relationship that can be captured and stored in a knowledge base. As a relationship matures, the knowledge base becomes more comprehensive and more accurate. Ultimately, the entire enterprise can benefit from this growing library of customer data, which is leveraged to provide customers with personalized and consistent service."[18]

Eventually, as the customer database becomes a nearly complete history of every customer's interaction with the company, managers need to be careful not to overwhelm customers with information about themselves. First and foremost, finding out that a company has been watching your every move can be quite unsettling to many customers, even if it is in their long-term interest. More important, however, enterprises must focus on delivering only data that is directly useful to customers at any particular moment. This requires more than just complete data collection and warehousing. Delivering only useful information in a timely manner requires an in-depth understanding of customer behavior and an appreciation for their needs.

So how should enterprises measure success in customer care/customer relationship applications? Traditionally, enterprises have measured customer service by metrics such as cost per transaction, number of inquiries handled per hour, and so on. Customer relationship management platforms, however, require a different measurement.

The single most important indicator of the effectiveness of customer management in an e-Enterprise is customer retention and repeat business. These factors measure the enterprise's ability to build long-term relationships and lock in buyers to own the whole customer—a cornerstone for success in the digital economy.

Personal computer, printer, and software manufacturer Hewlett Packard has recently aggregated all its post-sales customer support into a single branded site it refers to as HP Customer Care Web. Here, HP offers services such as software and driver updates, product returns, FAQs, warranty/repair information, and guides for installing and setting up HP products.

To encourage customers to take advantage of the services provided by the HP Customer Care Web, the company has incorporated an e-mail notification service to alert customers to the availability of new support offerings for their HP product. The site also includes user forums for individual products to encourage customer self-service and community-generated solutions to particular problems. Support and information pages are also categorized by product as well as by geographic location, so that customers can choose from non Web-based support options available in their location.

According to Doug Moore of HP's Product Support Division, HP Customer Care "plays an important role in increasing customer satisfaction by making support easier to access and understand. Increasingly, customers prefer the control and convenience they get with around-the-clock online support, and this site will be our key platform for providing future enhancements."[19]

Some examples of key customer care processes that should be automated by a customer management platform include: *one-to-one marketing, customer self-service/solution-centered support*, and *customer history/account management*.

One-to-one marketing

One-to-one marketing in a customer relationship management application is about providing customized cross-selling, up-selling, and bundle pricing. Before a sale has even taken place, the customer management application can begin recording and analyzing user buying habits in order to identify individual goods to promote and special services and pricing to offer. By extracting data from the customer database about past purchases, successful marketing promotions, and individual personal profiles, enterprises can present customers with a shopping interface and services that encourage the highest instance of repeat buying.

As we discussed in Chapter 3, forward-looking enterprises will resist the temptation to allocate resources to attract new customers and will instead focus on delivering a buying experience for existing customers that is robust, personalized, and pleasing. When the customer finally is ready to check out, the application can recommend additional purchases to her to offer a more complete solution, improve customer satisfaction, and plant the seeds for superior relationship management.

Customer self-service/solution-centered support

The combination of *customer self-service and solution-centered support* acts as the primary interface between customers and the enterprise.

Customer self-support is best employed in product comparison and post-sale support roles. Typically, customer self-service touch points such as automated call centers, online FAQs, and automatically generated responses to e-mail inquiries free customers to answer their own questions on their own time at their own pace. The result is both an increase in customer satisfaction, and a reduction in staffing of traditional customer support hotlines.

Traditional types of customer service, including warranty, product, account, and maintenance information, are most easily converted to a self-service format because the types of data that customers require are usually predictable.

According to customer management packaged application vendor Silknet, "a straightforward request handled on the phone costs a company between $25 and $30. By comparison, resolving the same problem through a Web-based self-service application costs between $2 and $3. Costs are compounded by the fact that call center operations offer little opportunity for economies of scale. Customers tend to ask the same questions over and over again. And service representatives answer them one customer at a time. Analysts estimate that repeat rates run as high as the 50 to 70 percent range."[20]

For more non-traditional customer support including call center and help desk integration, collaborative customer communities, and knowledge-based support systems, enterprises must invest in custom, solution-centered support components, including online chat, bulletin boards, and customer-driven content aggregation sites.

Customer history/account management

Managing individual customer accounts presents a combination of two challenges: the enterprise must collect as much information as possible and then deliver only what the customer needs at any give time. Usually, accomplishing this goal requires an intelligent invest-ment in technology and business know-how. Where does the data come from? First and foremost, it is collected from traditional cus-tomer care transactions, including buying history and problems the customer has had in the past. Also, however, the database can be pop-ulated with non-traditional customer information such as surfing habits within the company Web site, e-mail exchanges with customer care representatives, records of successful promotional campaigns delivered to customers, and so on.

Currently, most enterprises don't do a good job of collecting and leveraging the broad base of customer information available to them. According to Forrester Research, less than half of Fortune 1,000 com-panies use non-traditional data such as Web and e-mail tracking in their marketing and customer service departments.[21]

CRITICAL SUCCESS FACTORS

As companies continue to automate inter-organizational processes in the form of B-to-B e-Applications, they will face a number of key bar-riers to success. To build B-to-B platforms that overcome these pitfalls, enterprises should focus on conquering five crucial challenges: *application agility/flexibility*, *creation/improvement/integration*, *overcoming political obstacles*, *application and data integration*, and *putting the CEO in charge*.

Application agility/flexibility

In the 1960s, Intel co-founder Gordon Moore made a bold prediction that microchip capacity would double every 18 months. Although pundits of the time argued that pace would be impossible to maintain, in the ensuing 30-odd years, what has become known as Moore's Law has proven remarkably accurate. Furthermore, it has become apparent that "a variant of Moore's Law governs network development. Technological advancement continues to increase the speed with which Internet communication occurs and to reduce overall communication costs. The combination is driving down the price of doing business in the Internet economy."[22]

It's easy to underestimate the dynamics of change in a given marketplace. After all, it's quite a tempting proposition to believe that things always were and always will be exactly as they are now. However, the reality is that change is an inevitable part of every industry—especially when viewed in light of the Net. One look at industry leaders only a few decades ago provides irrefutable evidence that success today doesn't necessarily translate into success down the road. To survive the test of time, market leaders must recognize that the ability to adapt and evolve is essential.

Because of this constant change, B-to-B application development and deployment cannot be approached as a one-time thing. Enterprises that count on purchasing an end-to-end solution from a vendor, installing it, and being done with e-Application development are missing the point of doing business on the Net. e-Enterprise is about refocusing the enterprise around the customer, turning it on a dime to meet changes in the competitive landscape, and owning the whole customer by providing best-of-breed, complete solutions.

To succeed online, enterprises must above all be flexible to accommodate both business and technology change. In the Net economy, business models can change overnight. We've already seen ample evidence of this in the B-to-C area. Consider Amazon.com for example. In the space of a little more than a year, Amazon.com went from an online bookseller to an online book and music seller, to an online book/music/movie seller, to an online portal offering links to anything that's for sale on the Net. The same will happen in B-to-B environments.

New opportunities and competitors can spring up on the Web without a moment's notice. To take advantage of opportunities and ward off challengers, even the most entrenched businesses must be prepared to adapt. The e-Enterprise revolution is an age of opportunity and change. For companies without an agile business architecture, it'll also be an age of extinction.

To coexist with this trend, application developers must develop a technology architecture that is capable of changing to support the latest open standards without sacrificing interoperability with proprietary, legacy systems. An e-Application technology architecture must support adding new functionality, swapping out components that have become obsolete, and adopting support for new standard technology as it becomes available down the road.

Process creation, improvement, and integration

In order to support the continuous evolution of e-Enterprise business processes and technology architectures, companies must adopt a well-defined process improvement strategy that can continue to work and deliver effective results through even the most tumultuous change. It's not about just making changes and being done. Instead, it requires a continuous cycle of process creation, improvement, and integration.

In the creation stage, enterprises define new application requirements and determine what business processes the application will address. During improvement, managers examine how the unique advantages and capabilities of the Net enable enterprises to improve existing processes and streamline information. Finally, the integration stage is about making new processes work with other corporate procedures both within and outside the enterprise.

Because e-Enterprise business processes represent a continuous evolution rather than a static solution, changes to the e-Application platform must be implemented continuously with very short intervals between new updates. The creation, improvement, and integration process helps to support this incremental process improvement by segmenting development and allowing managers to begin designing new application elements even before the newest processes have been completely implemented.

Overcoming political obstacles

e-Enterprise is about process integration both within the enterprise and with suppliers, customers, and business partners. By definition, these processes connect entities with different management structures, goals, and priorities. In order to be successful, e-Applications must navigate this potential minefield of political obstacles.

Let's take, for example, an extended value chain application. Extended value chain applications' primary added value is the ability to integrate information from multiple supply chain entities: manufacturers, end-consumer markets, logistic providers, and SMEs. In order to build a platform that unites these very different organizations and individuals, however, application administrators must make some key decisions. Who will oversee and have final say over technology standards? Where will the decision-support databank be maintained? Which department within the enterprise will take ultimate responsibility for the maintenance and upkeep of the application?

When making these decisions, enterprises must balance control with cooperation to ensure that they have authority over their own investments in the systems and yet don't try to dominate other business partners.

Application and data integration

Another important challenge when uniting multiple business entities under a single application platform is overcoming application and data integration difficulties. Because every company maintains distinct business processes that add unique value to its business, packaged applications don't provide the level of support that enterprises need right out of the box. Because of this, e-Application development can't simply be about installing. Even when corporations purchase end-to-end applications, they should be prepared to spend a significant amount of time and money writing custom code to make enterprise applications work with each other and share common data sources—even across enterprise boundaries.

In the digital economy, e-Enterprises will function not as stand-alone entities, but instead as a node in a network of business partners who share data and process transactions in real-time. As these networks continue to strengthen relationships between corporations, the distinction between a business and its closest partners will blur.

This type of complete enterprise integration, however, isn't easy. During the past decade, the complexity and cost of ERP installations has given enterprises a healthy respect for the difficulty of integrating proprietary data and application systems from across the enterprise. Typical ERP installations require years of custom coding and often cost more than purchasing the application itself.

In e-Enterprise, the challenge is even more formidable. First, because multiple enterprises are involved in every B-to-B initiative, data exists in a wider variety of formats. More important, however, no single management team has control over data standards for the entire application. In an internal ERP installation, management could dictate that every department follow certain standards and conventions in order to facilitate integration. In e-Enterprise, however, there is no way that one enterprise can exercise that type of absolute control over another. Because of this, adherence to open standards such as XML and EDI and third-party regulations such as OBI and SET is absolutely critical for e-Enterprise. Again, how do you reach standards across an industry of competitors each reaching for an advantage?

E-ORGANIZATION

Finally, enterprises must recognize that becoming an e-Enterprise isn't simply a technology issue to be managed by an IT department. It isn't about choosing Java over ActiveX or COM/DCOM over CORBA for example. These are simply deployment discussions. Because it involves process engineering and improvement, becoming an e-Enterprise is a core strategic issue. It's about molding every part of the enterprise into whatever the market demands that it be and it's about setting long-term goals to refocus the business. It's about business as much as it is about technology, and as such it must be managed directly by a team of executives that can 'walk the line' between corporate strategy and IT issues.

Ultimately, this requires corporations to take new stock of the role of technology in the enterprise. It requires IT leaders to learn business, and business leaders to learn technology. In the complex B-to-B environment especially, enterprises must rethink internal organization and create new roles in management that are directly responsible for e-Enterprise initiatives. Oftentimes, this means forsaking traditional ideas about corporate org structure and building new, e-Organizations from scratch whose divisions report directly to the CEO.

In the digital economy, the CEO will have a new role. In addition to his/her traditional responsibilities, he/she will be in charge of overseeing the creation of the enterprise business architecture and for ensuring that the new e-Organization operates efficiently within the e-Enterprise.

PART 3

---

e-Enterprise Methodology and Architecture

5 Building e-Enterprises

E-TRANSFORMATION

The idea of clicks and mortar... suggests that the successful companies in the Internet Economy will be those that do everything well. They'll offer great products at low prices, great service, perfectly targeted marketing, friendly Web sites, beautiful retail spaces, flawless delivery, and so forth... In a clicks and mortar world, you have to do everything, do it fast, and do it right.[1]
— David Pottruck, co-CEO of Charles Schwab

In Chapter 1, I discussed how the Net is bringing about a fundamental change in the way corporations do business. For established "bricks-and-mortar" corporations, the Web was initially an afterthought, a place for posting static product information and accepting credit card numbers and shipping addresses to make purchases. We called this "e-Commerce."

In its second iteration business on the Net became more complex and specialized. Corporations began to appreciate the value of doing businesses with other enterprises, and to implement specialty business-to-business (B-to-B) e-Applications such as Maintenance, Repair, and Operations (MRO) procurement to automate simple online processes. On the business-to-consumer (B-to-C) side, retailers recognized the value of personalized content and dynamic product information. Online marketplaces became more interactive and efficient. "Bricks and mortar" had become "point and click." Because this stage was about more than simple transactions, we labeled it "e-Business."

Most companies have embraced e-Commerce by now. Some have taken halting steps toward e-Business. However, I predicted that another stage was coming, where corporations would recognize the Net for its true value: not a new distribution channel or customer touch-point, but a strategic tool that touches every aspect of the enterprise—both on the Net and in the real world, through process engineering, improvement, and integration. This third phase, e-Enterprise, isn't just brick and mortar and it isn't just point and click. Instead, it's a perfect fusion of the two: clicks and mortar.

In Chapters 2, 3, and 4, I introduced some important business models and described their relative merits, challenges, and effects upon overall enterprise operations. I discussed B-to-C and B-to-B initiatives, gave examples of successful pioneers, and talked about inter-organizational process engineering as the basis for e-Enterprise applications. In this chapter, I will outline the fundamentals of building an e-Enterprise.

Becoming an e-Enterprise doesn't happen on its own. It's the result of following a methodical, objective, results-driven approach that reflects the experience of industry leaders. Furthermore, developing an e-Enterprise strategy can't simply be outsourced to consultants. It represents the core of the enterprise, and no consultant—no matter how much of an expert he professes to be—knows more about your business than you do.

Making the transition from e-Commerce to e-Business to e-Enterprise means understanding and anticipating the changes that must occur in every aspect of the enterprise: *culture, people, business model, organizational model, application model, management processes,* and *technology* (see Figure 5.1).

Culture

Although corporate culture is largely an intangible asset, few would deny that it plays an essential role in shaping the character and effectiveness of the enterprise. In the earliest days of e-Commerce, the culture of most Web initiatives was marked by chaos (even when such

	e-Commerce	e-Business	e-Enterprise
Culture	Chaos, **.COM Mania**, **Reactive**, Individualistic Control, **Hype**	Business Model Focus, **Proactive**, Process Creation, Cooperation, **Branding**	Enterprise Focus, **Iterative**, Process Integration, Empowerment, **Mission Critical**
People	**Technology & Implementation Focus**, Hot Skills	**Process/Design Focus**, Core Competency	**Analysis/ROI Focus**, Strategy Orientation, Knowledge-based
Business Model	**Content Aggregation**, VC Funded, Pure Net Play, IPO	**Process Aggregation**, F1000 Spin Offs, Hybrid, Consolidation	**People Aggregation**, Inter-Enterprise Integration, Co-opetition, Virtual Corporations
Organizational Model	Function Focus, Isolated, **Founder Driven**, In-Sourcing	Cross Organizational Focus, Federated, **e-Business Czar Driven, Out-Sourcing**	Extended Enterprise Focus, Collaborative, **CEO Driven**, **Partner-Sourcing**
Application Model	**B-to-C** Focused On-line Marketplaces for Hard Goods	**B-to-B** Procurement, B-to-B Communities, Soft Goods, B-to-C Auctioning	Mission critical **Inter-Enterprise** applications for unique business processes
Management Processes	**Situation Driven**, Project Orientation, Disconnected	**Process Driven**, Program Orientation, Connected	**Method/Model/ROI Driven**, Enterprise Solution Orientation, Integrated & Extended
Technology	**Catalyst**, Client Driven, **Unique**	**Driver**, Server Driven, **Accepted**	**Enabler**, Network Driven & Distributed, **Commodity**

FIGURE 5.1

initiatives popped up in stable old-line companies). Although most employees had heard the hype surrounding the World Wide Web and the Information Superhighway, few had any real concept of where or how it would affect them personally, let alone the enterprise as a whole.

Early Net initiatives were led by individual visionaries who broke away (or sneaked away) from the pack and established the first corporate beachheads on the Web. Less farsighted pioneers quickly followed, playing catch-up the only way they knew how: imitation. This led to .com mania, where new Web businesses sprung up overnight, either fueled by radical vision or by fear. Hype ran wild. IPO's skyrocketed. Market capitalization went through the roof. On the whole however, the culture of e-Commerce was oddly reactive: People stood on the brink of a new age, knowing that change was coming but not really knowing what to do.

In the e-Business era, .com mania has begun to settle. More new initiatives are led by corporations taking proactive measures to harness the Net to their everyday business activities. Their focus is less on becoming an Amazon.com or eBay and more on developing a sound business model where carefully created internal and external processes embrace the Net.

In e-Enterprise, culture will come full circle back to the corporation as a whole. Instead of leading point projects that address one process at a time, managers will focus on the complete enterprise. Development of new architectures with supporting applications and processes will be iterative and ongoing. Special emphasis will be placed on processes that integrate internal and external business systems, thereby empowering business leaders to make strategic decisions based on the Net.

People

During e-Commerce, the focus was on the whiz kids of technology. Fortune 500 corporations hired seventeen-year-olds to do HTML coding. Twenty-one-year-old Java programmers could command astronomical starting salaries with little if any experience. Because Web site initiatives in most corporations had virtually no strategic value at this stage, executives were less hesitant to hand such tasks to green newcomers. The Net brought new technical skill sets to the forefront of computing, and the supply of programmers well-versed in these disciplines was inadequate.

Proving to be a perfect economics model, however, supply soon caught up with demand. Simultaneously, enterprise focus shifted from overcoming technology obstacles to process design. Suddenly, business knowledge and process engineering experience meant as much as programming knowledge. A new class of employee began to take charge: the enterprise developer whose core competency is modeling enterprise processes and developing e-Business applications.

In e-Enterprises, individual employees will view the Net much as they do any other strategic business thrust. Instead of isolated specialists leading the charge, careful analysis and return-on-investment (ROI) projections will guide e-Enterprise initiatives. Applications will be strategically focused. The most valuable asset will be the knowledge worker who can integrate business and technology into a coherent strategy.

Business model

Most early e-Commerce successes were startup companies with little if any presence in conventional markets. These pure Net plays built their reputations by aggregating content and wowing the market with numbers. Amazon.com rose to fame by becoming the world's biggest bookstore. eBay boasts millions of auctions every day. Content sites such as Time Warner's Pathfinder can post every story from every issue from every one of their magazines.

e-Commerce was also the heyday of venture capital funding. Entrepreneurs with little experience could get access to working capital like never before as investors clamored to get in on the next big thing before its inevitable IPO.

In the e-Business era, the startup craze has slowed and Fortune 1000 enterprises are leading the charge through business process aggregation. Still a bit unsure of where Net initiatives fit into their overall strategy, corporations will sometimes start new online commerce divisions only to spin them off.

Alternately, many Fortune 1000 companies are signing long-term agreements with pure Net plays to leverage their own brand recognition with the startups' perceived technology and niche position. Finally, we are seeing dramatic consolidation among Net companies as traditional software companies spend exorbitant sums to round out their product lines with new Net offerings and position themselves as Web players.

e-Enterprises, by contrast, will recognize that knowledge workers form the core for success on the Net. They will focus on aggregating the most talented and experienced personnel into process-oriented teams. These teams will then concentrate on integrating processes that flow between enterprises. The result will be co-opetive networks of virtual corporations that are linked in cyberspace to share information for mutual strategic advantage.

Organizational model

The role of the organizational model, or org model, in the e-Commerce phase depended on whether the enterprise considered itself primarily a player in conventional markets or a pure Net play.

Traditional corporations had learned the lessons of horizontal integration and were primarily focused on internal functions for individual product lines and departments. Because developing an early Web-presence was typically inexpensive and wasn't considered much of a strategic move, corporations often delegated Web site design and maintenance to small internal IT teams.

Startups often struggled to maintain an efficient org model through periods of dramatic growth and change. Many upstarts were entirely driven by the core founders, and maintained the loose models typical of young companies, even as they hired thousands of new employees and diversified into new and varied markets.

In the e-Business phase, corporations have taken the first steps toward a cross-organizational approach to Net initiatives. To manage these hybrid installations involving stakeholders from multiple departments and even multiple enterprises, some companies have taken a federated approach to ownership, maintenance, and upgrading.

Simultaneously, many organizations are recognizing the strategic value of e-Business and creating new internal divisions to lead their forays onto the Net. Directed by the CIO, an executive VP of e-Business, or a newly created e-Business czar, these divisions often report directly to the senior executive team while integrating their activities with multiple other entities inside and outside the enterprise.

As e-Enterprises complete this extension of the traditional org model, distinct lines between individual corporations will blur as processes become more entwined. Partner organizations will evaluate strategic opportunities in a collaborative fashion, responding to market demands and delivering complete solutions to customers. New e-Enterprise initiatives will reflect the shared ownership of multiple corporations through integrated partner sourcing and joint responsibility for design and development.

Because this kind of activity will represent the most critical strategic advantage for the enterprise, the CEO will take direct responsibility for overseeing e-Enterprise platforms and application design.

Application model

Early e-Commerce plays were primarily B-to-C commerce initiatives focused on building online marketplaces populated with consumer hard goods. Once again, Amazon.com and eBay come to mind. Both sought to aggregate customers and build community by selling a wide range of products and delivering personalized content.

In e-Business, the models for Net business have begun to diversify. A few focused application types such as B-to-B procurement and virtual marketplaces are getting most of the attention. However, other non-traditional models such as B-to-B online communities, software sales, multimedia, knowledge content areas, and excess inventory auctioning are also carving out presences on the Web.

e-Enterprises will complete this diversification by supporting a broad variety of mission-critical inter-organizational applications. Even the most unique enterprises in niche industries will use visual modeling tools and repositories of open software components to build applications for their particular needs.

Management processes

Because it was propelled by reactive rather than proactive forces, e-Commerce management was largely situation-driven. Managers were usually middle level employees with very little strategic responsibility. They focused on day-to-day projects that were designed, implemented, and rolled out one at a time. This led to a disjointed management view of e-Commerce initiatives.

e-Business, on the other hand, is business process-driven. Executive managers—typically from a distinct e-Business division—focus on uniting single-point applications into large e-Business platforms that share information and data in real-time. Simultaneously, they maintain a long-term view of the business that envisions not only the next revision of an application, but also the overall goal and direction of Net initiatives.

e-Enterprises won't be able to afford qualitative, hunch-based decision making for their strategy and application development. Instead, corporations will employ a methodology designed by industry experts. This process will be driven by methods, the creation and support of new business models, and continuously forecasting and measuring ROI on Net investments.

The goal will be complete solutions on an enterprise-wide scale. These platforms will be completely integrated with existing processes and systems. They will be flexible enough to support add-ons, reengineered procedures, and new business models as they come about.

Most importantly, development and modification of the e-Enterprise platform will be an ongoing effort intimately related to every part of the corporation.

Technology

Lastly, technology must undergo a massive change en route from e-Commerce to e-Enterprise.

In early e-Commerce, technology advances provided the catalyst for business opportunity. Consider the revolution brought about by the release of the commercial Web browser. Before Netscape released its Navigator product in 1995, public Internet access was limited to proprietary online services such as AOL, Prodigy, and CompuServe. Would-be online merchants had to strike deals with these gatekeepers before gaining access to individual surfers. Innovation was mostly limited to large firms signing long-term agreements to be featured on a particular online service.

The ubiquitous Web browser smashed barriers to entry on the Net and new .coms sprung up left and right. Simultaneously, an ever-widening audience moved online and became prospective customers.

In e-Business, technology is a driver that lets corporations automate and improve core business processes. In direct contrast to e-Commerce, which relied primarily on client-side technology advances to enable new features, e-Business innovation is driven by server-side technology advances such as Java servlets, full-featured application servers, and dynamic content generation through integration with corporate data systems.

Technology has begun to be accepted as the norm rather than a dangerous new resource by most organizations. Companies are less hesitant to support new industry standards and develop new tools and architectures.

In e-Enterprises, however, technology will play the role of a passive enabler. True change and innovation will come directly from strategic business leaders.

This technology environment will depend on a ubiquitous network supported by open, published standards. Enterprise technology resources will be distributed across this network. These resources will be an even mix of new, cutting-edge products and standards, existing safe choices, and left-over legacy systems surrounded by new wrapper code to make them Net savvy.

The changes in each of these seven areas are dramatic. Corporate leaders should not underestimate the preparation and resources that will be needed for a smooth transition to e-Enterprise. Systems vendors may offer guidance, but they have an ax to grind. Objective outside experts, with experience leading other corporations through the transformation, can offer proven methodology and independent verification and validation. But to be really successful, you must recognize that your own intensive knowledge of your business is the most critical success factor.

E-ENTERPRISE METHODOLOGY

Once the full engagement of the leadership team is ensured, the next thing required for a successful transition from e-Commerce to e-Business to e-Enterprise is an objective methodology for creating your e-Enterprise model. This, of course, begs the question: what exactly is an e-Enterprise model?

According to industry magazine *InformationWeek*, a model is a representation of business concepts that can be validated, that can be checked for rigor and robustness, that capture and communicate ideas, that can be changed, and that can provide 'what if' scenarios.[2]

e-Enterprise models should contain several primary components: business models, process models, application models, and application architecture. Each of these is driven by a combination of e-Vision and e-Strategy, which we describe later as the fundamental force behind e-Enterprise business and technology architectures.

The concept of modeling within the enterprise isn't new. In fact, the earliest modeling techniques were developed more than 20 years ago to describe how data resided in mainframe and database systems. Later, with the advent of object orientation and component-based development, new object modeling methodologies rose to aid developers building enterprise applications.

However, e-Enterprise modeling is quite different from these. The main distinction is the level of abstraction it enables. Unlike system-level approaches, e-Enterprise modeling tools can be used by both technology experts and business managers to model high-level business concepts that result in inter-organizational e-Enterprise applications. In fact, many corporations today have begun to use simple tools such as Microsoft PowerPoint and/or Visio to attempt high-level business modeling. It's a start, but it's not enough.

Despite the visual representations that are usually associated with modeling, it is important to note that e-Enterprise modeling is far more than just a collection of drawings. A robust e-Enterprise model includes a mechanism for cross-referencing business needs and IT capabilities, as well as a reusable repository of business and technology assets. This new form of modeling is sometimes confused with basic business process modeling. In fact, although business process is a part of an e-Enterprise model, it is only one element. The complete e-Enterprise model exists at a much higher level; it depicts the entire enterprise from strategy/vision all the way through to implementation.

e-Enterprise methodology is a structured, step-by-step approach that facilitates robust modeling of the entire enterprise through a series of rapid iterations. The methodology consists of the modeling process itself supported by facilities such as a reusable asset repository and modeling tool, and an additional set of techniques that can be applied to unique situations. This combination of elements enables step-by-step analysis of enterprise assets, business processes, and application development. It allows for organizational learning along the way and ultimately powers the transition to e-Enterprise.

During the first phases of the Net revolution, efforts at e-Commerce and e-Business were largely unorganized and impulsive. The first steps towards doing business on the Net, for example, were usually driven not by executive managers with an eye toward corporate strategy, but by individual members of corporate IT departments or fringe groups of developers. At this stage corporations were primarily concerned with issues such as employee usage, up-to-date content, and overall look and feel.

Because the Web wasn't really a strategic issue, many enterprises chose to bring in teams of independent consultants to staff development efforts and determine future directions.

Now that corporations have began to do real business online, however, the Net has became both more expensive and more closely related to overall enterprise strategy. As a result, many organizations have developed simple process guidelines to steer Web application development and manage the growth of e-Business resources. This includes tracking customer requirements, determining marketing focus, and developing strategies to increase transaction revenues.

During the transition to e-Enterprise, a more complex and robust methodology will be necessary. This methodology should include a suite of tools including an e-Knowledgebase of reference information, a modeling tool, industry leading research, training programs, and process templates to enable definition of e-Enterprise business, technology, process, and application models. At the same time, the methodology should encourage best-practice design decisions while outlining techniques to enable structured development and cycle-time efficiency.

It used to be that e-Commerce or e-Business development processes were marked by distinct phases that happened sequentially:

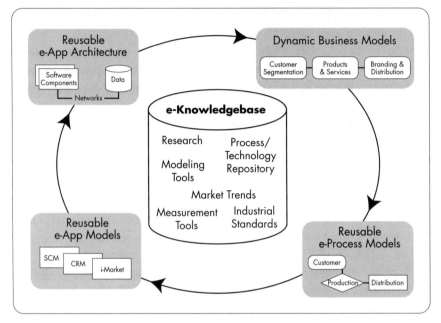

FIGURE 5.2

determine objectives, design, stabilize, manufacture, roll out, and analyze. However, e-Enterprise methodology advocates a continuous development life cycle where five different development stages— *e-Visioning and e-Strategy modeling, e-Process modeling, e-Application modeling, e-Architecture,* and *e-Knowledgebase*—occur simultaneously in a perpetual cycle of analysis and improvement. Throughout the entire process, e-ROI and e-Measurement are used to ensure that the new initiatives meet strategic goals. Figure 5.2 illustrates the stages of this methodology.

e-Visioning/e-Strategy

e-Visioning and e-Strategy is primarily about gathering and analyzing information to determine the overall focus and strategy of the enterprise. This creates the business model for the overall enterprise. Among other things, the business model outlines the required focus and priorities for strategic initiatives.

An essential component of this stage is analyzing market trends to determine how your corporation's business model fits in and will compete in the marketplace. The foundation of any market analysis is a databank of customer information and behavior as well as information about competitors' positions in the marketplace and the directions they plan to take.

Ultimately, you should define the target market for your goods and services through data collected from corporate and partner knowledgebases, market research from analysts and experts, customer focus groups, surveys, and acknowledged industry trends.

Another essential component of e-Visioning and e-Strategy is determining the e-Enterprise economic structure. Typically, this is a financial model that is based on a combination of predictable cost analysis—for example, staffing costs, distribution, and manufacturing—and also intangible costs. Intangible cost analysis incorporates qualitative assumptions and predictions about industry trends, customer acceptance of new products, and marketing program success.

Overall, e-Visioning and e-Strategy is about creating a corporate strategy that is driven by a combination of long-term goals and continuous e-ROI and e-Measurement. Sometimes, when feedback indicates that another overall strategy could be more profitable, you'll have to go back to the drawing board and start this stage over again.

Keep in mind, however, that like all stages in e-Enterprise methodology, e-Visioning and e-Strategy is characterized by fast cycle-times and iterative changes. It's designed to leverage existing business models and assets rather than encourage wholesale, long-term enterprise displacement. To reconcile this short-term, iterative approach with enterprise strategy down the road, it's necessary to balance long-term goals and the big picture with step-by-step success.

The most pressing danger during this stage is the tendency to forget enterprise core competency. Losing track of core strengths while flailing in new directions leads to disaster more often than not. According to James Ware and Judith Gebauer, "the failure to align a Web initiative with existing strategic direction and focus usually occurs when the Web team has not thought through basic marketing concepts like 'Who are our customers and why do they buy from us?'"[3]

e-Processes modeling

e-Process modeling begins once you're confident that the current iteration of e-Visioning and e-Strategy has produced an accurate and profitable business model for the enterprise. During this stage, you examine and determine what type of processes can support the required enterprise business model.

Once you've determined what type of e-Initiative you want to take, it's time to think about exactly what process model can support each initiative. Because process models are composed of business entities, use-cases, and process definitions, you first should define these in some detail. Once this is done you should employ a visual modeling tool and an enterprise repository of previously used entities, use-cases, and process definitions to allow business managers to take the best from previous initiatives and modify them to work for the new application.

e-Application modeling

e-Application modeling involves the business design of application models that support the overall enterprise business models and processes. Examples of application models include cataloging, requisitioning engines, and shopping carts. Typically, this stage involves getting stakeholder and customer feedback about the application through user interface mockups and application prototypes to define detailed application functionality.

During this stage it is essential to use an application-modeling tool for more nuts-and-bolts application design, such as what each module will contain and how the user will navigate through these modules. In preparation for the final implementation of the application, developers can also use this stage to identify required data structures and sources including legacy data sources and applications that can provide back-office functionality.

Like the e-Process modeling stage, e-Application modeling involves extensive use of the business repository to keep cycle-time short—all in all this stage should last no longer than two to three weeks.

e-Application architecture

e-Application architecture describes the design of the technology infrastructure that will support the final e-Enterprise applications. At this point, you must figure out the overall technology architecture and ensure that it meets the real business needs you have been defining.

e-Application architecture involves determining individual integration points between the application and data sources, the application and back-end installed software, and between multiple back-end systems. Every decision should be made with a good deal of attention toward not only the functionality of the application the day it is rolled out, but also the ability of the platform to scale up to support heavy usage, added business attributes, new users, and additional functionality in later revisions.

e-Application architecture design is also where developers determine which business and technology components will make up the final platform. However, it is important to distinguish between the description of this type of logical architecture and the actual planning of the physical architecture of the application. Logical architecture issues include how you will distribute the application to take advantage of networked resources, the network infrastructure you plan to employ, and the location and type of the data resources that the application requires. It does not, however, at this time require developers to select individual products and technologies for implementation.

Finally, this stage includes settling the final ownership issues for the application, data, business knowledge, hardware, and human resources necessary to support the application. Like the previous two stages, e-Application architecture modeling should be doable in approximately two to three weeks.

Modeling tools and techniques/e-Knowledgebase

So far, this methodology may seem quite complex, but then so is your business. High-quality e-Enterprise modeling tools and techniques can help guide you through the creation, definition, and communication of the overall e-Enterprise business and technology architectures. "Market research studies indicate that less than 2 percent of all IT shops use modeling tools of any kind ... Modeling isn't as widely used as programming-language tools ... but there's a big push on now, and a lot of attention is being paid to the use of modeling tools."[4] At this system level, such tools include UML-based data, object, component, and process modeling tools from vendors such as Popkin Software, Rational Software, and Select Software.

But e-Enterprise modeling requires quite different tools to unify business and technology architectures through a visual representation not just of system-level ideas, but of overall enterprise-level concepts. These tools will enable enterprises to reap the benefits of reusable business and technology assets.

As all industry moves toward e-Enterprise, a new generation of modeling tools will emerge that will facilitate this process on a whole new level. Just as computer-aided design and manufacturing software (CAD/CAM) revolutionized product innovation, so will visual simulation tools be used to draw the blueprints for e-Enterprise and lead you through business and technology innovation.

The final stage of e-Enterprise methodology culminates in the development of an extended enterprise e-Knowledgebase that makes employee experience, development assets, modeling tools, and market research available to shorten cycle-time and ease the development process. Fundamentally, the role of the knowledgebase is to act as a central nervous system for e-Enterprise architecture development that distributes information around the corporation wherever it is needed through an infinite cycle of development iterations.

The most important component of the e-Knowledgebase is the combination of the business and technology repository and the visual modeling tool. Both of these assets are 100 percent reusable across multiple applications and even across completely different e-Enterprise models.

E-ROI AND E-MEASUREMENT

One absolutely crucial aspect of e-Enterprise methodology is a carefully defined e-ROI and e-Measurement process that provides constant feedback to determine how the project is progressing with regard to financial and other key measurements.

The distinction between these two facilities is quite simple. e-ROI implies prediction and tracking of financial return on investments that have already been made. e-Measurement, on the other hand, is a broader approach to examining general impact on the corporation. Too often enterprises make the mistake of viewing and measuring strategic initiative—like e-Enterprise model definition and development—only in terms of short-and medium-term financial gains. This type of thinking rewards managers who deliver immediate results at the expense of the long-term strategic health of the division or group. Enterprises err by promoting managers who only deliver immediate gratification, and bringing a new manager in to face the consequences of their predecessor's short-sighted outlook.

Important intangible results are often the consequence of trends that are hidden within traditional financial metrics. For instance, measuring the financial return on an investment, although seemingly straightforward, can be a difficult proposition. For one thing, knowing the actual financial return doesn't necessarily mean that you can trace it back to the real source. It is essential that e-ROI and e-Measurement tools examine detailed information regarding the cost of the procedure, how often the process occurs, how essential it is to overall enterprise profitability, what other processes are affected, and what alternative processes may be available.

One conventional purpose of ROI and measurement analysis within the enterprise has been to set departmental and project budgets based upon the expected financial benefits. This system has been based on the profit center concept pioneered by General Electric in the 1960s. Naturally, this led managers to focus on investment in regard to short-term, financial rewards.

As a result, instituting a system for determining ROI often contributed to a general apathy for investments whose returns wouldn't show up on the balance sheet next quarter. Needless to say, this meant that enterprise divisions became less strategic, and overall enterprise performance down the road often suffered as a result.

Good enterprise ROI and measurement, then, can't only include things like revenues, cost, and overall profit. It also must encompass a wide range of business metrics that may be entirely unique to the division being evaluated and the aims of the evaluators. How should you measure success for e-Enterprise development? Quite frankly, it's completely different for every initiative in every division in every corporation.

Typically, e-ROI and e-Measurement evaluate a variety of enterprise assets and metrics, including cycle-time, division management, customer satisfaction, partner interaction, and, of course, cost, revenues, and the bottom line. The only prerequisite for determining what your measurement scheme should examine is that it include a variety of different information; tracking only one or two statistics gives a very limited view of the enterprise.

This approach is known as the balanced scorecard approach. Developed and published in the Harvard Business Review by Harvard professor Robert S. Kaplan and industry expert David P. Norton, the balanced scorecard was originally "organized around four distinct perspectives—financial, customer, internal, and innovation and learning. The name [reflected] the balance provided between short- and long-term objectives, between financial and nonfinancial measures, between lagging and leading indicators, and between external and internal performance perspectives."[5]

Today, a balanced scorecard for e-ROI and e-Measurement has come to mean any set of metrics that gauges success using a broad range of financial and non-financial metrics. Again, the prerequisite is that more than a few limited types of information be utilized.

To choose the appropriate metrics for an individual e-ROI or e-Measurement project, it is helpful to remember the essential customer-centricity of e-Enterprise models. Traditionally, most performance evaluations have focused on internal metrics such as revenue, cost, efficiency, employee understanding of strategic goals, etc. In e-Enterprise initiatives, however, you should view company success not from the point-of-view of an internal employee, but from the standpoint of an external business partner or more commonly a customer. Because the ultimate aim of the corporation is to meet client needs, it makes sense to evaluate the corporation from the standpoint of a customer with an eye towards competitive positioning in the marketplace.

This leads to another common mistake that managers make in evaluating the success of business units and their initiatives. Too often, ROI and measurement activities are undertaken with an enterprise blind spot. Results that look like a win may in fact be a relative loss compared to the actions of other players in the competitive landscape. Your corporation may have improved x percent during the latest quarter—a perceived win—but it is actually a dangerous loss if your competitor improved 10x percent.

Another major pitfall is pinning goals for every division to a single enterprise-wide standard. This can cause managers of divisions that enter the evaluation period in a strong position to become complacent. Conversely, divisions who enter the period on thin ice quickly realize that they will be unable to meet the enterprise goal and resign themselves to failure from the start.

e-Measurement and e-ROI, like e-Enterprise development on the whole, is a continuous process that measures success in every phase of the development methodology. This means that e-ROI and e-Measurement are strategic rather than just evaluative tools. At every stage, they can be used to focus efforts to keep that stage and the entire project on track. The measurement process is one of constant feedback and improvement, where results are managed in real-time.

Over time, this constant feedback fosters an entirely new corporate management technique. Rather than wait until a project is complete to evaluate the effort and institute changes for the next iteration, strategic managers can become directly involved in day-to-day operations through the real-time analysis of corporate data.

Instituting and managing continuous e-ROI and e-Measurement links the feedback process directly with corporate strategy. Kaplan and Norton do a good job illustrating this principle for the four enterprise measurement perspectives that they advocate:

- **Financial:** Financial metrics contribute directly to enterprise understanding of and planning for revenue growth, corporate asset management and investment, and internal productivity planning.

- **Customer:** Customer-centric measurements include market share, customer retention, customer satisfaction predictions for long-term and short-term profitability, and new customer acquisition.

- **Internal process:** Internal ROI addresses processes such as design and production innovation, operations efficiency, and service.

- **Learning and growth:** Learning and growth includes important metrics relating to internal employees, including personal and professional growth, job satisfaction, motivation to success, empowerment, and alignment with overall enterprise strategy.[6]

Each of these areas provides feedback to a common center—the executive management—responsible for determining the corporate vision and strategy for the enterprise.

REUSABLE ASSET REPOSITORY

Earlier in this chapter, we spoke about the principle of reusability in e-Enterprise business and technology architectures. To efficiently capture this reusability in e-Enterprise development, it is essential to have a repository for storing business-specific application models and technology assets for reference and modification in later iterations of the methodology. Other types of information that are typically included in a reusable asset repository include generic process models, definitions for customized business entities, and custom and purchased software components for use in new applications and upgrades.

These repositories are essential elements of the enterprise's overall knowledge management platform. Recognizing the value of aggregating all enterprise information such as sales data, customer lists, successful sales strategies, product designs, end-user feedback, financial balance sheets, and unit performance histories, corporations have begun to assemble and classify massive databases of corporate information. These databanks can then be made available over the Net to employees from multiple departments and even to external stakeholders.

This broad user base is one of the most important challenges of knowledge management; repositories must cross departmental or even enterprise boundaries to provide services to employees and business partners. Because no single database is large and flexible enough to manage the complete needs of a Fortune 1000 corporation, knowledge managers face the considerable challenge of integrating multiple databases, including information from legacy applications and Enterprise Resource Planning (ERP) installations, to provide a complete view of corporate information.

Another important challenge is getting users to adopt knowledge management techniques when they enter business data into the corporate network. Users are likely to consider small pieces of data irrelevant and throw them out rather than take the time to index them in the appropriate corporate databank. However, even tiny pieces of information can help knowledge managers track enterprise trends and deliver accurate and relevant information to decision makers.

Within the context of e-Enterprise applications, knowledge management enables enterprises to create repositories of business processes, technology components, and application models.

The corporate business repository stores information that managers can use to standardize definitions for business and process models. In addition, users can archive existing process components, including business entities such as purchaser and supplier, activities such as approval and requisition, and processes such as procurement and approvals. These archived entities can then be recalled later by managers in other departments to be reused or modified for new process models.

The technology repository serves a similar purpose. Instead of archiving business entities, however, this repository stores technology resources such as business objects, pre-built and purchased components, developer documentation, application design parameters, and enterprise technology standards.

It would be easy to simply consider a technology repository as an advanced version control system. However, by providing developers not only with program resources but also with user experience and enterprise know-how, technology repositories provide an essential and cost-saving service.

One example of the advantages that can be provided by a repository combined with a component-based development process is application and code portability. By archiving source code and data in a software repository, developers can quickly reassemble applications to run on new software and hardware platforms.

When creating a repository for either business or technology assets, enterprise knowledge managers would do well to anticipate and determine solutions for a number of important issues before beginning implementation.

First and foremost, information repositories within an enterprise knowledge management system should be codified according to the final business use that the information supports. To enable this specific segmentation, repositories should focus on a single particular need—e.g., UML processes for corporate customer care—and then expand the repository outward as the range of reusable assets grows. This strategy allows administrators to perfect management techniques on a small scale before the project gets swamped by the sheer size and breadth of collected data.

Another important issue is that of ownership. Because repositories are designed to be reused by employees in multiple organizational groups, repository administrators must determine early on who will own, manage, and maintain the information. In addition, repositories that employ advanced features must determine which departments and organizations have greater roles than others in determining archive techniques and standardization.

The end result of a successful business and technology repository is a reusable asset that enables corporations to share information to reduce e-Enterprise application costs. At the same time, a repository substantially reduces cycle-time for new versions of applications and process models, and provides strategic advantage in the form of faster time-to-market and responsiveness to customer needs.

E-ENTERPRISE ORG MODELS

Another essential component of an e-Enterprise methodology is attention to the fundamental revisions that will have to be made to enterprise organizational models.

The traditional concept of the enterprise org model—often depicted as a pyramid or upside down tree, has its roots in the earliest days of the industrial revolution. During this period, most employees were factory laborers or salespersons whose primary role was to carry out orders rather than to take initiative themselves. Consequently, management made a concerted effort to make sure that "thinkers were separated from doers, and it was assumed that all knowledge was captured and controlled from headquarters."[7]

Because of the general immaturity of techniques for communicating and coordinating across large distances, individual business units were once constrained primarily by geographical boundaries. The resulting structure was organized around fairly local units encompassing vertical functions such as manufacturing, design, sales, marketing, and accounting. First and foremost, this static hierarchy enabled managers to think for the entire unit and then mandate and monitor that their orders be carried out. Despite its rigidity and in some cases obsolescence, this model persisted for nearly a century.

During the business process-reengineering phase of the 1980s, however, management experts advocated a new basic structure. Corporations were encouraged to turn the traditional management hierarchy on its side to create a horizontal structure focused on individual processes such as managing a particular product rather than vertical functions such as marketing and sales. Enterprises quickly found, however, that although this philosophy increased collaboration and communication among employees with different roles, it limited the organization's ability to adopt dramatic changes.

As an example, consider a department focused on developing and marketing a new television set. By uniting engineers, marketing professionals, salespeople, and financial/accounting representatives in a single organization focused on the new product, the company captured new synergies in collaborative design, focused marketing, and market analysis. Furthermore, when the product was ready for a new revision, employees could pool their expertise to ensure that the new product would meet customer needs and be successful.

On the other hand, because the group was entirely focused on a single product, employees had trouble thinking outside the bounds of the particular process group. All changes in the corporate product line were the next version, rather than the next "big thing." Although the organization encouraged product evolution, it discouraged product revolution.

New e-Enterprise org structures, on the other hand, will be a radical departure from both of these traditional organizational models. The corporations of the future will be marked by six key trends: *vertical and horizontal integration, extended enterprise relationships, new roles and responsibilities for executive management, partner sourcing vs. outsourcing vs. insourcing, employee incentives and accountability,* and *empowerment and losing control.*

Vertical and horizontal integration

The virtual organizations of the future will use new technology and management techniques to create an org structure characterized by a combination of vertical and horizontal divisions. This will capture the efficiency of traditional structures as well as harness the improved focus of horizontal integration. The enterprise of the future will be defined by a highly fluid structure consisting of teams that come together to work on a particular project and then quickly disband and reform with other teams for new projects.

Like the horizontal integration approach, each of these teams will be composed of employees with a wide range of expertise. However, the dynamic quality of the team's place in the overall org structure will encourage employees to think from a complete enterprise strategic point-of-view, enabling out-of-the-box thinking and dynamic reorganization to stimulate revolutionary product changes.

These teams will also be more autonomous from the corporation's central management, to encourage entrepreneurial behavior by individuals. At the same time, however, they will be more highly integrated with other work groups than in today's organizations, even if only for a relatively short period.

Extended enterprise relationships

Another hallmark of e-Enterprise corporate structure will be the creation of extended organizations that include external partners known as complementors into the internal organizational structure. This movement will result in a good deal of blurring between enterprises. In this model the corporate relationship with complementors will be much the same as that with internal enterprise divisions. Rather than behave as individual organizations, e-Enterprises will move to grab business opportunities as complete networks of companies with integrated and shared business processes.

Why do you need to include external partners in the extended enterprise org structure? First, product lines are becoming more and more complicated, and customer demands for complete solutions are necessitating that corporations partner to deliver marketplace value. Also, networked corporations have access to planning and market data from a much broader base, which allows them to draw better conclusions about their own role in the overall marketplace.

The extended enterprise is fundamentally different from the conventional business organization in a number of ways. Conventional org structures are usually built around individual profit centers (which goes back to the quarter-by-quarter financial view we discussed previously), and are designed so that all important decisions are funneled to senior managers who make the call and allow instructions to filter back down the hierarchy. Networked organizations, on the other hand, are designed not to funnel and distribute decisions to and from managers, but instead to empower knowledge workers to make decisions independently. The overall structure of the e-Enterprise is driven not by strategy as it is in conventional org structures, but instead derives from an iterative, circular feedback loop that is driven by product development and communication with corporate customers.

In the e-Enterprise era, the idea co-opetition, where groups both within and outside the enterprise work together for mutual advantage, will become the focus of inter-organizational relationships. Within this context, however, it will be increasingly important for e-Enterprises to balance integration between groups with the ability to respond individually and quickly to innovate and add value to the business.

Co-opetition in the extended enterprise model is often misinterpreted to mean tight integration of enterprises at the strategic, executive level. Although co-opetive corporations will share strategic goals—for example Intel and Microsoft collaborate extensively to fuel momentum for their Wintel standard for personal computers—cooperation at this level mustn't lead to dependencies that make individual reaction or separation an impossibility.

Another danger of close integration is that high-level executives often have little understanding of or respect for the day-to-day nuances of individual product lines. Allowing managers to create inter-organizational dependencies, then, runs the risk of wiping out the unique value-adds that distinguish an individual product from its competitors in the market. This leads to too much enterprise collaboration, a condition that is known as "lockstep."

Instead of collaborating at the executive level, e-Enterprises will look to form close alliances at the level of middle managers who best understand product and marketplaces and can best appreciate potential partner contributions. This provides the organization with the strategic benefits of partnering with external corporations to round out product lines and share marketing information while still enabling a single group to act alone to achieve an important individual win.

New roles and responsibilities for executive management

The most important role of the executive in the e-Enterprise will be to promote the idea of coadaptation, or balanced integration between the customization and standardization promoted by horizontal and vertical integration respectively. Primarily this means balancing collaboration between enterprise teams and external groups with promoting individual wins. "The key to making coadaptation work," Shona Brown and Kathleen Eisenhardt explain in their book *Competing on the Edge*, "is to maintain a palpable tension between the collective and the individual win. This means clear accountability and reward for meeting individual business goals, as well as transforming groups of individuals into teams."[8]

Primarily, this will include breaking apart and matching new groups in real-time to respond to market demands. Managers will be responsible for both maintaining modularity within the enterprise to prevent groups from becoming irreversibly fused by delegating responsibility across the entire network. This means that every e-Enterprise executive must be well versed in helping disparate groups from far-flung backgrounds communicate and work together.

This type of cross-organizational cooperation has existed in Net initiatives in some form from the very beginning. Even the earliest Web initiatives crossed departmental boundaries to integrate IT and marketing. Now, however, groups from every part of the enterprise, including production, planning, logistics, finance, R&D, and sales, will have to be on the same page at all times to maintain product focus and win in the marketplace.

To bridge the communication gaps between these technical and business-oriented groups, executives, such as the CIO, who come from a technology background will find their roles becoming strategic. At the same time, CEOs and COOs whose previous role was entirely business-oriented will find that understanding and appreciating technology is an absolute must.

This isn't to say, of course, that technology issues will drive most business decisions the way they did during the early days of .com mania. Even in the most wired e-Enterprises, business functionality will rest on a network supported by technology standards. This isn't the same as network technology defining business processes.

Throughout the entire development, deployment, and usage life cycle of e-Enterprise initiatives, managers must constantly perform testing in the form of e-ROI and e-Measurement. From these quantitative, objective results, executives will work to craft a strategy that takes into account long-term enterprise positioning as much as short-term financial results.

Partner sourcing vs. outsourcing vs. insourcing

As we mentioned previously, early e-Commerce efforts were typically developed either completely in-house (insourcing) or by external consultants who were responsible for making strategic as well as implementation decisions (outsourcing). Both of these decisions were typically driven by cost issues; companies would choose to insource to prevent incurring expensive consulting costs or conversely would outsource to avoid having to build an expensive Web development department. In e-Enterprises, a third option will become widespread: partner sourcing.

Essentially, partner sourcing is an extension of the extended enterprise org model. Unlike either insourcing or outsourcing, partner sourcing adds direct strategic value to the enterprise by leveraging the technical know-how of consulting firms with the intimate strategic knowledge and focus of internal enterprise management.

The partner sourcing model is characterized by long-term relationships between consultants and clients where responsibility for initiatives are shared and delegated between the two parties according to their core competencies. This results in increasingly fluid partner relationships: there is more opportunity for long-term partnering, but organizations are less locked-in and will be able to exit from a bad relationship.

When selecting external partners, e-Enterprises should look for providers whose services are complements to their own. In direct contrast to a competitor, whose product or service makes your own less valuable, "a complement to one product or service is any other product or service that makes the first one more attractive," Adam M. Brandenbuger and Barry J. Nalebuff explain in their book *Co-opetition*. Some examples of obvious complementary products include "hot dogs and mustard, cars and auto loans, televisions and videocassette recorders, television shows and the *TV Guide*, fax machines and phone lines, phone lines and wide area networking software, catalogs and over night delivery services, red wine and dry cleaners, Siskel and Ebert."9

The classic example of complementary products in the technology industry is hardware—say an Intel processor—and software—Microsoft Windows for example. As Microsoft releases new versions of its operating system that require more processor power to take advantage of new features, consumers are motivated to make new hardware purchases. Similarly, when a new Intel chip is released, many customers upgrade to a new version of Windows to take advantage of their new computing power.

Employee incentives and accountability

Another aspect of the enterprise that will be fundamentally transformed during the transition to e-Enterprise will be employee incentives and responsibility.

During the .com mania, employee incentives were often tied to stock options and the promise of a get-rich-quick IPO. Although it lured many talented people to start-up companies, this method has proven inadequate for building long-term employee loyalty. As a result, many firms have begun to evaluate new compensation models that retain the lucrative aspects of stock options at the same time that they encourage employees to take a more farsighted approach to employment.

One such approach is to place less emphasis on salary and options in favor of a huge performance-based bonus system. This keeps base salaries competitive from the enterprise point-of-view. At the same time, it rewards the standout performers who typically produce large individual company wins like inventing a revolutionary new product. This is an expression of the concept of balance between team and individual success.

The metrics for determining the payout of this bonus system, however, should be based on different criteria than bonuses in conventional organizations. Today, most bonuses are directly tied to individual events such as signing on with a new company or completing a long-term project. This system, however, tends to reward employees who produce in fits and spurts, and emphasizes time and delivery over the quality of the end product.

In e-Enteprises, bonus distribution—and overall enterprise performance—will be determined by different metrics. "We have stressed ... that managers have been raised on the principle that productivity can best be increased by minimizing unit labor costs through higher throughput, by using better technology, or by work-based incentives," Jeremy and Tony Hope explain in their book, *Competing in the Third Wave*. "But this model of productivity improvement is now under serious question. In other words, the biggest improvements in productivity do not come from machines, technology, or incentives, but from how well managers use technology to improve the organization and quality of the workforce, and whether such improvements meet strategic objectives."[10] Bonuses in the e-Enterprise environment, then, should be based not on isolated events, but instead on the subjective quality of each employee's contribution to the overall strategic goals of the enterprise.

Empowerment and losing control

The final issue in the development of new organizational hierarchy will be that of empowerment and losing control. As we have already discussed, org hierarchy in the e-Enterprise will be marked by a balance between vertical organization that allows managers to retain control over workers and horizontal integration that encourages synergy between employees with different responsibilities.

A direct consequence of this shift is the need for managers to empower individual knowledge workers to take responsibility for decisions. These decisions usually occur at the middle management level, where executives are still close enough to individual offerings and product lines to understand the individual factors that directly affect customer demand. This is an expression of the movement towards customer-centricity in the enterprise. According to this thought process, the executive manager who would normally be charged with leading such decisions is too far removed from the actual marketplace to know what it is exactly that customers want.

At the same time that central organizations give up direct control, however, they must ensure that rogue, unsupervised employee actions don't hurt the enterprise as a whole. In e-Enterprises, central management must monitor its internal divisions and complementary partners closely to make sure that group directions correspond with high-level goals for the enterprise. Still, executive management going forward will be limited to purely strategic and not tactical management.

RESPONDING TO REAL-TIME DEMANDS

So what's the big deal about becoming an e-Enterprise? Why should you, as an organization, take the time and allocate the resources to follow a methodology to move from e-Commerce to e-Enterprise?

More than anything else, becoming an e-Enterprise is about using the speed, ubiquity, and power of the Net to run the entire organization in real-time. You may be wondering what exactly real-time means in this sense. Whose time, after all, is real-time?

In new virtual enterprises, customer-focus will be the ultimate byword, and real-time will mean exactly when the customer wants whatever it is that the customer wants. Marketing guru Regis McKenna describes this phenomenon as a future where "all information superhighways lead to service.... Real-time service is the key to winning the hearts and minds of new consumers," McKenna continues, "... it means being in touch all the time, creating an experience, adding information that addresses individual needs and circumstances, responding without delay, and gaining valuable feedback for new and improved offerings."[11]

In the Net future, real-time will be everything, and enterprises will learn to service their customers and run every aspect of their business—product design, marketing, product assembly, distribution, and customer support—accordingly or they will fail. If it doesn't happen in real time, it'll be too late.

Real-time product design

Real-time product design will be a combination of collaboration among part suppliers and designers as well as a deeper understanding of market conditions and exact customer needs. e-Enterprises will know more about their customers than ever before, and they deliver products and services to the marketplace with an individual focus and immediate attraction for their customers that hasn't been seen ever before.

Real-time marketing

Real-time marketing is about establishing long-term customer focus, determining which customers are most valuable to the enterprise, and marketing goods and services to customers with a perfect segment-of-one focus.[12] Because of this personalized approach, real-time marketing is both more effective than conventional market share-based approaches and more useful in delivering strategically loyal customers.

Real-time product assembly

Real-time product assembly allows corporations to manufacture and deliver individual products only after an order takes place. This cuts down on product inventory, and as a result reduces the incidence of overproduction, underestimation of demand, end-of-life-cycle product clearances, and inefficient logistics practices.

Already, many direct PC manufacturers employ this process. When a consumer places an order for a system over the phone or Net, the manufacturer assembles a system from in-stock parts that matches the user's preferred product configuration and ships the customized system.

Real-time distribution

Real-time distribution is ultimately about shaping the organization to respond to product demand in real-time through collaboration, co-opetition, and virtual organization. When distribution channels need new inventory for sale, the e-Enterprise system will recognize what products are needed and where, and will ship them out to replace goods that have been sold without the customer even noticing that inventory has turned.

Real-time customer support

Finally, real-time customer support means empowering customers to get answers to questions and product information exactly when they want it. In some cases, this includes online customer self-support such as a product FAQ. In more advanced cases, however, it means answering a customer's individual question before she even knows what to ask. Imagine the example of a PC that has developed a software configuration problem. In the future, the system will recognize the problem locally, connect to the Net, download the required software patches and updates, finish the installation, and fix itself without any customer intervention at all.

The ultimate goal for each of these real-time advantages, of course, is a satisfied customer. Today, customers already demand excellent service. In the age of the e-Enterprise, however, their requirements will only become more and more stringent. To meet these demands, corporations above all else must be able to change to meet individual customer demands, change to support new business models, change to partner with new external enterprises for mutual demand, and change to capture new internal efficiencies enabled by technology.

Right now, we stand on the brink of a new era, and it is an exciting time to be in business. In the coming years, every one of us will be faced with more opportunities to fundamentally change our markets than we've probably faced in all of our careers. Some of us will be fortunate enough to grab these opportunities and run with them. Others, however, will stumble.

The age of the e-Enterprise may not be entirely a zero sum game, but unfortunately, there will be missed opportunities and there will be losers. It will be absolutely essential to plan for changes before they happen by embracing an objective corporate methodology for harnessing the almost inconceivable power of the Net for your business by becoming an e-Enterprise.

6 e-Enterprise Architecture

INTRODUCTION TO E-ENTERPRISE ARCHITECTURE

So far most computer users still use the new technology only to do faster what they have always done before... But as soon as a company takes the first tentative steps from data to information, its decision process, management structure, and even the way work gets done begin to be transformed.[1]

—Peter F. Drucker

Before we can talk about e-Enterprise architecture, we have to explain exactly how it fits into the overall model of the enterprise. Business managers often mistake e-Enterprise architecture for a technology issue to be handed off to IT departments and development engineers. Technology-oriented employees, on the other hand, argue that executive management must be in charge of architecture. Both are wrong—and right.

A great deal of this book is about bringing business and technology together. In fact, we define the term "e-Enterprise" in Chapter 1 to mean a corporation that has successfully put the two together. However, we haven't yet said how we think the two should meet.

That's where an e-Enterprise architecture comes in. Using an abstract framework that represents both business and technology, companies in the new economy will finally bridge the gap between executive and technical leadership. Figure 6.1 illustrates the framework for e-Enterprise architecture.

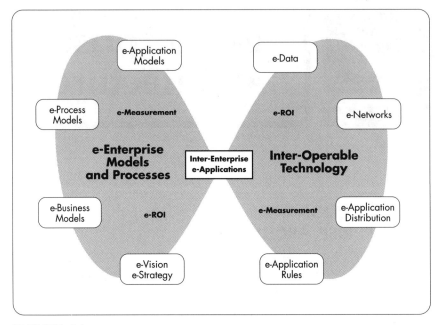

FIGURE 6.1

The first thing to notice about this framework for e-Enterprise architecture is its shape: like ∞, the universal symbol for infinity. In a virtual corporation, e-Enterprise business and technology development are both *continuous* evolutions.

To support this constant change, e-Enterprise architecture must embrace an iterative approach that makes changes to the overall architecture one piece at a time, yet is always conscious of the whole. The enterprise architecture can be divided into seven distinct elements. Some have been discussed at more length in earlier chapters, some are introduced for the first time with this framework. But each addresses different issues and demands a different focus:

◧ **e-Business models:** Define the high-level shape of the e-Enterprise derived from target market/customer analysis, financial modeling, inter-enterprise touch point examination, ownership, and resource analysis.

- **e-Process models:** Involve the creation of inter-organization processes that leverage the Net and are composed of business entities, use-cases, inter-organizational processes, reusable business processes, and business components.

- **e-Application models:** Define the actual application from a design rather than an implementation point-of-view. Typical e-Application models consist of a detailed application definition, user-interface mockups, application specifications, and business rules, as well as blueprints for how to include reusable functionality and application components in the final platform.

- **e-Application rules:** Governs the final application by utilizing business and application logic, a rules engine, the application framework, and component software.

- **e-Application distribution/integration:** Enables developers to allocate application resources across the network using multiple application servers, a distributed object architecture, technology components, middleware, and Enterprise Application Integration (EAI) software.

- **e-Data:** Refers to an abstracted data component that manages data for the entire platform. The e-Data layer includes application data, data management systems, data warehouses, legacy data, and ERP/MRP data repositories.

- **e-Network:** The network infrastructure for the e-Enterprise platform, typically driven by network security solutions, encryption, connectivity tools, a Network Operating System (NOS), and system analysis and management tools.

Throughout each of these components of enterprise architecture, it's essential to continuously monitor the success of the e-Enterprise applications. As we saw in Chapter 5, e-ROI and e-Measurement track the effects of new initiatives in terms of financial and strategic gains.

The framework does define an essential distinction and interface between the business modeling and technology development processes, labeled "e-Enterprise Models and Processes" and "Inter-Operable Technology" respectively in Figure 6.1. The business process modeling portion of e-Enterprise architecture guides the progress from corporate vision to e-Enterprise applications. Inter-operable technology guides development of technology solutions that support the output of the modeling phase. Tools and results generated by both of these processes must come together in the form of e-Enterprise applications.

This means that people from both business and technology backgrounds must learn to collaborate effectively. We all know, however, that getting managers and engineers to understand each other is usually no walk in the park. Here's where the concept of high-level abstraction comes into play.

Abstraction in the design phase of technology products is nothing new. Consider, for example, the role technology abstraction plays in the design of electronic devices. When I go to my local electronics retailer and purchase a new stereo, I actually take home an assembled group of end products from a number of different manufacturers. Within the stereo system are parts from many smaller, lesser-known electronics companies. Although these pieces provide essential contributions to the product's performance, the engineers and designers at the brand-name stereo manufacturer have little understanding of the design principles and construction of each component. This raises two questions: First, why wouldn't the engineers build the whole stereo from scratch? And second, how can they assemble a product from pieces they don't understand?

The answers are quite simple.

First, building from scratch would require stereo manufacturers to develop and perfect not only the overall design, but also the manufacturing processes for all of the components. This would be prohibitively expensive. As for the second question, the component manufacturer provides the stereo engineers with the technical information they need to design their finished product. The brand-name stereo manufacturer's engineers can focus on what they do best: building stereos, not designing electronic components.

The key to all this is abstraction. Inner workings of complex components are hidden from engineers, allowing them to assemble prebuilt pieces and focus on high-level design rather than nuts-and-bolts.

This same concept is crucial for technology enabling business managers to deal effectively with decisions that involve significant technical details, and for developers to deal with technical matters that also entail complex business issues. Left alone, managers tend to think purely in business terms. Engineers tend to view technology as the alpha and omega of their jobs. Without this abstraction, putting the two together can be like trying to mix oil and water. There's nothing more frustrating—or unproductive—than a team of business managers and a team of software developers locked in a conference room trying to make the other guys think the way they do.

e-Enterprise architecture can be an invaluable tool for bringing these disparate points of view together. By providing a level of abstraction between nuts-and-bolts business and technology, e-Enterprise architecture empowers managers and developers to work together on the same page to design e-Enterprise applications that add real value to the company.

Typically, corporations have been forced to relegate design, architecture, and application decisions either to business or to technology people. Abstraction in an e-Enterprise architecture, however, allows business managers and developers to adopt a common, simple vocabulary for modeling applications. The result is an e-Enterprise platform that provides a clear business benefit, supported by the latest technology standards and design principles.

ARCHITECTURAL CONSIDERATIONS

During e-Enterprise architecture modeling, it's essential to pay extremely careful attention to good design principles. Because architecture forms a complete framework for every e-Enterprise application from both a business and technology point of view, it directly determines the outcome of a business's Net initiatives more than any other single piece of the e-Enterprise puzzle.

For corporations that take the time to architect a platform that meets their current needs and allows for expansion to meet future needs, e-Enterprise will provide powerful leverage for every new e-Initiative. Corporations that fail to design a robust architecture will run into problems with each and every new application they try to build.

Let's take a closer look at the properties that must be taken into account when working through the e-Enterprise framework: *agility*, *interoperability*, *reusable assets*, *ownership*, *scalability*, and *cycle time*.

Agility

Agility—both in terms of business and technology—is an absolute necessity for any e-Enterprise architecture. In the technology space, agility often means the ability of developers to add new standards as they gain industry acceptance and remove legacy systems as they become dated and obsolete. Agility is about ultimate adaptability in changing business ecosystems and about responding to market change whether driven by competitors, new technology, or customers.

The key is developing an architecture that shares information and resources between applications without irreversibly locking them together. For new technology acquisitions, this is as simple as making decisions based on open standards. In many cases, however, agility means retrofitting legacy applications with wrapper code that allows them to communicate with platforms and standards that didn't even exist when they were designed and deployed.

Becoming an agile business, however, goes far beyond technology challenges. First, you've got to ensure that throughout even the most tumultuous internal changes, external stakeholders such as customers and business partners maintain a unified, consistent view of the enterprise. By severing ties with important partners, even inadvertently, businesses risk losing customers, alienating suppliers, and becoming lost in the marketplace.

Continuous change can lead to employee confusion regarding exact roles and responsibilities within shifting departments. The key is to support a program of managed change that includes continuous education of employees and business partners regarding their changing roles in the corporation—and the preservation of unique added value in the enterprise's offerings. Information sources that form the lifeblood of organizational knowledge must remain intact and stable through these strategic initiatives.

Employees in an e-Enterprise often are asked to adopt traits and techniques that haven't traditionally been rewarded. In the digital economy, corporations must reward entrepreneurial thinking across all levels, adaptability to function effectively in new and different business environments, and vision-based leadership by upper management.

Successful e-Enterprises must engage in constant customer dialogue to determine changes in market dynamics, foster team behavior between previously separate departments and business partners, and make its core business functions even more flexible to allow the enterprise to turn on a dime to respond to new competitive opportunities.

Interoperability

Interoperability from a technology standpoint means being able to closely integrate with every technology investment that the corporation has made. Because most enterprises support a wide variety of computing platforms and applications, including Enterprise Resource Planning (ERP) installations, custom-built legacy systems, custom-designed relational data base management systems (RDBMS), home-grown Web applications, client operating systems, and server platforms, designing an e-Enterprise architecture that is capable of incorporating almost any computing system is essential. Furthermore, the architecture must be able to evolve to support new technology standards as they emerge.

From a business perspective, interoperability means close communication between both internal departments and external stakeholders. As large corporations continue to diversify product lines to compete across many industries, interaction between internal departments with distinct product offerings, culture, and business processes will be indistinguishable from the way that corporations communicate and deal with partners outside enterprise boundaries.

The key to managing interoperability in the enterprise is striking a balance between too little and too much integration. In their book *Competing on the Edge*, Shona L. Brown and Kathleen M. Eisenhardt describe this balance as coadaptation, or "the process whereby systems of related agents take mutual advantage of each other in order to change more effectively, yet still be adaptive in each agent's particular situation. For example, any particular animal in a species can adapt to its own surroundings, but it can also learn from other animals in its species and coordinate with them in mutually beneficial activities—like hunting in packs. The result is complicated yet successful behavior. As in any edge-of-chaos process, coadaptation is most effective when poised on the edge of chaos between too much and too little structure."[2]

When companies err on the side of too much interoperability between departments and business partners, individual groups lose distinct competitive advantages and become irreversibly tied to the performance of other entities. This can lead to commodity product and service offerings. When inter-departmental integration is led by senior executives who have lost touch with the unique dynamics of each entity's value proposition, a condition known as lockstep can occur. Lockstep within the enterprise is a direct symptom of over-integration, and is marked by an inability of groups to change individually to pursue unique market opportunities.

Too little interoperability, on the other hand, results in individual corporate entities that duplicate enterprise processes in different departments and corporations unnecessarily. This condition makes it almost impossible for the enterprise to leverage even simple benefits of cooperation like volume discounts in corporate purchasing. Groups tend to rely on random, individual couplings for inter-departmental cooperation, which lead to poorly managed initiatives that require a lot of effort for a relatively small return.

Reusable Assets

Successful e-Enterprise architectures are marked by reusable assets that can be employed in e-Applications from internal accounting systems to complex value chain management applications. In fact, it is this idea of reusability that generates the concept of an enterprise architecture in the first place.

e-Enterprise asset repositories are extensions of the overall company knowledge management system. Knowledge management is a relatively new corporate discipline. In the past decade, however, many information-based corporations have recognized that managing corporate knowledge can be an essential tool for both internal use and external customer self-service. Some corporations have gone so far as to create a new division headed by the CKO, or Chief Knowledge Officer, whose sole purpose is to collect, codify, and publish corporate data. The earliest knowledge management systems were direct descendants of corporate computer networks that allowed employees in any location to store and query commonly useful information.

Across application boundaries of every type, platforms share common technology knowledge such as distributed resource connectivity, data management, and consistent user interface. Similarly, corporate applications tend to share common business knowledge and requirements such as user profiling, customized workflow, and reporting/analysis tools. e-Enterprises who learn to reuse this functionality in the form of flexible software components, rather than building them from scratch each time that they are needed, will enjoy reduced costs and faster times to market.

To store these reusable assets, the enterprise needs to make a concerted effort to develop repositories for business and technology components. As business managers design and perfect corporate modeling tools such as business entities, processes, and use-cases, they add the final products to the repository. When they need a new entity down the road, they can take a similar object from the repository and modify it rather than creating a new one from scratch.

Similarly, as application developers build software pieces, they populate a software object and component repository for later use or modification.

Ownership

Because e-Enterprise applications by definition cross departmental and corporate boundaries, ownership issues are critical. From the earliest design stages, enterprise partners must establish who is responsible for what part of the applications, from the databases that store customer information to the hardware that hosts the platform. Corporations may choose to institute a system of shared responsibility and ownership to ensure that even in the event of a complete severing of corporate ties, both businesses can salvage some tools from the initiative.

Ownership, however, isn't just an issue for technology assets. Consider, for example, two suppliers who have instituted a co-opetive selling application to enable them to bid for a large, long-term supply contract. If the two corporations decide to go their separate ways before the contract is fulfilled, who is entitled to claim the buyer relationship? Conversely, who should be saddled with the responsibility of fulfilling the contract to avoid a breach-of-contract suit?

Scalability

Scalability—both from a business and technology standpoint—is another essential aspect of successful e-Enterprise architectures. While predicting the usage requirements of an application is usually fairly straightforward in its first iteration, it can be difficult if not impossible to predict changes in registered users, site hits per day, and bandwidth requirements just a few months down the road.

For this reason, e-Enterprise architectures must be able to scale up easily and quickly to accommodate new usage requirements. By utilizing a distributed application architecture, corporations can simply add new resources—such as application servers, databases, and Net connections—as their requirements increase.

Cycle time

e-Enterprise application development shouldn't be marked by fits and starts. Instead, it should be a continual process. Corporate application planners and developers must institute an iterative development process that begins new changes before the previous revisions are completely implemented.

Manufacturers in technology industries where products evolve at an unbelievable pace have employed such a design process for years. In the microprocessor industry, for example, manufacturers are invariably working on multiple, next-generation processors even as they release a brand new model.

The result of such an iterative design method is short cycle times between releases that are marked by minor adjustments rather than full-scale replacements. This enables enterprises to function seamlessly even during the rollout of new e-Enterprise applications, and minimizes the employee learning curve for new versions of software.

E-ENTERPRISE BUSINESS ARCHITECTURE

e-Enterprise business architecture involves components of the enterprise architecture that are directly related to modeling the business functionality of the corporation. When designing business architecture, managers should be guided primarily by overall corporate vision and strategy. At the same time, business architecture design must remain grounded in the realities of enterprise execution, and should be shaped also by tangible issues such as go-to-market strategy, product development plans, customer focus, and post-sales customer care.

Once the infrastructure has been modeled, underlying architectural support structures, such as organizational structure and individual business processes, should be made to reflect the new high-level organization of the enterprise. Finally, business applications are developed that model corporate processes. The result is a business framework that is based on strategy and vision and implemented by technology architecture.

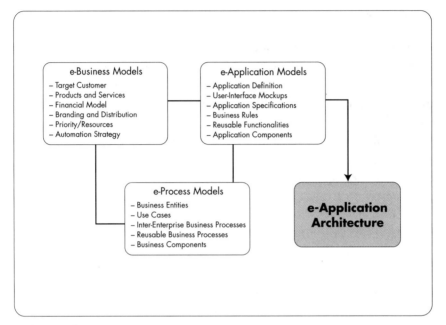

FIGURE 6.2

The three distinct pieces of e-Enterprise business architecture are *e-Business models, e-Process models*, and *e-Application models* (see Figure 6.2).

e-Business models

The corporation's e-Business model describes the overall structure of the business from a high-level perspective. Some important elements of e-Business models include determining the corporation's target market and primary audience for their goods and services. It also includes the optimal product and service mix for each market segment. The corporation must also predict the revenue streams that will be generated by this product/service/customer mix. Elements such as branding, sales channel, partnership strategy, and product delivery are also included in this model.

The issue of ownership of intellectual property such as processes, and physical assets such as e-Enterprise applications and hardware, must also be determined at this high-level stage. This will avoid any possibility of ambiguity during process engineering with external partners.

The e-Business model includes careful analysis of existing enterprise resources to ensure that the corporation reuses assets that provide value and discards those that have become outdated or just plain ineffective.

Finally, the e-Business model must define critical success factors, as well as the ROI analysis and measurement criteria to create a balanced scorecard to keep the enterprise on track.

e-Process models

The e-Process model describes the internal and external processes that define the company's day-to-day behavior. These processes must reflect both the corporation's e-Vision/e-Strategy and the individual business models that you choose to pursue.

Typically, e-Process modeling involves defining and working with business entities such as "customers," "suppliers," and "departments." These components are then assembled to form complete inter-organizational business processes that are reusable in multiple iterations of process engineering.

In order to visualize these processes after they have been defined, it can be helpful to employ use-cases that follow an "if-then" logical model. For example, "if the customer tries to make a purchase that exceeds his individual purchasing limit, then pass the PO to the purchasing manager for approval."

e-Application models

e-Application models are the direct descendants of e-Process models. Rather than simply represent the business processes, however, they aim to model the applications that will be developed to streamline business procedures.

e-Application models outline the overall application functionalities from the end-user perspective. These application functionalities are supported by a data and object model. Data and object models provide the underlining data structure and usage for a target application. e-Application models often include the development of a user-interface mockup. This allows users to step through the process using the application's navigation aids.

Because e-Application models represent the final platform from a design rather than an implementation point of view, they can include abstract concepts such as business rules and reusable functionalities that have yet to be implemented by software designers.

E-ENTERPRISE TECHNOLOGY ARCHITECTURE

The ultimate goal of e-Enterprise technology architecture is to translate the corporation's business vision into effective e-Enterprise applications that support reengineered intra- and inter-organizational business processes. This may sound like a straightforward proposition, but it is in fact very complex and can be nearly impossible without strict adherence to agile and open technology standards.

Even corporations that make intelligent technology architecture decisions looking forward will face crucial technology challenges. Most legacy systems—even fairly recent client-server and ERP apps, for example—weren't designed with true enterprise-wide interoperability in mind. They tend to be proprietary, closed systems that require extensive modification to work with the rest of the e-Enterprise technology architecture.

Custom integration can be especially challenging, as it involves understanding the business processes that each application addresses, plus the actual technology and the data manipulated by the platforms. Typically, application integration takes place at two distinct levels: data level integration and API-/method-level integration.

Data integration involves simply sharing a common data repository between two or more systems. It is considered a relatively inexpensive solution that is quick-to-implement, doesn't require new tools and technologies, and doesn't alter the custom business logic and so is non-invasive for sensitive applications. It suffers, however, in that it doesn't do a complete job of process integration.

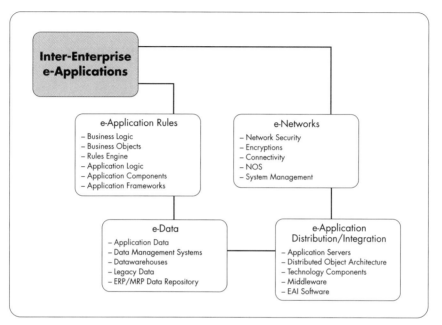

FIGURE 6.3

API-/method-level integration, however, takes advantage of outward facing software interfaces to applications that are included in some packaged solutions or added by corporate developers in the form of wrapper code. These interfaces allow other systems to communicate directly with the application rather than having to interface through a user-controlled GUI. Typically, API-/method-level integration involves direct access to internal systems such as process/workflow modeling, application objects, as well as application data.

This is at once API-/method-level integration's strongest attribute and most dangerous liability. By integrating directly with the internal framework of applications, developers can allow platforms to share common processes and can encourage system reuse. At the same time, however, they must be careful not to fundamentally alter or break the application's core functionality.

e-Enterprise technology architecture consists of four distinct stages: *e-Application rules*, *e-Application distribution/integration*, *e-Data, and e-Networks*, illustrated in Figure 6.3.

e-Application rules

e-Application rules are the technical mechanisms that enforce business rules.

Every business process has rules or "checks and balances" to govern the operation. For example, a large purchase requires a higher-level approval than a small purchase, an automatic transfer from a customer's checking account to his savings account can occur only if there are enough funds available, and a weekend traveler booking a flight two weeks in advance qualifies for a lower fare than a business traveler who suddenly has to make a one-day trip.

Typically, these rules are unique to each and every implementation. They must be modeled to each corporation's policies and specifications.

In terms of implementation, such rules are embedded within software of a "rules engine" that stores all necessary information about rules like purchasing limits, approval processes, airfare rules, etc. When a transaction is entered into the computer system, the rules engine is queried to see if it's okay to complete the transaction.

In this way, the application logic is made to mirror the business logic prescribed during the e-Process modeling phase of e-Enterprise architecture development. The components of e-Application rules that are typically modeled during this stage include application components, business objects, and app frameworks, all of which include at least some level of technical design.

e-Application distribution/integration

e-Enterprise platforms cross internal departmental boundaries and even bridge multiple enterprises, so they must by necessity work with a wide variety of existing technology implementations. For example, an enterprise with a large ERP installation as well as custom-built legacy systems for company financials and HR must be prepared for an extensive integration program to unite data and processes from these widely distributed—both geographically and technologically—systems.

The cornerstone of e-Application distribution and integration is a distributed architecture that allows application resources to be located on individual application servers that are connected by a network and that communicate using standards such as CORBA and COM/DCOM. In order to ensure communication between systems that don't support such distributed architectures, developers often utilize middleware standards such as IBM's MQSeries and BEA's Tuxedo to exchange standardized messages between applications.

Technology components are used to provide the e-Application's basic communication and distribution services. Also, Enterprise Application Integration, or EAI, software can be useful in extracting data from closed systems and making it available across the platform.

e-Data

The e-Data layer consists of data stored and manipulated by the e-Enterprise application. Because this data may be required by more than one application, it is often stored separate from any particular system in large data warehouses or data management systems that can be queried by any application through open standards such as JDBC/ODBC.

In most cases, the e-Data layer consists of more than just relational databases. Many enterprises find that business data is already stored in legacy applications or ERP/MRP applications with closed, custom data formats. In these cases enterprises must work to enable data abstraction from individual applications. On the other end of the spectrum, the newest data management systems include object databases that store data in encapsulated software objects rather than simple entries in a database.

However data is stored in the e-Data layer, it must be monitored and distributed to applications within the e-Enterprise in a manner that both anticipates data requirements and still enforces data access policies to what is often sensitive business information.

e-Networks

The e-Networks layer consists of the network infrastructure that provides a backbone of communication between the multiple distributed components of the e-Enterprise platform. e-Networks often employ a

Network Operating System (NOS) to provide and manage core network functionality.

In addition, most enterprises implement network-level component technologies such as firewalls to protect internal network investments or connectivity components to facilitate communication across networks with heterogeneous technology environments. Advanced networks also employ new technologies such as Public Key Infrastructure (PKI) encryption and digital certificates to ensure the integrity of data that is passed over the network.

PRE-BUILT BUSINESS AND TECHNOLOGY COMPONENTS

The key to reusable assets in e-Enterprise applications is the use of software components. These components are pieces of software that perform services through a specific, published interface. Although they can't be used as complete applications in a stand-alone manner, developers can glue together multiple components to create full applications in much the way that a builder assembles a complete building from multiple, pre-fabricated pieces. The fundamental value of the application is in how the developer chooses to piece together the components. Just as a builder can assemble the same steel girders, concrete blocks, and metal siding into any number of different buildings, developers can piece together almost any application from common software components.

Depending on whether the common service provided by a component solves a technology or business issue—database connectivity vs. user profiling for example—the software component is then referred to as either a business or a technology component.

Traditionally, the first design issue that Net application developers faced was the build vs. buy decision: Should I develop the application from scratch or purchase a pre-built software solution and customize that? Today, e-Enterprise application developers face a new dilemma: develop and populate a component repository from scratch, or purchase and assemble a mix of pre-built and business-specific components for their applications.

Develop a component repository from scratch

In the Net's earliest days, the complete absence of pre-packaged Web applications forced developers to write code completely from scratch. Although this allowed designers to meet precise application requirements, it also created a number of problems.

First and foremost, it takes a long time and costs a great deal to construct every component. Even with teams of developers working full speed on new application development, enterprises had to allocate months or years to go from design stage to final implementation. In addition, developers were forced to grapple incessantly with the difficult learning curve associated with implementing new technologies as they are developed and released by standards bodies.

This isn't to say that building components from scratch is a dying art, however. Today, the market for e-Enterprise components is still largely underdeveloped. In order to meet specific application requirements, developers often don't have many choices.

Purchase and assemble pre-built and business-specific components

The other option is to assemble applications from pre-built and business-specific components that encapsulate business or technology services. This solution allows developers to reduce development time and costs while ensuring that the final application meets the specific business rules that produce a unique competitive advantage.

Assembling applications from pre-built components gives developers the best of both worlds. It hides the underlying technology details and allows engineers to focus on application logic and implementing complex features that add unique value.

This may seem counter-intuitive—after all, how can a developer work with a piece of software without knowing how it works? Remember, however, the example of the stereo manufacturer. Developing a product—whether a stereo or software application—from pre-assembled components is analogous to driving a car without having to know how the engine works. Many people haven't a clue how to assemble a radiator or fuel injector from scratch, but are pretty good at taking advantage of them by driving their cars to and from work each day.

The single most important thing to remember about a component-based design strategy is the importance of adhering to standardized, open interfaces for interaction between components. Once this initial hurdle is overcome, every e-Enterprise application built in-house can begin to accrue savings in time and money, from drawing board to integration with other systems and maintenance after implementation. Furthermore, using components to assemble new applications allows the software engineering team to concentrate more on business goals and less on the new system's technical obstacles. Component assembly also allows corporations to mix-and-match individual "best of breed" services and applications from multiple vendors.

Already technology components play an important role in software development. For years, developers have worked with technologies such as ODBC drivers and more recently connectivity standards such as DCOM and Enterprise JavaBeans.

The market for business components—software that provides business services for e-Enterprise software—is a different story. For the most part, commercial pre-built business component products have been few and far between. With the maturation of standards for component interoperability such as CORBA, DCOM/COM+, and Enterprise JavaBeans, however, help seems to be on the way.

"Two years ago, when we started with components, there was not much for sale," explains Emery Worldwide Airline's Jeff McGlaun describing the hurdle that many application developers faced in the earliest days of pre-built components, "with the latest release of Enterprise JavaBeans, [however] the architecture just became mature enough to develop to. We look to purchase components for generic things. Things that are strategic and proprietary, like a costing component, we build ourselves."[3]

Gradually, as more software developers such as EC Cubed (a company I founded) and Theory Center begin to bring more pre-built business components to market, component usage of all kinds will skyrocket. Like electronic devices such as the telephone and fax machine that require a large installed base to become really useful, components won't deliver their full potential until pre-built offerings are mature and available for a wide variety of purposes.

Even when the market for components reaches its prime, enterprise developers will be forced on occasion to create new components to handle extremely specific business needs. Even in such cases, developers should be able to find a similar component in the repository and extend its functionality to provide even the most unique services to e-Enterprise applications.

Consider an example from EC Cubed and financial services provider MasterCard. In order to develop an Internet Commercial Card Gateway that would allow data entry from various front-end systems into MasterCard's purchasing card, or P-card, system, MasterCard chose to customize components from EC Cubed's ecWorks suite. By reusing the services encapsulated in EC Cubed's components, MasterCard developers predict that they'll cut their time-to-market nearly in half.

In addition to the important distinction between providing business and technology services, software components can be categorized as either vertical or horizontal depending on the services they provide.

Components that provide services that are valuable in multiple application categories are referred to as horizontal components. Typically, the services they provide aren't industry specific. An example of a horizontal component is a profiling component in a procurement application that is used to maintain detailed supplier information and deliver custom-buying experiences to different users of the application.

In a virtual marketplace application, this same component could be used to provide similar services—such as one-to-one marketing, targeted advertising, and tracking individual buying patterns—with a minimum of customization to account for the very different application type.

On the other hand, components that are highly specific to particular application types are referred to as vertical components. A prominent example of vertical components are those that support the HL7 standard for healthcare applications.

Developers often extend the functionality of horizontal components by customizing them to include unique business rules and support specific processes. In effect, this creates new horizontal components for the repository. For instance, some type of workflow is applicable to enterprises in almost every industry. Developers working on an application for the insurance industry could extend a generic workflow component to handle the processing of new policies, the receipt of new premium payments, and processing new claims and payments. Out of that effort would come a new, equally reusable vertical component for the insurance industry. The same original workflow component could also be extended in another direction to address manufacturer production lines and extended again to cooperate with components in another business to enable just-in-time production and delivery.

Already, the advantages of providing a simple interface to complex technology underpinnings are apparent in numerous industries. Simple, standard commercial tools like telephones, faxes, and, more recently, Web browsers, are acceptable, user-friendly faces of extremely complex technologies and massive electronic infrastructures. Eventually, as server-side component software evolves and standards for interoperability between components mature, component assembly will offer these same advantages to the e-Enterprise application development community.

By the end of the first year of the new millennium, industry analyst META group predicts that "most Global 2000 companies will use a 'software factory' model to implement new application systems, requiring developers to move from a 'craftsman' approach to a culture of assembly and reuse. These applications will be component-based, message-enabled, and event-driven, using [a multi-tier] design that will leverage enterprises' capacity-on-demand capability."

CONFORMING TO INDUSTRY CONSORTIA

Historically, most electronic data and transaction integration has occurred either completely within individual enterprise boundaries or with close business partners who either share common IT investments or whose business is valuable enough to warrant building from scratch applications to manage the relationship. Consequently, with the exception of a few technology standards such as EDI, open electronic business standards were largely the stuff of textbooks and theoretical discussion.

As more and more corporations move to the Net and look to do business electronically with organizations outside of their traditional electronic partners, however, this approach has proven to be outdated and ineffective. Open standards for sharing information, making transactions, and defining business processes have quickly become an absolute necessity.

At first, e-Business standards bodies met with some degree of resistance from IT workers and VARs who were concerned that establishing tightly controlled standards would limit the ability of software developers to innovate to gain competitive advantage. This outcry, however, was overshadowed by the collective need to define rules for doing business on the Net. "[Standards bodies] don't want to squash competitiveness and it's not to stop innovation," Fran Foster of the Software Publishers Association correctly points out, "but there is a certain level of agreement that needs to come on standards. That's the mission."[4]

Here, we'll introduce five industry consortia working to establish the standards and practices that will define e-Enterprise architectures for the twenty-first century: CommerceNet, RosettaNet, Open Buying Initiative, Open Financial Exchange, and Internet Content and Exchange.

CommerceNet

CommerceNet was one of the first e-Business industry consortia and a very early Net pioneer. (See www.commerce.net.) CommerceNet opened its doors in April of 1994. To put that in perspective, the first commercial Web browser, Netscape Navigator, wouldn't be released for another six months.

Since 1994 CommerceNet has positioned itself as an "e-Business chamber of commerce" of sorts. It aims to aggregate and integrate standards to form a single, interoperable architecture for doing business online. In this way, the consortium isn't so much about defining standards as collecting and managing multiple efforts.

Today, there are over 500 members of CommerceNet, including "leading banks, telecommunications companies, VANs, ISPs, online services, software and services companies, as well as major end users."[5] As of mid 1999, CommerceNet offers four membership levels ranging in price from $5–$50,000.

CommerceNet's research offerings are highlighted by GIDEON (Gateway to Internet Demographics Online), a joint venture with Nielson Internet Demographics Studies that collects and summarizes marketing data from the Net. GIDEON contains complete demographics extending all the way back to 1995 and is available at the CommerceNet Web site to members only.

Another important component of CommerceNet's research offerings is its archive of custom research reports by member organizations and leading industry analysts. Finally, the consortium offers research briefings and opportunities for collaboration and networking at its quarterly meetings.

To ensure that the standards they support are adopted by a wide variety of industry players, CommmerceNet actively engages in a variety of public relations campaigns that are available for consortium members.

But CommerceNet's most important impact on Net commerce, of course, is its member-led projects and pilots to define standards and overcome technology and compatibility problems. One of the most influential and important programs is CommerceNet's Global eCommerce Forum, or GeCF, which aims to produce e-Business solutions for the financial industry such as Secure Electronic Transactions (SET), digital certificates, and smart cards. Some other ongoing projects sponsored by the consortium include the Catalog Interoperability Project (standardizes catalog Web catalog formats for easy integration and data exchange), the eCo framework (encourages interoperability among multiple industry standards), International Cross Certification, and the CommerceNet Privacy Research Initiative.

Lastly, CommerceNet representatives contribute to other industry consortia such as RosettaNet and OBI to provide "CommerceNet Certification," a stamp-of-approval of sorts for open Net commerce standards that can be adopted across technology and industry boundaries to define the future of Net commerce.

RosettaNet

RosettaNet borrows its name from the Rosetta Stone. (See www.rosettanet.org.) Discovered in 1799 in the Nile Delta by an officer in Napoleon's invading French army, the Rosetta Stone is considered the key piece of evidence that led modern scholars to decipher ancient Egyptian hieroglyphics.

Like its namesake, RosettaNet aims to facilitate the translation of disparate tongues—in this case custom business processes. The consortium's slogan, "Lingua franca for eBusiness," conveys its primary goal: enable enterprises to exchange commerce information through "a set of industry-wide electronic business interoperability standards."[6] Ultimately, RosettaNet aims to make exchanging business data and integrating inter-organizational processes on the Net—what they describe as server-to-server communication—as easy and intuitive as human-to-human communication in the real world.

RosettaNet was founded in 1998 by IT executives frustrated with their inability to reuse custom-developed integration tools. The Consortium's Partner Interface Processes, or PIPs, are best practice business data models and process workflows that are geared towards the B-to-B market with special emphasis on supply chain environments.

Members can choose four membership types depending on their role in promoting RosettaNet standards: coalition partners work to enlarge the support base, architect partners provide subject expertise in the form of developers for consortium project teams, execution partners support standard implementation in commercial products and home-grown applications, and solution partners provide tools and services that support RosettaNet interfaces. There is no cost to join as a coalition, execution, or solution partner, but architect partners must contribute to at least three projects a year and board members must pay a yearly membership fee.

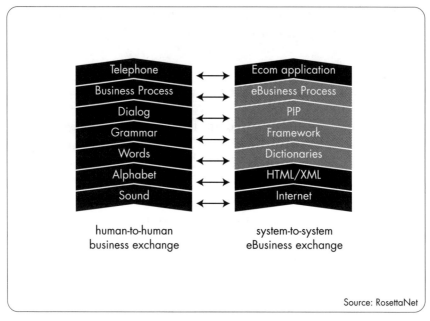

FIGURE 6.4

Figure 6.4, taken from the RosettaNet homepage, illustrates the services that it provides in the context of an entire electronic partner dialog.

Because the variety of processes that enterprises could aim to model is almost endless, RosettaNet bases its PIP definitions on common dictionaries of properties that PIPs can contain. This ensures that when creating custom PIPs business partners can guarantee that they are speaking the same language.

Open Buying Initiative

The Open Buying Initiative (OBI) is another industry attempt to standardize e-Business processes. (See www.openbuy.org.) Unlike RosettaNet, whose focus is to define an entire framework for all inter-organizational processes, OBI concentrates exclusively on making B-to-B purchases on the Net.

OBI was founded in October 1996. OBI's founding members were Fortune 500 companies whose early Internet procurement programs suffered from a lack of established standards for interoperability. Currently, over 60 organizations including buying and selling corporations, aggregators, systems integrators, and software vendors are members of the OBI consortium.

The group conducts pilot programs of new methodologies and interfaces, actively promotes market acceptance of OBI standards, and releases benchmarking and "best practice" standards for electronic commerce. OBI aims to automate the enterprise buying process, which it describes as the requisition, approval, order confirmation, and payment processes. The actual standard is made available in the form of public documents available for download free of charge at the group's Web site: common business requirements, a supporting architecture, technical specifications, and guidelines for implementing an OBI-compliant solution.

For buyers, OBI promises a number of important advantages. First, the standard enables purchasing departments to develop long-term, strategic buying relationships with preferred sellers to increase volume discounts and lower costs. OBI also provides a model for complete supplier integration with the buying application, and defines easy-to-use process templates to model e-Business applications before they are actually developed. Suppliers too benefit directly from the OBI standard. Primarily, OBI enables suppliers to meet specific buyer requirements in the form of cost-effective customer service.

The initial version of the OBI standard, v1.0, was released in March of 1997 and updated to v1.1 in June 1998. However, the industry showed considerable hesitation to invest in a standard that was expensive to implement and as of yet had no direct participants. Although industry watchers believed the standard was solid, OBI suffered from a very real inability to achieve a critical mass of implementation.

Recognizing this growing concern, the board of directors transferred control and management of the OBI Consortium to CommerceNet in June 1998 in a concerted effort to leverage the wide industry acceptance that CommerceNet had begun to build. Today OBI standard continues to evolve—v2.0 was released in January of 1999—and the consortium continues to sign up new members to boost industry acceptance of their buying standard.

Open Financial Exchange

Open Financial Exchange (OFX) specializes in standardizing the electronic exchange of financial information between consumers, businesses, and financial institutions. (See www.ofx.net.) OFX was created and continues to be managed by three of the software industry's and the Net's most high-profile and powerful players: Microsoft, Intuit, and CheckFree.

Founded in 1997, OFX began as a simple initiative to enable consumers and small businesses to exchange financial information in much the same way that large businesses had used EDI for decades. The consortium quickly added leading financial institutions, brokerage companies, and technology solution providers to broaden the scope of the standard. Currently, the OFX standard addresses consumer/small business banking, electronic bill presentment and paying, and investments in stocks, bonds, and mutual funds.[7] These transactions are supported not only through Web applications, but also thin client and personal finance software such as Intuit's Quicken.

OFX offers members and general users a variety of services related to the OFX standard. The specification, of course, is available free of charge from the OFX Web site. In addition, the group provides a comprehensive certification and training program and makes lists of certified OFX solution providers available online.

OFX offers users a number of important benefits. Most importantly, support for the OFX standard reduces the importance of making technology decisions and allows developers to concentrate on the financial issues of the exchange process between partners. The standard also enables financial institutions to support a wide variety of interfaces and client models with minimal customization and integration.

Internet Content and Exchange

Internet Content and Exchange, or ICE, is a relative newcomer. Originally submitted to the World Wide Web Consortium (W3C) in late 1998, ICE aims to provide a standard for organizations to exchange, supply, update, and control data on the Net.

The need for a comprehensive business data exchange format like ICE was so drastic, in fact, that over 80 companies—including industry giants CNET, Adobe, Microsoft, Sun, and Vignette—collaborated to submit the standard to W3C in just ten months.

The ICE uses platform independent open standards to provide a mechanism to define and then exchange business data and also unique add-ons such as pricing and terms for a contract. Because the protocol is concerned only with the mechanism for data exchange and not the information itself, ICE can be used to share business information in any format.

The ICE protocol includes two main roles: a subscriber and syndicator. The role of the syndicator is to produce and store content, and to initiate interaction with subscribers in the form of a subscription establishment. This causes a new subscription—which typically includes information such as delivery policies, usage reporting, presentation, etc.—to be added to the subscriber's catalog of potential subscriptions. When the subscriber chooses to view a subscription, the data is converted and delivered over the Net.

PART 4

—

Enabling
Components

e-Enterprise Business Components

In the Internet Economy the big won't beat the small—the fast will beat the slow.[1]
 —John Chambers, President and CEO, Cisco Systems

The real driving factors behind the new economy are flexibility, agility, and time to market. Obviously, this means speeding the desired e-Applications to market in the first place. However, speed also involves how quickly your company can respond to market changes by rolling out new, iterative versions of e-Enterprise platforms. Sometimes emerging technology standards that enable exchange of information between partners and stakeholders drive these changes. Sometimes they are driven by shifts in the external business landscape such as new market opportunities. Still other times they result from concerted analysis and process engineering driven by internal corporate forces.

As discussed in Chapters 5 and 6, the key to enabling this perpetual business, application, and technology change is a reusable repository of operating models and infrastructure that embody the common functionality shared by multiple e-Applications. Therefore, this repository must store the high-level business services that provide cross-functional business/application functionality and the technology components that aid in producing the underlying technology infrastructure. These high-level business services are known as application or business components. The combination of business and technology components provides the backbone not only for the repository, but also for the iterative design and deployment methodology that is integral to the concept of the e-Enterprise.

Although the concept of technology components has been around for some time, the concept of business components is still in its infancy. During the coming years, the Net commerce software industry will continue to develop and deploy business components to ensure that enterprises have the tools that they need to fashion a complete repertoire of business services with a minimum of custom-coding. This chapter will focus on some business components that are fundamental in creating an architecture reflecting reusable common business processes integral to enterprise-wide e-Applications.

In Chapters 2, 3 and 4, a wide variety of e-Application business models, application functions, and their similarities were highlighted. In this chapter, we will examine the most common business processes and application functions. These define the core business components that form the basis for an agile e-Enterprise business architecture that can be quickly configured over and over again.

Like a technology component, which will be discussed in greater detail in Chapter 8, a business component consists of larger grain objects, data structure, published APIs, and extensive configuration/ administrative tools for a faster development and deployment cycle. Unlike a technology component, a business component focuses on facilitating critical business rules and functions. It primarily deals with a user's need to access, facilitate, and perform business functions. In contrast, a technology component focuses on accessing, facilitating, and performing system functions.

As discussed in Chapter 6, these components can be cross-application, cross-industry or industry, and application-specific. However, in order to create an agile and holistic e-Application architecture that can continuously evolve, application architecture must begin with cross-application inter-enterprise business components.

Rather than focusing on the technical details of the implementation strategy or the architecture of these components, this chapter will instead highlight business functionality in order to provide a better

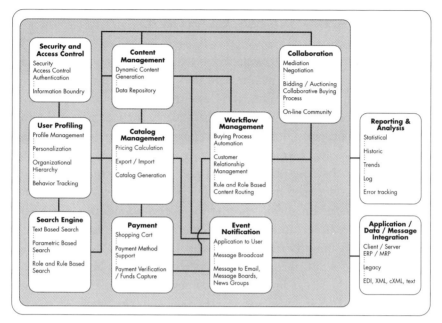

FIGURE 7.1

understanding of the fundamentals of defining common business components. This is important not only for building a reusable repository, but also to use as an architectural guideline for selecting pre-packaged application solutions. It is essential for a pre-packaged application to be built upon these business component principals in order to ensure the agility required for an ever-changing e-Enterprise.

During the course of this chapter I'll highlight ten business components: security and access control, user profiling, search engine, content management and cataloging, payment, workflow management, event notification, collaboration, reporting and analysis, and data/message integration. For each, I'll briefly describe the functionality that each business component contributes to an e-Enterprise architecture and, where applicable, how it interacts with other business components to solve business problems. Figure 7.1 depicts the common architecture that business components create and the inter-relationships between them.

SECURITY AND ACCESS CONTROL

One of the barriers most frequently cited by corporations and consumers who hesitate to do business on the Net is the perceived lack of
security on the Web. As such, it is essential that any e-Application
that contains potentially sensitive information such as personal profiles, internal corporate documents, or payment information includes
a comprehensive and confidence-inspiring security and access control
component. At its core, the security and access control component
establishes trust between parties by providing three key services to the
application: establishment of information access boundaries, authentication of remote users, and authorization according to user profile.

Information boundaries manage who can see and do what—and
when—in an e-Application. They allocate privileges to access protected areas of the site, content, and business functions, as well as control access rights to applications on other computer systems. To ensure
that an access control component can protect a variety of digital
resources, information boundaries should be defined down to a particular level of granularity. The most advanced solutions not only protect
single files, but can even extract and protect parts of files to ensure
that confidential information remains safe. An access control component establishes individual information boundaries for each individual
user or user group in concert with a user-profiling component. Some
examples of the types of information that are protected by information
boundaries include confidential bids to fulfill a posted RFQ, custom
negotiated pricing agreements, and profile information that can be
accessed and modified by selected administrators and users.

User authentication refers to the process of ensuring that a user or
program that is attempting to access the platform over the Net is who
the user claims to be. Generally, this involves securely transmitting
confidential information such as a username and password, a digital
certificate, or a public key for encryption from the user to the system.
Robust security and access control components should support a
number of different technology components for authentication in
order to ensure that authorized users employing a wide variety of
technology can access the system with a minimum of difficulty.

One of the key elements to this underpinning technology is single sign-on, which allows users the ease of signing on to an enterprise-wide application infrastructure once and being able to access user-specific systems, applications, and content without having to log on over and over again. Single sign-on technology infrastructure must support management of log-on facility and user-specific information carry-over across many system domains. With the growth of extended enterprises, users must have the ability to travel from corporate intranet to extranet to Internet without multiple sign-on requirements. Therefore, authentication and security business components must be supported with single sign-on functionality.

Once the user is confirmed to be authentic, the system can begin the process of authorization, or determining what application resources the user has access to. Typically, authorization involves several other business components, including the personalization/profile management and workflow modules. If the user is determined to be allowed to view the selected file, execute the selected program, or modify the selected data, then the security component delivers it automatically.

In addition to ensuring that end users do not receive access to pages and data that are confidential, the authorization process also serves another purpose. Increasingly, as consumers make purchases from specialized Net merchants with less brand recognition and established trust than an Amazon.com or Cisco Systems, it is becoming more important for consumers to be able to ensure that the application host is indeed who it claims to be. Moreover, that it is a reputable and respected partner for business. The security and access control component enables this through an association with technology components such as digital certificates, which operate on a two-way basis and the digital signature.

A typical exchange between an end user, the access control component, and an e-Application could go as follows. The transaction would begin when the user sends a request for a page. Since the information boundary module indicates that the page is protected, the access control component would send the user a notification page requiring her to log into the system. The user would enter her login information—for instance, username/password combination—and then would

transfer the information securely across the Net to the authentication module. If the login information corresponds to a registered user, the authentication module would pass the request to the authorization module. The authorization module is responsible for working with the user-profiling component to determine if the selected user has access to the protected page or resource.

Once users are logged into the system, the access control component remembers what resources they have access to, and allows them to access protected pages and data, and execute programs. This allows the user to change network resources automatically until the user logs out of the application or a pre-defined period of time goes by. Advanced access control modules also employ some type of business rules module (including role, authority, privilege level, spending limits, etc.) to manage access at a higher level than simply on a page-by-page or file-by-file basis.

To identify possible breaches in security, the component must automatically include intelligent logging and reporting features that identify security faults as well as otherwise invisible unauthorized attempts to access the system. Without a security component, e-Applications would be vulnerable to a number of different security breaches. Threats range from theft of a customer's credit card number to breaking into online systems and committing fraud or misappropriating funds. Criminals or competitors may even attempt to steal confidential information for sale to other corporations or for their own competitive advantage. Of course, the greatest threat to an e-Enterprise is the complete failure of the platform. Such a large-scale outage can irreversibly damage the reputation and long-term viability of the platform in the eyes of users.

To provide this wide range of services and features, it is essential to select a security/access control component that is flexible enough to handle security for a wide range of applications while at the same time being closely enough integrated to ensure that information is completely secure. By combining a robust security/access control business component with technology components such as digital certificates, cryptography, and so on, e-Application developers can prevent interception of data and ensure proper access to content by the right person at the right time.

USER PROFILING

Since most users tend to interact with the enterprise through a number of distinct applications—e-Tailing and customer care for example—it is absolutely essential that individual profiles be shared across application boundaries. Traditionally this has proven difficult, as most hand-built or off-the-shelf applications incorporate their own distinct profiling mechanisms that are not intended to share information with other systems. A business component that is employed by multiple applications, however, can easily and seamlessly share information input through one application with any number of other e-Enterprise installations.

Often, the easiest way to generate an individual profile for a user is asking the user to provide information about himself. In many cases, however, requiring such user information at the get-go can drive potential customers away. In this case, the component can create a new profile from scratch with default profile information. This can then be added to and modified as the user interacts with the site by searching for a particular product, clicking on a pop-up advertisement, or purchasing a product. The range of techniques and tools available to provide this profile information is wide and varied. Some prominent examples include existing customer databases, user registration, guest books, cookies, interaction tracking, and customer feedback through forms, surveys, complaints, and correspondence through customer care for instance.

In addition to automatically logging and collecting profile information, the user-profiling component provides application administrators the ability to import and integrate profiles from other customer databases. Also, as the user becomes more experienced in using the site, it can be advantageous to allow users themselves to edit their own profile information to ensure that it accurately reflects what they perceive to be their own unique interests.

In a B-to-C environment, the most obvious uses for a user-profiling component are one-to-one marketing and authentication for the purposes of payment. As users navigate and use the site, their activity is logged and saved so their latest profile persists into all future inter-actions with the platform. Once a complete profile of a user has been collected, it can then be automatically grouped according to demo-graphics or common interest in order to target advertising or promo-tions. For example, a healthcare site may choose to group users who have searched for information about a specific condition, let's say arthritis, with users who have clicked on pain reliever advertisements in order to specially advertise a new content section on the latest arthritis research and treatment developments.

A B-to-B user often requires personalization features that are more robust in order to maximize their efficiency in utilizing the application. Unlike consumers whose activity within a site is usually relatively unpredictable, most business users behave quite pre-dictably when using an e-Enterprise system. Consider for example, the case of a purchasing manager charged with re-supplying MRO goods for a corporation. After only a few iterations of purchasing spe-cific goods in predictable quantities in regular time intervals, it can be quite easy for a profiling component to determine what the user is likely to be looking for at any given time. If it is time to re-stock paper clips or re-supply pens, more often than not the application can predict it and offer goods that minimize the user's search time and maximize efficiency.

Another essential driver for a personalization component in the B-to-B area is the flexibility of purchase conditions. In most B-to-C initiatives, prices are fixed regardless of volume purchases or repeat business. In B-to-B where most prices are negotiated individually, however, it is essential that the application be able to track buyer information such as custom pricing for preferred clients, preferred method of shipping, and time demands for specific products. A B-to-B user-profiling component must be able to add value to the information it gathers and often works in conjunction with a reporting component to determine such things as aggregate pur-chasing behavior of a group.

Since organizational positions and responsibilities rather than individual tastes dictate many individual permissions and profiles in a B-to-B environment, it can often be advantageous to attach profiles not to individual persons but instead to their roles. This role-based profiling allows individual users to change company positions and assume different responsibilities within the system without dramatically rebuilding the profiles.

Also, because B-to-B buying is usually more process intensive than B-to-C buying, a user profiling component may at times be necessary to record a user's progression through a requisitioning process so that even if the process is interrupted it can be easily restarted where left off.

In many e-Applications, the access control and personalization services are very closely connected to each other. This not only is a good way of providing access control, but it also assures that changing business rules or user privileges don't require large overhead costs or time investments. Numerous products exist to enhance the personalization of access control capabilities of a site, including sophisticated analysis of profile information for every request for an application resource.

SEARCH ENGINE

Since many e-Applications employ catalogs or knowledgebases that by their very nature contain a broad variety of goods, services, and information, it is essential to employ some type of search component to allow users to easily locate the information that they want. The easier it is to search and find, the more satisfied the user will be.

Product catalogs, support knowledgebases, and information/content repositories are some of the most prominent e-Applications that require searching components. In fact, almost every application requires some degree of accurate and efficient searching capabilities. Although different types of content are by nature better suited to certain searching techniques, usually a combination of two basic techniques—search by content and search by parameter—suffices.

Searching by content is perhaps the single most common functionality on the Net today. In an e-Enterprise environment, searching by content can be used in any number of different situations. Some examples include searching by product description or type (electrical products, tools, products of a certain color or manufacturer, products below a certain price, new products, related products, etc.); by application (for example, an oil rig part as distinct from a car part); by classification or category (for example, a hierarchical structure such as a standard industry code); by industry reference number/code (some industries have unique product coding systems dating back to before fast, computerized searching of random-sized alpha-numeric strings); or visually, searching a string of drawings or photos (particularly helpful for products whose names are not known but that are recognizable on sight).

Searching by parameters differs from content-based searching in that it is based on how the content is organized rather than what it actually contains. Parametric searching requires a more sophisticated approach that allows users to search across multiple products each with multiple specific properties. For example, in cases when one or more known properties can be entered to search the database for all the products possessing that combination, i.e., a product of a particular type, less than a certain size, exceeding a particular level of output, possessing a specific feature, and falling below a certain price. Common types of parametric searching include searching by alphabetical order, by information hierarchy, by keyword, by fuzzy logic, and by natural language.

The most common type of parametric searching is searching by hierarchy. This involves searching a tree or parent-child structure, starting with a few broad choices and splitting them into larger numbers of more specific types, until the desired object is singled out. The effect is one of drilling down from less specific to more specific choices of product categories. Doing a search at Yahoo! for the category "car" when searching for the home site of "Ford" is a simple example of a hierarchical parametric search.

Fuzzy logic is another category of parametric searching. Put simply, it allows a parametric search to be qualified by prioritizing the different properties in the search and allowing the searching component to return near matches in addition to perfect matches. These results are then pre-ranked and displayed according to suitability. For example, a shopper at a CD e-Tailer may search for "jazz" and have not only results categorized specifically as "jazz" but also "ragtime," "new age," and "swing" returned to them.

A keyword search could be useful for searching among several thousand employee profiles in a global HRIS system through the organization's intranet to identify an employee who may have specific, unique training or expertise that the organization may wish to leverage.

Search engines create a virtual safety net for a user. They are often used as a last resort when the regular navigation features fail, thus, a poor search engine leaves the user literately lost—not a good business goal.

CONTENT MANAGEMENT AND CATALOGING

Almost without exception, e-Applications of every type must include some form of content management and cataloging components. Whether building this component in house or purchasing an off-the-shelf product, it's essential to consider three baseline functionalities: 1) how the user benefits from optimal content distribution and content organization, 2) how the application takes advantage of this component to dynamically transform content from vast e-Enterprise data resources into useful information for the user, and 3) how do content/application/system managers define and organize criteria and rules.

In some cases—as with the e-Tailer, for example—this is self-evident. Even less traditional models, however, usually require this functionality as well. Applications such as healthcare and EBP informational sites must manage dynamic databases of consistently evolving data, and extended value chain platforms must aggregate intelligence from disparate applications and databanks to present a single, unified view of the value chain in real-time.

The most obvious use for this type of business component is, of course, the online catalog employed by e-Tailers, virtual marketplaces, and most procurement platforms. In the early days of e-Commerce, it was sufficient to create static pages of HTML to present product information on the Net. Today, however, e-Applications must employ a content management and cataloging tool that handles multiple authors with multiple roles to help manage increasingly large and complex catalogs of information. Content management coordinates and helps accelerate the rapid life cycle within the Web site. Without this coordination, innovation is impeded and overall content issues are at risk.

One of the Net's key advantages in both the B-to-B and B-to-C arena is its ability to deliver massive amounts of information in a manner that can be dynamically customized to individual preferences and tastes. A content management and cataloging tool, in concert with some type of user profiling and product configuration component, enables catalog publishers to easily include personalized and individually relevant information with a minimum of overhead customization costs.

Typically, content is generated dynamically from a database that has been populated with individual product information such as related graphics, SKUs, and product descriptions that link database queries to spaces on a Web page template. This means the design is separated from what might be a mass of fast-changing data, such as stock prices. A simple change to the template can thus instantly change thousands or even millions of Web pages, even while the content of each of those pages is itself constantly changing. The same content may thus be presented in a variety of forms, by using different templates for different users.

In addition, individual database fields such as product category, sub-category, price, product code, part number, and physical specification are included for use by the product configuration and searching components. To deliver this raw information in a form viewable over the Net, page templates must be designed to query a database that includes text and graphics specific to each product. In such an architecture, the content management/cataloging component provides a layer of abstraction between the raw data on one side and the presentation layer on the other.

In the B-to-C area, the cataloging component queries the user profile component and the product database to return dynamically generated product information pages that correspond to each viewer's personal profile. This enables application managers to continuously update information and deliver the latest content for a superior buying experience. This leads to one-to-one relationship marketing that delivers a unique and dynamic mix of product offers and information that the system knows from experience is of interest to each individual buyer.

In B-to-B environments, the online cataloging component should be utilized to make enterprise buying more efficient. Since most B-to-B purchases are somewhat predictable and repetitive, the system, in concert with a user profiling component and product database, can be used to find supplies that match criteria of previous purchases, at the right price and on the right terms. The virtual marketplace sites can also report relevant market intelligence data to catalog managers and marketing executives.

In addition to customizing information available to potential buyers, a cataloging component must provide individual interfaces to enable a multi-vendor procurement/resource management environment where custom content from individual seller catalogs can be aggregated into a common format according to the buyer's specification. Each individual vendor can then manage its own content and have changes automatically reflected in the aggregated catalog. In some cases, catalog managers can even allow individual vendors to customize the look and feel of their product pages within the aggregated catalog. This gives individual vendors a greater measure of control and responsibility for ensuring that their products are presented in the most favorable manner.

A third case where individual content generation is essential is when catalog managers allow individual buyers to participate in populating the catalog by adding their own content, taking part in discussion threads, and so on. In such cases, however, it is essential that the cataloging component be flexible enough to extract, deliver, or publish information intelligently according to individual preferences. It also requires that the system be extremely easy to use.

In simple cataloging environments, publishing the content is a complex procedure in its own right, independent of the creative and marketing processes that determine the messages and design. The abstraction layer provided by a cataloging component enables catalog managers to publish a wide variety of information in a wide variety of data formats, with minimal physical alteration and cost overhead. A robust cataloging platform supports the widest range of data types (from simple text to complex multimedia) and access methods within the context of a single page template. This separation of data and presentation allows the quick integration of Web offshoots like WebTV and Web access via PDAs.

Consider, for example, an e-Tailer specializing in selling CDs and DVDs to end users. With a minimum of effort, the content manager would be able to ensure that the product page for the latest U2 album would include sound clips of popular tracks. At the same time, the page for the new Steven Spielberg thriller could include clips from the film's trailer.

In addition to enabling this essential functionality, the content management/cataloging component must integrate directly with back-end inventory management, ERP, supply chain, and other enterprise applications to ensure that managers have the most up-to-date information.

An excellent example of this type of interaction is the integration of the product marketing and individual consumer information databases into an e-Tailing environment. To ensure that repeat customers from conventional channels (such as telephone and mail order) are accounted for in new Web distribution centers, the e-Enterprise platform must dynamically include information from multiple databases and multiple applications.

In fact, a full-scale e-Application infrastructure must be able to extract information from a limitless range of systems including other legacy systems, tools for authoring content, and standalone databases. For this to work, open architecture and modularity of a content management tool are essential.

Since most e-Applications include some degree of customization in the goods, services, and information made available to the end user, many cataloging components utilize a product configuration module. Put simply, product configuration is the act of choosing an appropriate feature set for a given product or service.

The primary piece of a product configuration module is the business rules engine that defines what features may be customized and determines what potential combinations are valid. The configuration process is usually conducted on the fly, following rules to ensure the end product is feasible. Consider, for example, a configuration tool that defines a build-to-order personal computer. If the machine is equipped with only one expansion bay capable of adding an external drive, and the user attempts to include a DVD as well as a removable cartridge drive, the configuration engine will return an error and the user will be prompted to try another configuration.

Such a specific tool may at first seem to be a niche product; after all, what if the application sells goods in pre-configured packages and no customization is required? In the network economy, shrinking inventory levels and real-time product construction have enabled organizations to build more flexibility and customizability into their product offerings without increasing overhead costs. Customers then benefit from enhanced freedom of choice, especially when compared to the old days of pre-configured products that might partially satisfy some while fully satisfying none. Customers can also benefit from a product configuration engine when alerted to necessary add-ons and accessories of which they otherwise might be unaware.

Despite their apparent simplicity, configuration engines require sophisticated software capable of quickly handling and analyzing millions of feature combinations in extreme cases. As build-to-order and real-time inventory become a fact of life in every industry, their importance will only increase.

PAYMENT

Payment is at the heart of any commerce platform. One of the key distinctions between B-to-C and B-to-B business and e-Application models is the form of payment utilized and accepted.

In a B-to-C environment, the buying and selling process is much simpler than in the B-to-B environment. In B-to-C, the virtual world of consumer spending is much like in the physical world—largely unregulated, often fraught with impulse purchases, and most obviously credit card driven. In B-to-B, the buying process, the product mix and services, and the payment process is much more complex. Except perhaps for MRO procurement, an individual does not normally pull out a corporate credit card to pay for large volume orders. Instead, a purchase order or electronic funds transfer is normally required. The terms of B-to-B purchases are generally predefined, regulated, vendor-specific, and customer and/or account-driven.

One similarity does exist between the two different processes for online purchasing—both utilize shopping carts. Shopping carts allow a buyer to pick and choose goods and services from a catalog offering and put them into a virtual basket that ultimately gets checked out after the buyer chooses an appropriate payment method.

Another type of payment emerging in the marketplace is digital wallets and electronic checks. The digital wallet and electronic checks are payment methods that are tied in with customer-specific financial institutions and that have the ability to "carry cash" while you travel in virtual marketplaces.

To support a wide variety of payment methods for either B-to-C or B-to-B environments, you need more than just software components. You need the involvement of financial institutions, third party brokers, credit card vendors, issuing banks, and online payment service providers. Hence, unlike other components discussed in this chapter, payment isn't just a software component that you buy from a vendor and integrate into your overall e-Application platform. Rather, you would approach one of these financial institutions or online payment gateways that enable an enterprise to create supplier and customer trading partnerships.

Choosing the right service provider(s) depends upon the e-Application payment model, which defines the extent to which the application platform must support simple credit card transaction processing or a complex electronic fund transfer. It also depends on the application system and network-level technical flexibility that enables the service provider(s) to be well integrated with the existing e-Enterprise system infrastructure. Finally, the ability to work with other business components such as workflow engines, content management, search engines, and data/messaging integration is another key factor in making the right selection.

WORKFLOW MANAGEMENT

In every e-Enterprise platform, application flow is dependent upon a number of distinct business parameters. Consider the example of an online procurement application. A purchasing manager is probably able to make a simple, low-volume purchase of routine goods—let's say light bulbs, pencils, or printer toner—with a minimum of supervision. In order to place a large order for hundreds of PCs, however, it is likely that some degree of approval is required.

To manage this variability in process flow, e-Applications must incorporate a workflow component that acts as a vehicle to pass a process from one stakeholder to another according to a predefined set of business rules. The business rules should be modeled by executive management in order to ensure that the application is optimized to deliver tangible, strategic advantages to the enterprise. Since optimal workflow tends to change over time, the component must be capable of modifying processes independent of other parts of the system.

Software components that define and route workflow processes enable businesses to engage in a continuous process of self-evaluation and evolution of procedures. Similarly, when business partners and suppliers make changes to their external-facing processes, the e-Application can quickly respond without altering the existing system underpinnings and unrelated functions.

An e-Enterprise workflow component must consist of three basic modules: the workflow definition module, the business rules definition module, and the workflow engine.

The role of the workflow definition module is to visually model the application workflow. This tool should be intuitive and easy to use so that business managers as well as technology developers can participate in the modeling. To speed the development of these processes, most workflow components include several templates for basic processes that can be easily modified to incorporate business-specific values and logic.

Like the workflow definition module, the business rules definition module is used prior to the rollout of the application. This tool is primarily responsible for defining the business rules that govern workflow decisions that are made by the component. For example, a virtual marketplace application may have a business rule that if the customer purchases X dollars worth of goods she should receive a volume discount. The business rules module would record this preference and automatically incorporate it into the workflow engine.

The final piece of the component is the workflow engine. This piece intercepts requests for pages and determines where each process must move to next in order to match both the process and business rules definition. To some extent, this rules engine holds the entire e-Application together and gives it a distinct form. As processes are dynamically updated during the course of continuous process engineering, the workflow engine must respond in real-time to transform conceptual models into real, working e-Enterprise systems.

Event Notification

Since many e-Applications are event-driven, it is essential to include a component that is capable of notifying users of important occurrences such as a contract award, winning an online auction, or a request for purchase authorization. Since Net users are always within contact distance, it is possible to stay closer in touch with business partners during a transaction than ever before. In traditional businesses, staying in touch has meant costly phone calls or personal contacts. On the Net, however, it is possible to dispatch a personalized electronic message for little, if any cost.

When a customer sets a process in motion within the e-Application, a vital atmosphere of trust must be maintained and enhanced by keeping the customer notified of progress at every stage of the relationship. Handling this well is one of the important value-added functions distinguishing e-Enterprises. Luckily, it is relatively easy and effective to automate user notification when the system relies on a number of standardized electronic methods of communication including e-mail, fax, pager, and message queues.

An event notification component requires software that is capable of monitoring the status of e-Application processes, registering individual events, and automatically communicating clear, well-designed information to the customer in real-time. Messages are delivered using templates for short or long messages and may include variable information values that are supplied by the application. Each of these templates has distinct functional roles. Short messages may carry all of a pager message, or the header of a fax or e-mail. Long messages provide more detail for the fax or e-mail. The user notification component must also work with the workflow component to monitor existing processes, as well as with the user-profiling component to determine individual users' preferred methods of notification.

To ensure that the user is not caught in a deluge of unwanted messages, it is essential that the user notification component include facilities allowing users to choose to be exempted from certain messages. At the same time, it should allow department managers to set group notification standards and track messages to ensure that employees are acting upon information delivered by the system.

COLLABORATION

One of the Net's key differentiators over other business media is that it lets users confidentially share information and collaborate in real-time to provide the most complete and competitive services possible. Some common examples of this Net-based communication include bid/ask boards, online auctions, chat rooms, and online negotiation platforms.

Collaboration has always been a hallmark of successful business. In fact, before the e-Enterprise revolution, people doing business gathered to trade items, negotiate positions, bid and counter-bid in commodity exchanges, brokers' offices, and bid/ask boards. It is only logical, then, that e-Enterprises provide similar places of business where players can collaborate on the Web.

To support this activity, collaboration components will include functionality such as secure, verifiable, undeniable and unambiguous bids, explicit agreements, contracts, requests for quotations and proposals (RFQs and RFPs), and flexible instruments that allow parties to define their own types of deals. Facilities necessary to manage these include automatic locking and version controls, copying of original specifications and other documents to all interested parties, and broadcasting events such as RFPs or new boards and new bids. Parties must be able to collaborate, conduct customer surveys or market research, and organize into logical groupings such as dealing rooms and trading networks for specific commodities, industries, or functional areas.

Also, the software will need to provide negotiation and collaboration functionality between combinations of buyers, sellers, middlemen, and other parties. This includes electronic bid boards, trading exchanges, auction houses and places to discuss requirements, negotiate, reach compromises, and lodge agreements. Ideally, these facilities should interface with existing corporate systems to seamlessly integrate with back-end legacy applications and other e-Enterprise business and technology components.

Negotiations and trading may take place on a single board or in multiple threads. It may be open-ended, subject to deadlines, or dependent on external or subsidiary events. The application must allow access to databases and filing systems to maintain information and draw upon it, deliver user profiling in conjunction with that component, and impose access controls so only known and accepted participants can take part.

Information resources also need to be managed and audible to allow for regulatory and legal oversight. This allows basic information to be available equally, for collaborators to choose to share sensitive information privately, and for the complete privacy of some information (for example, in a sealed-bids situation, or where the identity of bidders may be hidden from those evaluating the bids). Event notification should also be used to ensure that participating parties are fully up-to-date on the progress of the transaction.

Finally, virtual negotiation applications of this kind demand strong administrative facilities, especially the ability to provide audit trails, logging of events and other information, and ongoing monitoring of system performance to ensure that it behaves effectively.

One of the chief barriers to establishing this type of system is building the trust and confidence of all parties involved. A bidder who loses an important deal due to a technical glitch or inadequate system design is likely to, at best, take the business elsewhere. At worst, such situations will undermine the trust of every party involved—including all current and future customers.

Collaboration components must also include some type of facility to provide for differences in legal jurisdiction between the parties to a negotiation or deal. Ultimately governments will have to legislate to ensure level playing fields wherever Net commerce participants may be.

Other business components such as user profiling and workflow modules will have a key role to play in building these virtual exchanges and forums by including such important properties as well-defined business rules and protocols for exchanging sensitive transaction information.

REPORTING AND ANALYSIS

To monitor the success of an e-Application on a business level, a platform must incorporate a reporting and analysis component. The concept of a reporting tool for Net commerce isn't a new idea. Since the earliest days of the Net revolution, systems managers have analyzed traffic and surfing patterns in order to ensure that hardware and software resources are capable of handling traffic.

As the e-Enterprise emerges, the need for reporting and analysis becomes mission-critical, and it must do much more than just count hits and track referring pages. It must be able to put together an overall picture of how an e-Application is being utilized, how it is impacting the target audience, how trading partners are performing, how success is measured, and how it is increasing overall efficiency.

To deliver the desired critical information, vast e-Enterprise data resources must be translated into a concise, intelligent, user-defined report that is sorted for high-level analysis on a real-time basis. Let us consider a customer relationship management application (CRM). A loyal customer accesses a CRM e-Application repeatedly to place orders, track account information, find new product information, and interact with customer service functions. In a B-to-C scenario, this type of CRM functionality could be quite simple. However, in a B-to-B CRM scenario, it is quite complex.

In either case, a reporting and analysis component must gather and present user-specific information utilizing other components such as data and messaging, content management, workflow, user profiling, and event notification to provide the above described CRM functionalities.

A reporting and analysis component for any e-Application platform must include traditional online analytical processing (OLAP) functionalities. It must contain the ability to define and generate event-driven reports, conduct multi-dimensional data mining, and establish priority management.

e-Enterprises are quickly moving beyond hype to continuous ROI measurement. Without having the ability to analyze a variety of data from manufacturing to finance and transforming them into hard information on a real-time basis, e-Application platforms cannot add value.

Traditionally for decision support, enterprises have used a slew of predefined reporting templates supported with application-specific query engines. But because agility and adaptation are key to fast growing multi-platform e-Applications, enterprises need to define a common reporting and analysis component that can be implemented as an independent, smart software agent for accessing, defining, and manipulating a wide variety of raw data into profitable information. Development of these generic, common, off-the-shelf reporting and analysis components has already begun. As the e-Application platform matures, these components will be used to conduct user behavior analysis from sales tracking to customer account inquiry to inventory management.

DATA/MESSAGE INTEGRATION

At their core, e-Applications are about sharing information between multiple partners for mutual advantage. Since most players in a robust system utilize at least some degree of proprietary software for data storage or internal corporate applications, it is hardly surprising that most platforms require some type of integration component to ensure that information flows from one stakeholder to another with a minimum of disruption.

Even within the context of a simple B-to-C transaction, a large degree of back-end data integration is necessary to ensure that the right information reaches the right place at the right time. From the customer's side, the transaction is simple: select a product, provide payment information, and check out. Under the surface, however, a number of steps must take place.

First, the appropriate funds must be requested from the payment provider. Once the component has received payment authorization, it begins to clear the transaction with the internal corporate legacy systems and ERP installations. Actual payment is triggered after shipment when the ERP system confirms fulfilment to the transaction server, which asks the payment clearance center to debit the customer's credit card company account.

In a B-to-B transaction, the process can be even more involved. The transactional component must authenticate the buyer's identity and check it against a list held by the selling company of authorized requisitioners. The transaction can then cross to the transaction server. Low-cost products such as computer supplies and stationery may well be ordered over the Internet, but high-value transactions involving volume purchases such as materials and components for the production process may well be ordered through the buyers' MRP system using traditional EDI links.

When you analyze the above B-to-C and B-to-B transactional examples, it becomes fairly clear that these transactions within the e-Application framework are driven by messages and data integration. These messages and data contain a vast variety of old and new information encapsulated with ERP messages, payment systems, legacy data, EDI transactions, XML data streams, and home grown data types.

A data/message integration component that provides business functionality must enable e-Application developers (and sometimes e-Application users) to define rules and criteria to construct these message and data types. Additionally, it must enable e-Applications to construct and to parse data and messages that are understandable by disparate application infrastructures.

Traditionally, system developers perform these tasks at a system or network layer by utilizing message-oriented middleware (MOM). However, at the dawn of e-Enterprise, the need for dynamically defining, creating, and understanding transactional and e-Application messages is forcing e-Enterprises to create a new breed of data/message integration components that are far more agile, user friendly, and flexible.

These intelligent components generate application-specific "wrapper code" around the user-defined messages to provide real-time e-Application communication and integration. This "wrapper code" then integrates with system and network infrastructure via predefined APIs. Without defining this new breed of data/messaging integration components, it is next to impossible to achieve the agility necessary to take advantage of personalization, real-time workflow management, and extended enterprise collaboration. Combined with the enterprise application integration (EAI) components discussed in Chapter 8, these data/messaging components enable e-Enterprises to create the technical underpinnings for an extended enterprise.

CONCLUSION

The objective of this chapter was to identify and articulate the key business components that define a common application framework for diverse e-Enterprise business and e-Application models. In the early part of this book you were introduced to several types of B-to-C and B-to-B e-Application business models, including e-Tailing, auctions, virtual communities, customer relationship management, and supply chain management. As any e-Enterprise must be built upon these functions of e-Application models, a common application framework must be defined that enables agility, speed, adaptation, reusability, and cost efficiency.

The goal of this chapter was to highlight the most common business components that are the underpinnings for any of the e-Application models discussed throughout the book. When a B-to-C or B-to-B e-Application is developed, most of the business components discussed in this chapter must be utilized. For example, for e-Tailing, the key business components for the underlying application framework are access control and profiling for personalization. Then, cataloguing and content management for content delivery, payment services, and event notification for selling tools, collaboration, and workflow for online community, reporting an analysis component for customer behavior tracking, and a data and messaging component for back office integration.

The same conclusion can be drawn if a B-to-B e-Application model is analyzed. For example, to create an e-Procurement platform, authentication and profiling components are required for user management, a content/cataloguing component for vendor information management, and workflow and collaboration for buying tools. Also, an event notification, reporting and analysis component for measuring vendor performance, and data/messaging component for ERP and back office integration are required.

Reusable off-the-shelf components have matured over the last five to seven years. However, the development of the business components discussed in this chapter is fairly young yet. It is difficult for e-Application developers to pick and choose the appropriate business components from Net commerce vendors. However, to maximize agility and continuous adaptation in an e-Enterprise, it is critical that e-Application developers define an enterprise-wide common application framework utilizing business components and leveraging the technology components discussed in the next chapter.

These business components are being developed by a slew of emerging Net commerce vendors, including Interworld, Open Market, Broadvision, EC Cubed, enCommerce, AlphaBlox, Sterling Software,

Microsoft, BusinessObjects, CyberCash, and eCash as well as by pack-aged ERP application vendors including SAP, Baan, PeopleSoft, Siebel, i2 Technologies, and Oracle. The true challenge of creating a common business component framework from this maze of vendors lies within the ability of individual enterprises to combine off-the-shelf business component selections with home grown development, while lever-aging ERP packaged solutions. Therefore, this common business com-ponent framework must be architected with independent validation and verification by performing a thorough gap analysis between cur-rent and future enterprise-wide e-Application architecture.

e-Enterprise Technology Components

Our goal is not to be a visionary, but to get people to take advantage of what technology is available today.[1]
　　　—Scott McNealy, Chairman & CEO, Sun Microsystems

We want everybody who works on the Internet to think of Internet Explorer technologies as a platform that they can build on, a platform that they can take advantage of.[2]
　　　—Bill Gates, Chairman & CEO, Microsoft

If you listen to Scott and Bill, all you have to do is to choose between Sun and Microsoft to define your e-Enterprise software infrastructure. I wish the answer was that simple. Au contraire, thanks to the IT industry, choices are unlimited and go far beyond Sun, Microsoft, and Oracle. As a matter of fact, choosing the right implementation strategy from the vast architectural and vendor options is becoming increasingly difficult.

In Chapter 6, I have outlined a high-level, logical technology architecture that contains high levels of abstractions such as e-Application Rules, e-Application Distribution/Integration, e-Data, and e-Networks. In Chapter 7, you learned the driving business components that primarily define the reusable e-Application Rules. In this final chapter, I will introduce some of the emerging technology components that should be utilized to implement these higher-level abstraction layers from a pure technology perspective.

Although this chapter discusses a few selected emerging technologies, it is not intended to be a recipe for physical implementation. Rather, it is intended to explore important standard technologies that should be understood, considered, independently verified, and validated for each e-Initiative.

You learned in Chapter 6 that components are pre-developed pieces of application code that can be assembled into working systems. Now consider the following issues:

- e-Enterprises need new capabilities to add to existing production applications at a faster rate and at a lower cost. These new applications must integrate with existing systems into a pervasive infrastructure used both internally and outside the organization by its partners, customers, and suppliers.

- The growth in the deployment of large-scale distributed systems is fundamentally changing the way in which applications and the underlying system software must be designed, developed, and used. Today's organizations have a variety of heterogeneous hardware and software systems that must continually evolve to meet emerging business requirements.

- There is an increasing need for application integration to enable heterogeneous e-Applications to communicate and interact among themselves. Enabling these diverse applications to cooperate and integrate seamlessly requires open standards or consensus. Standards are evolving through the formation of consortia whose aim is to promote standardization in a particular area. Some examples of standard bodies are Open Software Foundation (OSF) and the Object Management Group (OMG). However, from an application point of view it is also important that any such standard be open—that is, it may be implemented by multiple vendors. This frees users from the tyranny of proprietary systems that lock them into a particular vendor solution.

- Software developers are faced with significant challenges as they attempt to mold their current solutions to take advantage of the benefits of distributed objects. The cost of architecting and building the next generation of applications seems to be difficult for many software vendors due to their lack of skills in this area of development.

■ The promise of component-based applications is to enable developers to build applications by mixing and matching pre-fabricated "plug & play" software components. This promise has been realized for the desktop application, the leading examples being drag & drop grids, charts, figures, images, forms, word processing, and presentation. However, enterprise component-based applications have yet to emerge.

This chapter highlights emerging technology components and standards that begin to mitigate these challenges.

TECHNOLOGY COMPONENTS

In Chapter 6, you were introduced to the concept of pre-built business and technology components. This section focuses on emerging technology components that are the underlying implementation infrastructure for new generation e-Applications. These technology components also provide the backbone for business/application components that were identified in Chapter 7. At the core, each tries to manage complexity and provide various system level services to quickly assemble application functionality.

In Chapter 6, you also learned about architectural concepts that differentiated business and technology architecture. The logical technology architecture is comprised of e-Application rules, e-Application distribution/integration, e-Data, and e-Networks. In this section, the technology architecture will be discussed more from an implementation perspective. The logical architecture is supported by physical infrastructure that directly correlates to emerging technology components that will be discussed.

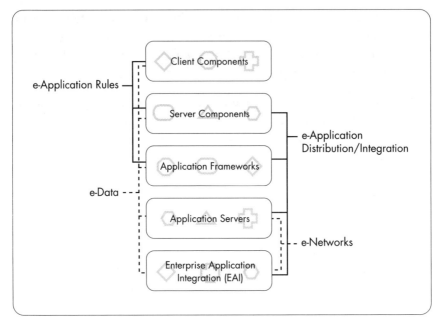

FIGURE 8.1

For example, e-Application rules are typically implemented with client/server components and application frameworks. Server components, application frameworks, and enterprise application integration (EAI) components are used for e-Application distribution and integration. Figure 8.1 depicts these relationships and introduces the concepts of client, server, application server, application framework, and enterprise application integration (EAI) components.

- **Client components:** Manages the user interface and some of the application logic. It determines how the user navigates the application. The client component typically sends messages to the server components to perform user specific tasks. For example, the client component may focus on a scenario where a certain part of the application module (such as a purchase order) is displayed depending on the user's interaction with the system after an online order is placed and verified.

■ **Server components:** Implements the server side business logic. For example, a server component could facilitate how a purchase order (PO) will be created and what kind of data it needs to extract from the user's profile. It may also create various POs depending upon the types of user (all types of users having been previously defined in the business logic). Server components may also be used to distribute business logic appropriately across the network for load balancing and application performance.

■ **Application servers:** Provide facilities and services to create application management, distribution, scalability, and reliability. For example, in an online superstore, an application server could connect to various components depending upon the number of users logged onto the site at a particular time, thus performing load-balancing tasks to ensure optimal system performance. Application servers often physically host and manage client and server components as well as application frameworks.

■ **Application frameworks:** A collection of business functionality generally used to provide a framework for an overall system. For example, an application framework could provide user management, search, work routing, and so on. The difference between an application framework and a component is that an application framework is a collection of large objects or applications whereas a component is a collection of small objects, which may be used to create various applications.

■ **Enterprise application integration (EAI):** Describes the development of a new set of integrated systems that are created by combining existing legacy applications, custom applications, and packaged applications with new Web functionality. This approach to integration uses standardized middleware frameworks and object technology to securely integrate functionality from disparate applications. These middleware frameworks provide connectivity among multiple applications through open interfaces, messages, and common processes regardless of their underlying technology infrastructure.

Client Components

The client can be viewed as a process (program or application) that sends a message to a server process (program or application), requesting that the server perform a task (service). Client programs usually manage the user-interface portion of the application, validate data entered by the user, dispatch requests to server programs, and sometimes execute business logic. The client-based process is the front-end of the application that the user sees and interacts with. The client process contains user-specific logic and provides the interface between the user and the rest of the application system. One of the essential elements of a client workstation is the graphical user interface or GUI. Normally a part of a desktop operating system or a browser, it detects user actions, manages the content display, and invokes a data extraction process.

For e-Applications, client components provide a standard infrastructure for user interface design, server communication, messaging, and platform independence. Client components are used to create both "thin-clients" and "thick-clients." A thick-client usually contains part of the business logic and application processing to provide greater functionality. These thick-clients do not use a browser, but rather they are stand-alone applications that are specifically dedicated to a particular application. They are equivalent to clients of the client/server era. A thin-client can be accessed from a browser without having a dedicated client software platform.

In general, client components enable implementation of client programs or applications with optimal development time, agility, interoperability, and reusability that maintain industry standards. Two dominant client components and architectures that have emerged over the last few years are JavaBeans from Sun MicroSystems and ActiveX from Microsoft.

JavaBeans

A JavaBean is platform-neutral, component-based software architecture for the Java platform. Designed by a partnership of industry leaders, JavaBeans are device- and operating system-independent.

JavaBean components are primarily used for client complements and user interface. However, they can be used to create full-scale server side applications as well. Because JavaBeans are core to the Java Platform, when a JavaBean component is written it runs on any platform that runs the corresponding Java Virtual Machine. This component, once created, can be used just about anywhere, on any platform. And because JavaBeans are device-independent, JavaBeans-based solutions can be deployed on everything from mainframes and personal computers to network computers and embedded devices to cellular phones and Personal Digital Assistants. The JavaBean component software integrates with other industry component models such as ActiveX, with no additional development required.

JavaBeans attempt to provide a smooth migration from existing platform-specific solutions into 100 percent pure Java based solutions, allowing developers to preserve their investment in legacy applications. This reduces the cost and time to deploy and develop distributed applications tremendously.

ActiveX

ActiveX is Microsoft's component technology for distributing applications over the Internet. ActiveX controls are Web-enabled Windows applications. One of the strongest arguments for developing with ActiveX is its language-independence. Controls can be written in C++, Visual Basic, or even Java. ActiveX fits into Microsoft's Active Platform, a range of technologies for building active Web content. In addition to using ActiveX controls as components built with C++, Visual Basic, Java, etc., developers can use ActiveX with Visual Basic Script or JavaScript. For intranets, ActiveX also allows MS Office pages to be embedded as active documents in the Web pages.

In addition, Active Server technology controls dynamic content, server-side controls, and scripts. One of the key drawbacks to this technology is its tight coupling with the Windows platform. Macintosh and UNIX are not catered to at this time although it is expected that they will be in the near future.

For Windows developers, ActiveX can serve as a handy way to export custom Windows applications to the Web. Existing client/server applications can be wrapped in ActiveX controls, offering a quicker path to Internet distribution than rewriting the same application in Java, for example.

Server Components

A server process (program or application) fulfills the client request by performing the task requested. Server programs generally receive requests from client programs, execute data retrieval and updates, manage data integrity, and dispatch responses to client requests. Sometimes server programs execute common or complex business logic. The server-based process may run on another machine on the network that acts as the host operating system or network file server. The server can then support either application level services and/or system level services. The server process acts as a managing agent that manages shared resources such as application distribution, application access, application communication, and load balancing.

For e-Applications, server components provide the infrastructure to implement business specific logic. Business specific logic typically contains common application components wrapped around e-Application specific business rules. Along with this business logic, server components enable object management, distribution, and scalability. Server components are also used for application frameworks, application components, middleware, and system level services. Middleware and system level services provide operating level functionality for communication, integration, and data transportation.

In a complex e-Enterprise environment, in order to support inter-enterprise processes through multiple e-Application models, a complex network infrastructure is essential both from an application and systems perspective. Mixing and matching distributed server components, like those I will discuss in the next section, enables this complex system distribution and integration to occur. These components are neither mutually inclusive nor mutually exclusive. Their uses are situation-specific based on the organization's current and future system/application goals. The following section briefly discusses some of the emerging server-side component technologies, namely Common Object Request Broker Architecture (CORBA), Distributed Component Object Model (DCOM), Enterprise JavaBeans (EJB), Object Transaction Service (OTS), and Microsoft Transaction Server (MTS).

CORBA

New generation e-Applications place additional demands on the enterprise information system infrastructure. They bring along two particular challenges in addition to others. First, they must be able to perform under high-user load, and second, they must integrate with the existing enterprise information system investment.

CORBA helps to achieve these goals. CORBA architecture is a specification of a standard architecture for Object Request Brokers. An Object Request Broker (ORB) is a middleware technology that manages communication and data exchange between objects. ORBs promote interoperability of distributed object systems because they enable users to build systems by piecing together objects from different vendors that communicate with each other via the ORB.

A standard architecture allows vendors to develop ORB products that support application portability and interoperability across different programming languages, hardware platforms, operating systems, and ORB implementations. According to Object Management Group (OMG), "Using a CORBA-compliant ORB, a client can transparently invoke a method on a server object, which can be on the same machine or across a network. The ORB intercepts the call and is responsible for finding an object that can implement the request, passing it through the parameters, invoking its method, and returning the results of the invocation. The client does not have to be aware of where the object is located, its programming language, its operating system, or any other aspects that are not part of an object's interface."[3]

COM/DCOM

Component Object Model (COM) refers to both a specification and an implementation developed by Microsoft that provides a framework for integrating components. This framework supports interoperability and reusability of distributed objects because it enables developers to build systems by assembling reusable components from a variety of vendors that communicate via COM.

COM defines an application-programming interface (API) to allow the creation of components for use in integrating custom applications or to allow diverse components to interact with each other. But for this integration to happen, the components must adhere to a structure specified by Microsoft. This enables applications written in different languages to inter-operate seamlessly, thus offering developers the ability to build maintainable and adaptable systems on a proven desktop component architecture. COM is therefore an effective toolset for a significant class of applications, but has not yet emerged as an enterprise technology.

Organizations that are predominantly Windows-based will find COM the best choice for application development. Once developers learn COM for single-system integration, they can leverage this knowledge later to build distributed applications. Other Microsoft services such as Microsoft Transaction Server (MTS), Microsoft Message Queue (MSMQ), and integration tools will certainly make COM a desirable infrastructure. However, COM is not a multi-platform solution; it is a Microsoft proprietary technology that poses an impediment to organizations that intend to link applications from various vendors and partners running on multiple platforms.

Distributed Component Object Model (DCOM) is an extension to COM that allows distributed component interaction. While COM processes can run on the same machine but in different address spaces, the DCOM extension allows processes to be spread across a network. With DCOM, components operating on a variety of platforms can interact, as long as DCOM is available within the environment. It is best to consider COM and DCOM as a single technology that provides a range of services for component interaction, from services promoting component integration on a single platform, to component interaction across heterogeneous networks.

DCOM's location independence greatly simplifies the task of distributing application components for optimum overall performance. Suppose, for example, that certain components must be placed on a specific machine or at a specific location. If the application has numerous small components, network loading can be reduced by deploying them on the same LAN segment, on the same machine, or even in the same process. If the application is composed of a smaller number of large components, network loading is less of a problem because they could be put on the fastest machines available, wherever those machines are.

A common issue during the design and implementation of a distributed application is the choice of the language or tool for a given component. Language choice is typically a trade-off between development cost, available expertise, and performance. As an extension of COM, DCOM is completely language-independent. Virtually any language can be used to create COM components, and those components can be created from even more languages and tools. Java, Microsoft Visual C++, Microsoft Visual Basic, Delphi, PowerBuilder, and Micro Focus COBOL all interact well with DCOM.

A critical factor for a distributed application is its ability to grow with the number of users, the amount of data, and the required functionality. DCOM provides a number of features that ease application scalability. In spite of all the advantages and desirable features that DCOM provides to developers, it still locks them into Microsoft's proprietary technology. On the other hand, OMG's CORBA relies on implementation by vendors resulting in a more varied technology platform. Fortunately, a few CORBA vendors have begun to address COM/CORBA interoperability. For example, IONA, Visual Edge, and Noblenet have released implementations that support mixed COM/CORBA environments.

Enterprise JavaBeans (EJB)

Enterprise JavaBeans (EJB) technology defines a model for the development and deployment of reusable Java server components. The EJB architecture logically extends the JavaBeans component model to support server components. Server components are application components that run in an application server. EJB technology is part of Sun Microsystems's Enterprise Java platform, a robust Java technology environment that can support the rigorous demands of large-scale, distributed, mission-critical application systems. EJB technology supports application development based on a multi-tier, distributed object architecture in which most of an application's logic is moved from the client to the server. The application logic is partitioned into one or more business objects that are deployed in an application server.

The Enterprise JavaBeans architecture provides a server component container model. The model ensures that Java platform server components can be developed once and deployed anywhere, in any vendor's container system. Even though the container systems implement their runtime services differently, the Enterprise JavaBeans interfaces ensure that an enterprise bean can rely on the underlying system to provide consistent life cycle, persistence, transaction, distribution, and security services.

The EJB architecture is completely independent from any specific platform, protocol, or middleware infrastructure. Applications that are developed for one platform can be picked up, moved, and redeployed to another platform without any effort from the developers. The Enterprise JavaBeans environment automates the use of complex infrastructure services, such as transactions, thread management, and security checking. Component developers and application builders do not need to implement complex service functions within the application programming logic.

It is also highly customizable and supports customization without requiring access to source code. To the IT manager, this translates into having the ability to assign different people to different tasks that match their skills, and to model the application around recognizable objects of functionality that resemble their corresponding physical-world business processes. This, in turn, translates into a greater degree of manageability of an overall project, and the greater possibility of reusing components in future projects. Those who have adopted Enterprise JavaBeans in their IT architecture are finding complex applications take less time to develop than non-Java applications, and complex projects are being completed on schedule.

Object Transaction Service (OTS)

By sitting above the operating system, middleware provides a common abstraction to the underlying system usually in the form of numerous co-operating services that provide useful functionality to an application such as naming, remote access, security, and so on. The CORBA architecture is one such example of middleware. As an industrial consortium-derived standard, it promotes the production of interoperable applications that are based upon the concepts of distributed, interoperable objects. The architecture contains many components and one of those components is known as Object Transaction Service (OTS).

OTS provides interfaces that allow multiple distributed objects to cooperate in a transaction such that all objects commit or abort their changes together. However, OTS does not require all objects to have transactional behavior. Instead, objects can choose not to support transactional operation at all, or to support it for some requests but not others. The OTS is simply a protocol engine that guarantees that transactional behavior is obeyed but does not support all of the transaction properties that are out there. Therefore, it requires other cooperating services to provide complete transactional functionality including persistent service, concurrency control service, and other relevant transaction-oriented services.

Microsoft Transaction Server (MTS)

Microsoft Transaction Server (MTS) is not a specification, but rather a product embedded in NT 5.0 (better known as Windows 2000). MTS is designed to support server-based transaction processing applications. But unlike the EJB specification, MTS was designed to run only on the Microsoft Internet Information Server (IIS) and in conjunction with Microsoft's own Distributed Transaction Coordinator (DTC). In other words, MTS is more like a proprietary product to make Windows 2000 a viable platform for distributed computing.

Unlike EJB, MTS does not conform to any open standards. While EJB provides the flexibility of using containers and servers from any vendor, MTS restricts its components to run only within the MTS executive container built in Windows NT. Moreover, MTS uses DCOM instead of CORBA to link disparate platforms. This certainly restricts the developer's ability to integrate legacy applications running on any UNIX platform with MTS applications. However, an MTS component could very well be written with any language that supports COM, like C++, Visual Basic, Java, etc.

The MTS component model looks very similar to the EJB model published in the September 1998 issue of *Component Development Strategies*. At the heart of both models is a container that manages the server-side components. However, the EJB model is based on a specification that many different vendors have implemented while the MTS model is a product incorporated into the Windows NT operating system and is only available from Microsoft.

Application Servers

An application server is a deployment platform that provides application scalability, reliability, security, and manageability. Application servers make the deployment and manageability of Web applications over Internet, intranet, or extranet easier by providing functionality geared to the Net. The challenge of building e-Applications with reliability, scalability, stability, and manageability is just now being addressed.

Application servers have gained momentum from the release of such successful products as IBM's WebSphere Application Server and BEA's WebLogic Server. They are called application servers because they form a clear level of separation between the Web server and data access layers. e-Applications built using the application server model should consist of three back-end layers: the Web server layer, the application server layer, and the data layer. In this model, most or all application logic exists in the middle tier, with application servers handling all data manipulation and HTML page-creation functions.

All application servers offer some basic features, including connection management, state and session management, business-logic hosting, load balancing and fail-over, database connectivity, and transaction management. These features relieve developers from low-level details and provide them with most of the development and deployment infrastructure, enabling developers to focus on business processes and logic.

BEA's WebLogic is a Web application server for developing, integrating, deploying, and managing large-scale, distributed Java applications. It enables companies to deliver high performance, scalable Net applications that leverage Java and EJB. WebLogic Server provides a comprehensive and widely used implementation of the Enterprise Java APIs.

WebLogic Server provides scalability, expandability, and high-availability through clustering support that does not require any special-purpose hardware or operating system services. It provides both Web-page and EJB component clustering. Web-page clustering handles transparent replication, load-balancing, and fail-over for the presentation logic that generates responses to Web clients (for example, the contents of a shopping cart).

IBM WebSphere, another popular Web Application Server, provides the software and tools for building and deploying Web-based applications. Combining the distributed object and business process features with transaction processing features that it offers, WebSphere can be used for the development, deployment, and management of heterogeneous business-critical applications. It uses open standards-based technologies like interoperable CORBA and EJBs to provide comprehensive, high-quality, middleware runtime services for distributed component applications.

Application Frameworks

The concept of application frameworks is the result of three major barriers faced by the developer community over the years as they attempted to keep their products viable in the ever-changing technology-driven market. One barrier was the problem of how to retrain developers to effectively use object-oriented technology. This task was greater than just learning another programming language. It required extensive knowledge in object-oriented analysis and design, which unfortunately was not a common skill set in the industry. Therefore, a new approach to building systems had to be learned, and a new set of skills and tools used.

A second barrier was the risk involved in moving to a new technology. Often the first solution that is built with a new set of skills and a new technology is less than perfect. A poor design will manifest itself in problems such as code that won't function properly, poor performance, or a solution that is hard to use. This type of result is a necessary step to learning how to apply a new technology, but the number and magnitude of the problems must be kept at a level that will allow a business to keep operating while adaptations can be made to the new approach.

A third barrier associated with moving to object-oriented technology was the cost of making the change. Organizations realized they needed some basic infrastructure upon which to base their applications. Many of them could not afford to develop this infrastructure by themselves. They also could not afford to rewrite their entire product line at one time. They needed to be able to spread the cost of upgrading their applications over time by having the object-based portions of the application interoperate with portions that had not yet been updated.

Frameworks that address these barriers such as those offered by IBM's San Francisco Project and EC Cubed's ecWorks help solve these problems. They offer solutions that provide an object-oriented infrastructure, a consistent application-programming model, and default business logic that can be used to jump-start building e-Applications. Developers can design their solutions using a proven programming model instead of developing a unique approach, and the use of a shared architecture will make it easier to integrate solutions from different software vendors.

The business components provide the most common business logic that can be enhanced and extended instead of having to build the entire application from scratch. Developers can build their applications by modifying and extending the default business objects and logic instead of having to start their applications from raw requirement statements. This allows developers to focus only on their business logic, not on lower-level details because the framework addresses most of them.

The IBM San Francisco Project is building three layers of reusable code for use by application developers. The lowest layer, called the Foundation, provides the infrastructure and services that are required to build industrial-strength applications in distributed, managed-object, multi-platform applications. The middle layer, called the Common Business Objects, provides definitions of commonly used business objects that can be used as the foundation for interoperability between applications.

The highest layer, called the Core Business Processes, provides business objects and default business logic for selected vertical domains. Initially, IBM San Francisco is delivering business components in the domains of accounts receivable, accounts payable, general ledger, order management (sales and purchase), and warehouse management. Over time, these components will be extended and enhanced with additional business processes, objects, and access to more framework interfaces providing greater application flexibility.

San Francisco provides flexibility to developers in building applications. At the lowest level, application developers can utilize the base infrastructure to provide a consistent programming interface and structure for building distributed multi-platform applications. Application developers may also choose to use parts of the next layer of Common Business Objects (CBO) as the basis for application integration. CBO provides a common foundation for building interoperable business solutions. At the highest level, application-specific business components will provide core business processes that can be easily extended to provide a complete business solution. San Francisco is implemented using the Java language thus making it inter-operable. It also allows developers to use many tools and class libraries that the industry is producing for Java development.

EC Cubed's ecWorks application components provide rapid e-Application development, enterprise-wide consistency of business rules, and quick response to changing business requirements. The components are self-contained modules that have clearly defined, open interfaces that offer high-level business services. ecWorks Internet-enabled e-Applications extend from inside the enterprise outward through the Internet to suppliers, distributors, partners, and customers, while maintaining unique business processes.

The ecWorks suite is composed of five different self-contained components that provide common cross-industry business services, enabling developers to focus on business logic rather than dealing with low-level system details such as managing transaction and connection pooling and so on. Each of these components caters to specific needs or services. Currently the suite consists of five components: ecProfiler, ecAdvisor, ecWorkRouter, ecTrademaker, and ecDataBuilder, providing services that include authentication, business events notification, inter-enterprise work routing, and data integration.

Organizations can use the suite as a whole to create and build complete e-Applications by leveraging each of the components to accelerate the development effort. For example, developers who are building an application that requires notification upon the occurrence of certain events can simply use the appropriate published APIs to accomplish the task. This not only reduces the cost and time requirement for development, but also enables developers to focus entirely on the application logic.

Enterprise Application Integration (EAI)

With the advent of complex e-Applications and the inherent need for seamless integration between business partners, organizations are burdened with the daunting task of integrating cross-platform, inter-enterprise applications and continually evolving business processes.

Moreover, the recent surge of mergers and acquisitions and higher customer demand has also contributed to the need for integrating enterprise applications into a unified set of business processes and a unified data model.

Enterprise Application Integration (EAI) provides a solution to this enormous task faced by today's organizations. EAI is considered the answer to the problem created by the islands of business automation over the past couple of decades. These mission-critical systems are either running on mainframes or are using proprietary data formats that are quite difficult to integrate, and the cost to modify these systems is phenomenal. Forrester Research estimates that 35 percent of development time is spent on creating interfaces and points of integration to provide seamless operation between disparate intra-organization applications.

The key to EAI is standardized middleware frameworks and by using distributed object technology that acts as a platform for functionally integrating disparate applications. Traditional systems integration enables unified views by creating one-to-one custom links among application servers, new packaged applications, and legacy applications. As the breadth of desired functionality increases, so too does the number of interfaces. A tangle of custom connections results and is complicated by the fact that few of the elements are static. New application functionality is always desired, new functionality is added to legacy systems, and packaged enterprise applications may be upgraded. Therefore, increasingly large percentages of the company's IT budget are devoted to interface maintenance, not new development.

New application development in such an environment becomes prohibitively complex and expensive. EAI replaces the multiple custom interfaces with a single layer of standardized inter-application middleware components—the application integration framework. This framework can be used repeatedly for new application development and enhancement of existing applications. The cost and complexity of new development is reduced, while the speed of new feature and application deployment is accelerated.[4]

Technically, EAI middleware is a combination of two basic types of middleware technology. The first type of middleware facilitates the communications between components of different applications and components of the same application. The second type of middleware helps simplify and consolidate separate instances of data and business logic into logical objects, and provides specialized services.

The Inter-application middleware enables programs from different applications to communicate with one another in three basic ways depending on the requirements of the new business solution. Messaging Oriented Middleware such as IBM's MQ Series or Microsoft's

MQS supplies asynchronous communications. Synchronous communications can be handled by distributed object-oriented technology such as products that conform to CORBA or COM, which were discussed earlier in this chapter. Transactional communications can be provided by such products as IBM's CICS or Encina, Microsoft's MTS, BEA's Tuxedo, or an emerging class of object-oriented transaction processing software such as Orbix OTM or Inprise ITS.

EAI, instead of creating custom interfaces between programs, relies upon a re-usable middleware framework as a common layer sitting between disparate applications. This framework, once built, can be used repeatedly in building future business-critical applications. Therefore, developers only need to build an interface to this framework instead of building multiple interfaces for various existing applications. This not only reduces development time significantly, but also reduces the cost of resources. The systems, in turn, also become maintainable, reliable, and easily expandable.

Because of this realization, a new category of EAI vendors has emerged in the application integration marketplace. These vendors focus on providing application process level integration to further automate these integration issues. Such vendors include CrossWorld, Extricity, and TSI Soft. CrossWorld's United Applications Architecture (UAA), Extricity's Extricity Alliance, and TSI's Mercator all attempt to integrate legacy systems with Enterprise Resource Planning (ERP) packaged applications and/or homegrown client/server applications that leverage the Net infrastructure.

The challenge of leveraging this approach is that many vendors emphasize their own standards, and it can be difficult to evaluate whether the standards used are the "right" standards for your organization's specific needs. While each vendor preaches cross-application/cross-platform solutions, the reality is that most of the time these solutions are not "plug and play." They tend to require a certain amount of customization to enable them to function in the existing infrastructure. For example, they way you would integrate SAP's ERP applications with Hyperion financial applications is not the same way you would integrate BAAN's ERP applications with Hyperion.

TECHNOLOGY STANDARDS

In the previous section of this chapter, some of the emerging technology components were highlighted. In this section, I will introduce some of the technology standards that must be considered in order for every e-Application implementation to maintain inter-operability, system security, and cohesive cross-enterprise processes.

These architectural and system level standards focus on issues that go beyond standard technology components. Reusable e-Enterprise architecture must be based upon standards that focus on cross-systems issues, and these standards must be considered regardless of the selection of CORBA versus DCOM or MTS versus ITS. The standards that are discussed in this section are UML for object modeling; PKI, digital certificates, and digital signatures for security; WFMC and SWAP for workflow; and XML for messaging. Some vendors have already started to embed these standards in their solutions, however many have not even begun. Therefore, it is incumbent upon e-Application developers to make sure some of these standards are deployed within the overall architecture.

Unified Modeling Language (UML)

As the strategic value of software increases for many companies, the industry looks for techniques to automate the production of software and to improve quality and reduce cost and time-to-market. These techniques include component technology, visual programming, patterns, and frameworks.

Businesses also seek techniques to manage the complexity of systems as they increase in scope and scale. In particular, they recognize the need to solve recurring architectural problems, such as physical distribution, concurrency, replication, security, load balancing, and fault tolerance. Additionally, development for the World Wide Web, while making some things simpler, has exacerbated these architectural problems. Unified Modeling Language (UML) was designed to respond to these needs.

Unified Modeling Language (UML) is a language for specifying, visualizing, constructing, and documenting the artifacts of software systems, as well as for business modeling and other non-software systems. UML represents a collection of best engineering practices that have proven successful in the modeling of large and complex systems.

Although UML does not guarantee project success, it does provide significant benefits to organizations and especially to developers. It lowers the perpetual cost of training when changing between organizations or projects.[5] It also provides the opportunity for new integration between tools, processes, and domains.

It specifies a modeling language that incorporates the object-oriented community's support on core modeling concepts. The developers of UML had many objectives in mind including to provide sufficient semantics to address certain future modeling issues related to distributed computing, frameworks and component technology, and to provide sufficient semantics to facilitate model interchange between a variety of tools.

Rational Software and its partners developed UML, which is the successor to the modeling languages found in the Booch, OOSE/Jacobson, OMT, and other methods. Many companies are incorporating UML as a standard into their development process and products, which cover disciplines such as business modeling, requirements management, analysis & design, programming, and testing.

One of the primary goals in designing UML was to provide a standard language for visualizing, specifying, modeling, and documenting the architecture of a system. A main benefit of UML is that e-Application developers gain control over the architecture they are building. UML is more expressive yet seems more uniform than Booch, OMT, and other methods. With respect to other visual modeling languages, including BPR, E-R modeling, and others, UML provides improved expressiveness and holistic integrity.

Privacy and Security

The lack of security over the Internet was a critical impediment preventing transaction-based commerce from existing until Netscape's

Secure Sockets Layer (SSL) was introduced. SSL enables users to interact with a server confidently without having to worry about eavesdropping, through the use of Public Key Cryptography.

In this section, I will introduce you to the various security and encryption technologies that exist today. There are several aspects of security to be aware of before discussing these technologies: authorization, authentication, privacy, and integrity. Authorization refers to a user's list of credentials that determine what the user is capable of doing when authenticated, while authentication verifies that the user is who he is claiming to be. Privacy and integrity refer to protecting the user's data from exploitation and interference.

Public Key Infrastructure (PKI)

Information security has historically relied on shared secrets. Passwords and PINs are shared between you and the computer or ATM machine you want access to. But sharing secret passwords depends greatly on trust between the parties sharing the secret—consequently, not the safest method to use in a world of unencrypted internetworking. Most computer break-ins are due to compromises by system users or by a hacker that uses a legitimate account to gain access to general security.

Some individuals and companies are replacing shared secret security (also called symmetric security) with the Public Key Infrastructure (PKI) approach. PKI uses a standardized set of transactions that use asymmetric public key cryptography, a more secure and potentially more functional mechanism for limiting access to digital resources. The same system could also be used for securing physical access to controlled environments such as your home or office.

In a PKI world, everyone is issued at least one cryptographic key pair. Each key pair consists of a secret (private) cryptographic key and a public cryptographic key. These keys are typically a 1024-bit or 2048-bit string of binary digits with a unique property: when one is used with an encoding algorithm to encrypt data, the other can be used with the same algorithm to decrypt the data. The encoding key cannot be used for decoding. A responsible party, such as a notary public, passport office, government agency, or trusted third party certifies public keys. The public key is widely distributed, often through a directory or database that can be searched by the public. But the private key remains a tightly guarded secret by the owner.

A public and private key pair alone provides a good means of establishing a secure channel in a transaction, but a lack of personal binding creates the need for a package that not only allows this security but also contains a personal reference and other credentials that help in authorization.

Authentication and authorization are very distinct properties that must be deeply considered before rolling out a public key infrastructure. To help solve some of these issues, keys can be stored in packages called certificates that provide additional information about the user. This additional information could consist of a name, office number, or even a list of privileges a user has when being authorized for a particular task.

Digital Certificates

Digital certificates verify the identity of the sender, place a tamper-resistant seal on a message, and provide proof that a transaction has occurred. Digital certificates give the Internet a high level of certainty, much the way a passport or driver's license verifies a person's identity. They also provide a level of safety and reliability similar to what certified mail provides for document delivery.

A digital certificate is an electronic identification card that establishes credentials when doing business or other transactions on the Net. It contains the holder's name, a serial number, expiration dates, a copy of the certificate holder's public key used for encrypting and decrypting messages, and the digital signature of the certificate-issuing authority so that a recipient can verify that the certificate is real. All this information is digitally signed and sealed by the Certificate Authority. Every time users send an electronic message, they attach their Digital Certificate to sign and encrypt that message. The recipient of the message first uses his or her own digital certificate to verify that the author's public key is authentic, then uses that public key to verify the message itself.

Digital Certificates bring a sense of privacy and confidentiality to the minds of consumers and companies engaged in commerce activities over the Net. They enable businesses to deploy secure departmental or inter-enterprise applications over the Net, to control access to restricted information, and to secure business-to-business services such as EDI. However, at this early stage of development, administrative functionalities to support digital certificates for a large volume of participants are immature.

Digital Signatures

A digital signature is an electronic signature that can be used by someone to authenticate the identity of the sender of a message or of the signer of a document. It can also be used to ensure that the original content of the message or document that has been sent is unchanged or has not been tampered with during its transmission. Digital signatures are easily transportable, cannot be easily repudiated, cannot be imitated by someone else, and can be automatically time-stamped. They can be used with any kind of message, whether encrypted or not, so that the receiver can be sure of the sender's identity and that the message arrived intact.

Digital signatures are created and verified by cryptography, the branch of applied mathematics that concerns itself with transforming messages into seemingly unintelligible forms and back again. Digital signatures use public key cryptography, which employs an algorithm using two different but mathematically related keys. The complementary keys used for digital signatures are arbitrarily termed the private key, which is known only to the signer and used to create the digital signature. In contrast, the other is known as the public key, which is ordinarily more widely known and is used by the receiving party to verify the digital signature and the correctness of the content.

Workflow Technologies (WFMC and SWAP)

People have historically used the term "workflow" to describe a type of application. The term usually says more about what an application does than how it works or how it was built. Modern workflow technology has much more to offer. In a business environment where it is critical to establish a direct relationship with customers and to cooperate in business-to-business transactions, embedding workflow capability in a variety of applications delivers important benefits. For an e-Enterprise business model to succeed, it is critical that core business processes of the organization be visible and directly accessible to customers. Customers expect and demand that they be able to initiate business processes, view their status, and modify them while in progress.

In addition to increasing customer demands, requirements for increased speed, reduced cost, and efficiency translate into taking advantage of business-to-business transactions. Supply-chain management demands a high level of control over inter-operable and flexible business processes. Applications must allow for rapid and constant change of business process without program code changes. Standards such as XML are rapidly accelerating the capability of automated business systems to interact. With a workflow-based architecture, partitioning an application to enable this sort of interaction is natural.

Several efforts are underway to define important standards for workflow interoperability. The Workflow Management Coalition (www.aiim.org/wfmc) has been working on interoperability standards for vendors of workflow systems. OMG (Object Management Group) has recently released its first workflow standard. This standard is based on the work of WFMC (Workflow Management Coalition) but is focused on workflow as a CORBA-based interoperability standard.

Other efforts, such as SWAP (Simple Workflow Access Protocol), are also underway to standardize how workflow-based systems would interact with each other over large networks, especially the Internet. The existing Web protocols have no inherent support for automated change notification, handoff of control, or initiation of human and computer-executed activities. In essence, there exists no standard mechanism for service requests to trigger a workflow process and monitor it across platforms and between organizations.

SWAP is being designed to allow for interoperability between different workflow systems and the applications they support. The scope of SWAP is limited to the interactions and requirements between a requester and a workflow service. This approach leverages existing Internet protocol designs and avoids the harder problem of prescribing a general interoperability workflow definition or interchange format.

Extensible Markup Language (XML)

Throughout 1998, Extensible Markup Language (XML) was a popular industry buzzword, making its mark as an extension to HTML. After realizing its potential power, flexibility, and extensibility, it has now become a dominant feature required by just about every e-Application. A subset of Standard Generalized Markup Language (SGML), it is defined by the World Wide Web Consortium (W3C) to ensure that related data can be transmitted and exchanged in a structured manner over the Web. It provides a more precise definition of data and provides more meaningful search results across multiple platforms.

Most of the hype that surrounds XML today is regarding its extensibility and the ability to display the same data via multiple delivery channels without writing an entirely new user interface from scratch for each. For example, an application that is available to users via the Web can easily be extended to a kiosk environment without writing any additional code for the user interface. This not only reduces development time and the need for additional resources, but it also provides the "write once, run anywhere" kind of flexibility to e-Application developers and organizations.

Unlike HTML, which is being used to convert text stream into the presentation of a page, XML's goal is to convert text stream into a data object with a complex inner data structure and leave the presentation separate. This separation of structured data from presentation allows seamless integration of data from diverse sources. Purchase orders, catalog data, medical records, and other similar information originating from disparate sources can easily be converted to XML on the middle tier, and be pushed to the users either through the Web browser or could be handed off to other e-Applications for further aggregation and processing.

The power and flexibility of XML is propelling it into a new dimension. Recently, Novell has announced its new XML-based directory services called DirXML. DirXML is a metadirectory software that uses XML to link data stored in disparate sources, from network operating systems to network devices and other business applications. This will certainly revolutionize e-Application development and would provide easy interoperability among various systems across multiple domains as well as enhance communication between multi-tiered application architectures.

The need for extensive telecommunications capability posed a major barrier to widespread Electronic Date Interchange (EDI) implementation. Beyond the computer itself, a basic requirement of EDI is a means to transmit and receive information to and from a variety of customers or suppliers. This required a heavy investment in computer networks.

Unlike the mail, to send electronic documents there must be a specific point-to-point electronic path for the document to take. So, companies were either required to develop extensive and expensive networks or rely on intermittent point-to-point modem communication.

However, some of these impasses have been addressed with the advent of XML/EDI. It is nothing but the fusion of XML technologies with EDI. The vision of XML/EDI is to facilitate organizations of various sizes to deploy cost-effective, efficient, and more maintainable systems to the global audience.[6]

Old EDI is captive to its proprietary structures and inflexibility. The XML/EDI group has added the following three additional key components to overcome these obstacles:

- Process Templates
- Software Agents
- Global Entity Repositories

These three components transform old EDI into XML/EDI that allows dynamic electronic commerce between business partners. In the past, EDI was very static, but XML/EDI provides a dynamic process that can be infinitely extended.

Organizations that have Web browsers and Internet connections can easily deploy XML/EDI-based applications. This certainly reduces the phenomenal cost of infrastructure cost that was associated with the traditional EDI. It replaces both simple HTML-based Web commerce and legacy systems, and is backward compatible with the older applications in place.

A new protocol, called Commerce XML (cXML) is being pushed by electronic procurement vendor Ariba Technologies and has gained the support of a number of other procurement vendors and leading electronic commerce companies in this effort.

It is described as a lightweight version of Extensible Markup Language (XML) that supports all supplier content and catalog models, including buyer-managed models, supplier-managed models, and Internet marketplaces. It also incorporates a request/response process for the exchange of transaction information, which provides a mechanism for the exchange of purchase orders, change orders, ship notifications, and other similar business processes.

cXML will help build open trading communities across all industries because it solves critical business-to-business Net commerce challenges. cXML provides support for multiple catalog management paradigms, real-time information exchange, and end-to-end transaction integration over the Internet. cXML also has a lower cost of implementation than does EDI because of its XML base and ability to leverage the existing HTML Net commerce infrastructure and software.

CONCLUSION

The objective of this chapter was to articulate and identify the key technology components that define an e-Application architecture. I have defined those technology components as belonging within the categories of client components, server components, application frameworks, and application integration. In each of these areas, I have highlighted standards and implementations of those standards by market-dominating vendors. The objective of doing so was to provide you with a basic understanding and introduction to the complex underlying technology components that are used to actualize e-Application models. These technology components provide a foundation on which to, first, implement business components as discussed in Chapter 7, and second to integrate these components into e-Applications that define the e-Enterprise.

As mentioned in the beginning of this chapter, these components were selectively discussed because of their relevance, popularity, and recent impact in the e-Application industry. These were not discussed to suggest that these are the only technology components that can or should be used to create enterprise specific e-Applications, but certainly these are technologies that must be considered.

In the technology standards section, I specifically discussed standards for object modeling, security, workflow, and messaging. These four areas of standards are the backbone for any e-Application. Regardless of specific technology components, these technology standards must be considered for defining and selecting appropriate architecture and implementation strategies. These standards are still emerging and many new standards will emerge within the next 12-24 months, however the standards chosen for discussion here were done so because of their maturity, utilization, and vendor acceptance. Furthermore, these standards were not defined by one vendor, but rather through the joint effort of technology leaders to create interoperability among diverse system infrastructures.

The types of technology components discussed earlier, leveraged with the technology standards outlined later in this chapter, create the implementation, architecture, and infrastructure for reusable e-Applications for an agile e-Enterprise.

Afterword

Who Will Be the Great e-Enterprises?

L et's say you've absorbed all there is to be learned about developing the next successful e-Enterprise. Perhaps you've already moved your learning into the marketplace, and the results have been the best you could have hoped for.

What you have won is the right to compete again.

If there's a bottom-line lesson to everything we know about e-Enterprise, it is this: if you haven't created business and technology architectures that enable you to win and win again—if they aren't robust and repeatable in terms of producing success—then you haven't arrived at e-Enterprise yet.

The right tools in this environment are the ones that allow business leaders to replicate—even automate—business and technology analysis and decision making, iteration after iteration. How else can you stay abreast of market opportunities and ahead of your competitors in today's relentlessly competitive environment? As Tom Trainer, CIO of Citigroup, said in the Foreword, you have to think about business and technology architecture as "a repository of reusable strategic assets that allow your e-Enterprise to evolve as rapidly and continuously as today's fluid markets." Only that, meshed with an organizational culture and people endlessly motivated to learn more and push ahead, offers an unbeatable combination.

It should be abundantly clear that this book has not been about telling you how to be the next Amazon.com. In fact, we believe that the glory days of the Net-only business model may be coming to an end. Instead, we are witnessing the ascendancy of the e-Enterprise, where electronic business capabilities are married to strengths normally associated with traditional, FORTUNE 1000, bricks-and-mortar, sometimes boring corporations.

Dale Kutnick, chairman and CEO of META Group, reminds us that "the Internet has produced a handful of spectacularly successful new companies that came out of nowhere. But 25–30 percent of the more traditional companies—those with real assets, real profits, integrated channels, and an array of other real strengths—will exploit the e-Commerce transition to become even more dominant in their industries. These leaders will be remembered as the great e-Enterprises."

Some individuals undoubtedly will argue that none of this has much relevancy to their own industry. Such individuals probably haven't made it to the end of this book. Nevertheless, let's ask ourselves if there is any chance that they are right.

Remember in Chapter 2 we discussed the Amazon.com executive who, when asked what that company would not consider selling, answered "cement"? Is this an example of a business that can never be an e-Enterprise? Well, companies that provide basic construction materials have their own suppliers and customers, just like any other business. As the high-volume customers implement online B-to-B applications, their materials' suppliers are forced to go there too. Indeed, they may well develop a competitive advantage by doing so quicker or better than their competitors. Furthermore, a load of wet cement may have been the original "just-in-time" commodity. It is still that today, which suggests opportunities to combine traditional assets (for instance, a fleet of cement mixer trucks) with Internet-based applications (for instance, fleet control systems).

What about cars? We're certainly not going to download them on the Internet, and produce them on a color laser printer. Yet early online movers like Auto-by-Tel and Microsoft's CarPoint have shaken up auto marketing enough to send the major manufacturers rushing to create their own e-Enterprise concepts. Thus, we see Ford entering an alliance with Microsoft to allow car buyers to search online for the exact car and equipment they want, or to order it custom-built that way. GM is so committed to becoming e-GM that a board member was appointed to recruit the talent they would need to ensure its success.

If you're still thinking of the energy utilities as sleepy businesses resistant to the kinds of change that e-Enterprise demands, take a look at PG&E Corporation. It now operates with a self-imposed four-week time limit whenever decisions need to be made regarding new business initiatives. Deregulation and Net opportunities have combined to demand that kind of speed. "In its new four-week time frame, the San Francisco utility recently completed a business plan for the potential companywide deployment of Web procurement of manufacturing materials," according to *InformationWeek Online*.[1]

What is the common theme behind each of these scenarios? Satisfying customers in real-time.

As we learned in Chapter five, becoming an e-Enterprise means using the speed, ubiquity, and power of the Net to run the entire organization in real-time: whatever the customer wants, whenever the customer wants it.

Real-time product design involves a deeper understanding of market conditions and exact customer needs than ever before possible. Real-time product assembly enables corporations to manufacture and deliver individual products only after an order is placed. Real-time marketing is the epitome of customer orientation, determining which customers are most valuable to the enterprise, and marketing goods and services with perfect "segment-of-one" focus. Real-time distribution means recognizing what products are needed where, and shipping them out before the customer even notices that inventory has turned. Finally, real-time customer support means empowering the customers to get answers and product information exactly when they need it— maybe even before they know it.

If you have an existing or a potential competitor who is sensing, understanding, and profitably responding to such customer needs before you do—and if you allow your competitor to replicate that success at will—you're history. Exercise your options, sell your shares, get out now.

In his book *Business @ the Speed of Thought*, Bill Gates says, "If you asked your friends whether they'd adopted 'the electricity lifestyle,' they'd think you were downright nuts." Imagine, however, a business still thriving today although it had failed to take advantage of all the great business innovations of the past 50 to 100 years. One that made no effective use of telephone or computers. Of air travel or overnight delivery. Of public relations or advertising. Of modern organizational theory, management science, or accounting or auditing standards. A company like that might still exist somewhere, on a very small scale. But it could not be a major player in any major industry that I know of.

Sooner than you may think, that is how we will come to see corporations that did not move fast enough up the e-Enterprise learning curve. That is, if we see them at all.

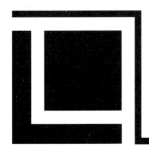

References

Chapter 1: From Net Commerce to e-Enterprise

1. Byrnes, Nanette and Judge, Paul C., "Internet Anxiety," *Business Week*, 28 June 1999, <http://www.businessweek.com/1999/99_26/b3635001.htm>.

2. Byrnes, Nanette and Judge, Paul C., "Internet Anxiety," *Business Week*, 28 June 1999 <http://www.businessweek.com/1999/99_26/b3635001.htm>.

3. "MR Research: Survey on Manufacturing," *Management Review*, September 1999, pp.18-21.

4. META Group, Inc. 19 December 1999 <http://www2.metagroup.com/index.html>.

5. Gartner Group Interactive Home. 19 December 1999 <http://gartner12.gartnerweb.com/public/static/home/home.html>.

6. META Group, Inc. 19 December 1999 <http://www2.metagroup.com/index.html>.

7. *The Association for Electronic Commerce*. 1 July 1999 <http://www.eca.org.uk/>.

8. *CommerceNet*. 1 July 1999 <http://www.commerce.net/>.

9. *CommerceNet*. 1 July 1999 <http://www.commerce.net/resources/pw/chap1-9/pg2.html>.

10. *Economist*, 10 May 1997.

11. Wilder, Clinton, "E-Transformation," *InformationWeek*, 13 September 1999, p. 48.

12. Wilder, Clinton, "E-Transformation," *InformationWeek*, 13 September 1999, p. 50.

13. Hammer, Michael and Champy, James, *Reengineering the Corporation*, HPF Harper Business, 1993.

14. META Group, Inc. 19 Demember 1999
     <http://www2.metagroup.com/index.html>.

Chapter 2: e-Application Models

1. Grove, Andrew. *Only the Paranoid Survive*. New York: Currency and Doubleday. 1996. p. 37.

2. Keen, Peter G. W., "Secret to e-commerce," *Computerworld*, 14 June 1999
    <http://www.computerworld.com/home/print.nsf/all/990614AD62>.

3. McKenna, Regis. *Real Time*. Cambridge: Harvard Business School Press. 1997.

4. Dell, Michael and Fredman, Catherine (contributor). *Direct from Dell: Strategies That Revolutionized an Industry.* New York: Harperbusiness, 1999. ISBN: 0887309143.

5. Electronic Commerce. 19 December 1999
    <http://infolab.kub.nl/general/e-commerce.php3>.

6. "Increase in Ad Spending Predicted," *Internet.Com*, 25 March 1999
    <http://www.cyberatlas.com/segments/advertising/emark.html>.

7. Meltzer, Michael, NCR Corporation, "Using the Data Warehouse to Drive Customer Retention, Development, and Profit,"
    <http://www.crm-forum.com/crm_forum_white_papers/crpr/ppr.htm>.

8. Peppers, Don and Rogers, Martha, Ph.D. *One- to One Future*. New York: Currency and Doubleday. 1993.

9. Seybold, Patricia. *customer.com*. New York: Times Business. 1998.

10. *What Is ORM?* Ariba Corporate Homepage. 1 July 1999
     <http://www.corp.ariba.com/corp/ORMVision/what_is_orm.asp>.

11. Schwartz, Matthew. "Extending the Supply Chain," *Software Magazine*, November 1998 <http:www.softwaremag.com/Nov98/sm118eb.htm>.

12. Kelly, Kevin. *New Rules for the New Economy: 10 Radical Strategies for a Connected World*. New York: Viking Press. November 1998.

13. "Healtheon Company and Investor Information," *Healtheon*, 27 July 1999
     <http://www.healtheon.com/com/index.html>.

14. Junnarkar, Sandeep. "Drkoop takes a dose of e-commerce," *News.com*.
     <http://www.news.com/News/Item/0,4,37695,00.html>.

Chapter 3: B-to-C e-Application Models

1. Dell, Michael with Catherine Fredman. *Direct from Dell*. New York: Harper Business. 1999. p. 157.

2. "Keynote – Neosphere98 Bob McCashin," *Centrobe*, 27 July 1999 <http://www.centrobe.com/news/keynotes/neosphere98.asp>.

3. "Keynote – Neosphere98 Bob McCashin," *Centrobe*, 27 July 1999 <http://www.centrobe.com/news/keynotes/neosphere98.asp>.

4. Melmon, Rich, Partner, The McKenna Group, "Real-time Marketing versus One-to-One Marketing," <http://www.mckenna-group.com/realtime/rt/index.html>.

5. Cox, Beth, "Report: Electronic Bill Payment to Grow Rapidly…" *Internet.Com*, 5 March 1999 <http://www.internetnews.com/ec-news/article/0,1087,4_76381,00.html>.

6. Peppers, Don and Martha Rogers, Ph.D. *The One to One Future*. New York: Currency and Doubleday. 1993. p. 12.

7. Tapscott, Don. *Blueprint to the Digital Economy*. New York: McGraw-Hill. 1998. p. 301.

Chapter 4: B-to-B e-Application Models

1. Brandenburger, Adam M. and Nalebuff, Barry J. *Co-opetition*. New York: Doubleday. 1996. pp. 16-22.

2. Truog, David. "The End Of Commerce Servers," *The Forrester Report*, March 1999.

3. "Cisco Fact Sheet," *Cisco Systems, Inc.* <http://www.cisco.com/warp/public/750/new_corpfact.html>. August 1999.

4. Joachim, David, "Cisco And e-Commerce: Like White On Rice," *Internet Week*, November 10, 1997. <http://www.techweb.com/se/directlink.cgi?WIR1997111003>.

5. Joachim, David, "Cisco And e-Commerce: Like White On Rice," *Internet Week*, November 10, 1997. <http://www.techweb.com/se/directlink.cgi?WIR1997111003>.

6. "Operating Resources Management – Leveraging the 'Total Spend' of a Company," *Summit OnLine*. <http://www.summitonline.com/tech-trends/papers/killen1.html>.

7. "Impact of ORM," *Ariba Corporate Site*. <http://corp.ariba.com/corp/ORMVision/impact_of_orm.asp>.

8. Treese, G. Winfield and Lawrence C. Stewart. *Designing Systems for Internet Commerce*. Reading, Mass.: Addison-Wesley. 1998. p. 54.

9. Rhineelander, Tom, Blane Erwin, and Michael Putnam, "Fourth Channel Purchasing," *The Forrester Report*, September 1997, p. 4.

10. Rhineelander, Tom, Blane Erwin, and Michael Putnam, "Fourth Channel Purchasing," *The Forrester Report*, September 1997, p. 11.

11. Booker, Ellis and Richard Karpinski, "E-Commerce Conundrum – It's Speed Vs. Comfort When Integrating Commerce With ERP," *InternetWeek*, May 3, 1999. <http://www.techweb.com/se/directlink.cgi?INW19990503S0001>.

12. Schwartz, Mathew. "Extending the Supply Chain," *Software Magazine*, November 1998. <http://www.softwaremag.com/Nov98/sm118eb.htm>.

13. AMR Research. September 1999. <http://www.advmfg.com/exec/exec9812s.htm>.

14. Anderson, David L., Frank E. Britt, and Donavon J. Favre, "The Seven Principles of Supply Chain Management," *Logistics Online* 1997. <http://www.manufacturing.net/magazine/logistic/archives/1997/scmr/11princ.htm>.

15. Jones, Dennis H. "The New Logistics," *Blueprint to the Digital Economy*. Tapscott, Don ed. New York: McGraw Hill. 1998. p. 228.

16. Langhoff, June. "Chain of Command: Forging New Partnerships, Building Bigger Profit Margins," *Oracle Magazine, Profit,* November 1997. <http://www.oramag.com/profit/97-Nov/chain.html>.

17. McNabb, Paul and Mike Steinbaum. "Reclaiming customer care: The Milkman Returns," *Cambridge Information Network*, 1999.

18. McNabb, Paul and Mike Steinbaum. "Reclaiming customer care: The Milkman Returns," *Cambridge Information Network*, 1999.

19. "HP Press Release – HP Launches Improved Customer Care Web-based and Call-Cente Support Capabilities," *Hewlett Packard*. <http://www.hp.com/pressrel/may98/28may98c.htm>.

20. "The Object Web Paradigm for Enterprise Applications," *SilkNet*. <http://www.silknet.com/resource/whatitmeans.asp>.

21. Gormley, III, J. Thomas. "Web-Centric Customer Service," *The Forrester Report*. February 1999.

22. "E-Transformation: Creating a Virtual TransactionNetwork," IXL Corporation. <http://www.ixl.com/whitepapers/e-transformation.pdf>.

Chapter 5: Building e-Enterprises

1. Weber, Jonathan. "Clicks and Mortar," *The Industry Standard*. <http://thestandard.com/articles/display/0,1449,5636,00.html>.

2. Gill, Philip J. "Business Snapshot – Business Modeling Tools Help Companies Align Their Business and Technology Goals," *InformationWeek*. <http://www.techweb.com/se/directlink.cgi?IWK19990419S0001>.

3. Ware, James, Judith Gebauer, Amir Hartman, and Malu Roldan. *The Search for Digital Excellence*. New York: McGraw Hill. 1998. p. 362.

4. Gill, Philip J. "Business Snapshot – Business Modeling Tools Help Companies Align Their Business and Technology Goals," *InformationWeek*. <http://www.techweb.com/se/directlink.cgi?IWK19990419S0001>.

5. Kaplan, Robert S. and David P. Norton. *The Balanced Scorecard*. Cambridge: Harvard Business School Press. 1996. p. vii.

6. Kaplan, Robert S. and David P. Norton. *The Balanced Scorecard*. Cambridge: Harvard Business School Press. 1996. p. vii.

7. Hope, Jeremy and Tony Hope. *Competing in the Third Wave*. Cambridge: Harvard Business School Press. 1997. p. 88.

8. Brown, Shona L. and Kathleen M. Eisenhardt. *Competing on the Edge*. Cambridge: Harvard Business School Press. 1998. p. 87.

9. Brandenbuger, Adam M. and Barry J. Nalebuff. *Co-opetition*. New York: Currency and Doubleday. 1996. p. 12.

10. Hope, Jeremy and Tony Hope. *Competing in the Third Wave*. Cambridge: Harvard Business School Press. 1997. p. 192.

11. McKenna, Regis. *Real Time*. Cambridge: Harvard Business School Press. 1997. p. 52.

12. Stern, Carl W. and George Stalk Jr, eds. *Perspectives on Strategy from the Boston Consulting Group*. New York: John Wiley and Sons, Inc. 1998. p. 135.

Chapter 6: e-Enterprise Architecture

1. Drucker, Peter F. "The Coming of the New Organization." *Fast Forward.* Champy, James and Nitin Nohria, eds. Cambridge: Harvard Business Review Press. 1996. p. 4.

2. Brown, Shona L. and Kathleen M. Eisenhardt. *Competing on the Edge.* Cambridge: Harvard Business School Press. 1998. p. 60.

3. Radding, Alan. "Fast Track to App Success." *InformationWeek*, 26 July 1999, p. 3A.

4. Clark, Tim, "Pushing e-commerce standards," *News.com*, 19 March 1998. <http://www.news.com/News/Item/0,4,20235,00.html>.

5. "About CommerceNet," *CommerceNet*, August 1999. <http://www.commercenet.com/about/>.

6. "RosettaNet – an Overview," RosettaNet, August 1999. <http://www.rosettanet.org/general/index_general.html>.

7. Rodriguez, Celso. "Introduction to OFX," Electronic Bill Presentment and Payment (EBPP) + Open Financial Exchange (OFX) Security. <http://www.cs.nyu.edu/ms_students/rodr7076/ebpp/sld010.htm>.

Chapter 7: e-Enterprise Business Components

1. "Meet Mr. Internet," *BusinessWeek*, September 13, 1999. p. 1.

Chapter 8: e-Enterprise Technology Components

1. Sun Microsystems. September 1999. <http://www.sun.com/corporateoverview/news/mcnealy-ctam.html>.

2. Microsoft. 19 December 1999. <http://www.microsoft.com>.

3. Object Management Group. 19 December 1999. <http://www.omg.com>.

4. Tallman, Owen and Kain, J. Bradford, "COM vs. CORBA," *Distributed Computing*, Jan/Feb 1999.

5. Tallman, Owen and Kain, J. Bradford, "COM vs. CORBA," *Distributed Computing*, Jan/Feb 1999.

6. Webber, David R.: "Introducing XML/EDI Frameworks." In: Schmid, Beat F.; Selz, Dorian; Sing, Regine: *EM - Electronic Transactions. EM - Electronic Markets*, Vol. 8, No. 1, May 1998. <http://www.mediamanagement.org/netacademy/publications.nsf/all_pk/804>.

Afterword: Who Will Be the Great e-Enterprises?

1. Wilder, Clinton, "E-Transformation: The Internet is triggering more profound change than anything that has come before it," *InformationWeek Online*, September 13, 1999.

Index

organizational model, role in effectiveness of enterprise, 144–145
Out of Control: The New Biology of Machines (Kelly), 53
outsourcing, in e-Enterprise, 166–167
ownership, in e-Enterprise architecture, 182

P

parametric searching
  in e-Enterprises, 214
  in e-Tailing, 62
Pareto's Law, 42
Partner Interface Processes (PIPs), 197, 198
partner sourcing, in e-Enterprise, 166–167
Pathfinder (Time Warner), 58, 143
payment options, in virtual marketplaces, 97, 99–100, 219–221
payment processing
  in B-to-B purchasing, 39–40, 46, 111–112, 219, 220
  in B-to-C purchasing, 219–220
  in Electronic Bill Payment, 72
  in e-Tailing, 63, 64
Paymybills.com, 73
P-cards, use for electronic payments, 100, 105, 193
PC Week, 39
PC World, 39
PDAs, Web access via, 218
people, role in effectiveness of enterprise, 142–143
PeopleSoft, 96, 97, 114, 230
Peppers, Don, 48, 76
personalization
  in bidding and auctioning, 66
  in B-to-B buying, 212–213
  of customer care, 124
  in e-Tailing, 63
PG&E Corporation, 263

pharmaceutical companies
  procurement applications of, 106
  virtual marketplaces of, 91–92
pharmacies, online, 54
physicians, Net use by, 55–56
pizza delivery business, one-to-one marketing in, 78–79, 80–81
PlanetRX, 9, 55, 60, 61
political obstacles, in B-to-B e-Applications, 130
Popkin Software, 154
Pottruck, David, 139
PowerBuilder, 241
PowerPoint (Microsoft), 148
Priceline.com, 9, 65, 67–68
  success of, 89
privacy issues, in Net marketing, 31, 252–253
Privacy Research Initiative (CommerceNet), 196
process creation/improvement/integration, in B-to-B e-Applications, 130, 132–133
procurement/resource management
  benefits of, 102–103
  in B-to-B applications, 50, 51, 53, 91, 100–107
  in e-Business, 10, 11
Prodigy, 146
product comparison, in B-to-C purchasing, 37, 38, 40, 43–44, 62, 63
product identification, in B-to-C purchasing, 37–38, 40, 41, 62, 63
production planning/fulfillment, in value chain applications, 122
profile management, in customer care, 69
Public Key Cryptography, 253
Public Key Infrastructure (PKI) encryption, 190, 251, 253–254
purchase order (PO) generation, in B-to-B purchasing, 39, 40, 45, 110–111
purchase phase, in B-to-C purchasing, 37, 38, 40, 44, 62